PENGUIN  W9-CBE-001

MEDITATIONS

MARCUS AURELIUS ANTONINUS was born in AD 121, in the reign of the emperor Hadrian. At first he was called Marcus Annius Verus, but his well-born father died young and he was adopted, first by his grandfather, who had him educated by a number of excellent tutors, and then, when he was sixteen, by Aurelius Antoninus, his uncle by marriage, who had been adopted as Hadrian's heir, and had no surviving sons of his own. Aurelius Antoninus changed Marcus' name to his own and betrothed him to his daughter, Faustina. She bore fourteen children, but none of the sons survived Marcus except the worthless Commodus, who eventually succeeded Marcus as emperor.

On the death of Antoninus in 161, Marcus made Lucius Verus, another adopted son of his uncle, his colleague in government. There were thus two emperors ruling jointly for the first time in Roman history. The Empire then entered a period troubled by natural disasters, famine, plague and floods, and by invasions of barbarians. In 168, one year before the death of Verus left him in sole command, Marcus went to join his legions on the Danube. Apart from a brief visit to Asia to crush the revolt of Avidius Cassius, whose followers he treated with clemency, Marcus stayed in the Danube region and consoled his somewhat melancholy life there by writing a series of reflections which he called simply *To Himself*. These are now known as his *Meditations*, and they reveal a mind of great humanity and natural humility, formed in the Stoic tradition, which has long been admired in the Christian world. He died, of an infectious disease, perhaps, in camp on 17 March AD 180.

MARTIN HAMMOND was born in 1944 and educated at Winchester College and Balliol College, Oxford. He graduated in Literae Humaniores in 1966, and since leaving Oxford has taught in England and in Greece. He was Head of Classics at Eton College for six years from 1974, and subsequently Master in College. In 1984 he was appointed Headmaster of City of London School, and thereafter was Headmaster of Tonbridge School for fifteen years from 1990. He is married, with two children. He has also translated *The Iliad* (Penguin, 1987) and *The Odyssey* (2000), and is now working on a translation of Thucydides.

DISKIN CLAY is Professor of Classical Studies at Duke University. His BA degree is from Reed College, in Portland, Oregon (1960), and his PhD from the University of Washington in Seattle (1967). He has taught at Reed College, Haverford College, The Johns Hopkins University, The City University of New York, and in France, Greece and Italy. His main publications have been in the field of ancient Greek philosophy. His *Lucretius and Epicurus* appeared in 1983; *Paradosis and Survival: Three Chapters in the History of Epicurean Philosophy* in 1998; *Four Island Utopias* (with Andrea Purvis) in 1999; and *Platonic Questions: Dialogues with the Silent Philosopher* in 2000. His study of *Archilochos Heros: The Cult of Poets in the Greek States* appeared in 2004. He is now working on two studies of Dante and his influence: *Dante's Parnassus: The Pagan Poetry of the Commedia* and *The Art of Hell*.

MARCUS AURELIUS

Meditations

Translated with Notes by MARTIN HAMMOND
With an Introduction by DISKIN CLAY

PENGUIN BOOKS

PENGUIN CLASSICS

Published by the Penguin Group
Penguin Books Ltd, 80 Strand, London WC2R ORL, England
Penguin Group (USA) Inc., 375 Hudson Street, New York, New York 10014, USA
Penguin Group (Canada), 90 Eglinton Avenue East, Suite 700, Toronto, Ontario, Canada M4P 2Y3
(a division of Pearson Penguin Canada Inc.)
Penguin Ireland, 25 St Stephen's Green, Dublin 2, Ireland (a division of Penguin Books Ltd)
Penguin Group (Australia), 250 Camberwell Road, Camberwell, Victoria 3124, Australia
(a division of Pearson Australia Group Pty Ltd)
Penguin Books India Pvt Ltd, 11, Community Centre, Panchsheel Park, New Delhi – 110 017, India
Penguin Books (NZ), cnr Airborne and Rosedale Roads, Albany, Auckland 1310, New Zealand
(a division of Pearson New Zealand Ltd)
Penguin Books (South Africa) (Pty) Ltd, 24 Sturdee Avenue, Rosebank, Johannesburg 2196, South Africa

Penguin Books Ltd, Registered Offices: 80 Strand, London WC2R ORL, England

www.penguin.com

First published in Penguin Classics, 2006
030

Translation and notes copyright © Martin Hammond, 2006
Introduction copyright © Diskin Clay, 2006
All rights reserved

The moral right of the editor has been asserted

Set in 10.25/12.25 pt PostScript Adobe Sabon
Typeset by Rowland Phototypesetting Ltd, Bury St Edmunds, Suffolk
Printed in England by Clays Ltd, St Ives plc

ISBN–13: 978–0–140–44933–4

www.greenpenguin.co.uk

Contents

Preface

The writings of Marcus Aurelius, conventionally known as the *Meditations*, are unique in Classical literature – the personal and philosophical diary written in Greek by an intellectual Roman emperor without any thought or intention of publication – and remain of unique interest and relevance to the modern world. *To Himself* is the better title given in the manuscript used for the first printed edition in 1559 (this manuscript is now lost: there is only one other complete manuscript): but neither this title nor the convenient division into 'Books' and 'chapters' has any authenticity. Marcus wrote for himself, probably without title and certainly without planned overall structure: and he wrote in Greek because in the second century AD Greek was still the language of philosophy, read, written, and spoken with facility by most educated Romans. Marcus' Greek – lively, taut, spare, sometimes crabbed – is both a joy and a challenge to the translator.

In a striking passage Matthew Arnold described Marcus Aurelius as 'perhaps the most beautiful figure in history. He is one of those consoling and hope-inspiring marks, which stand for ever to remind our weak and easily discouraged race how high human goodness and perseverance have once been carried and may be carried again' (*Essays in Criticism: First Series* [London, 1865]). Though Marcus himself would have rejected the extravagance of this praise, there is some truth in Arnold's rhetoric: truth likewise in G. M. A. Grube's more recent characterization of the *Meditations* as 'a strange, noble, and sad book' (*Marcus Aurelius: The Meditations* [Indianapolis, 1983]). What is certainly true is that the range, diversity, and honesty of

Marcus' reflections on human life and death in the perspective
of eternity – doubt and despair, conviction and exaltation all
equally intense – have enduring power to challenge, encourage,
or console. And there is the constant interest of the personal
preoccupations, problems, and prejudices which give sharp life
to Marcus' writing. All this is informed by a passionate moral
commitment, the philosophical conviction of the unity of all
things, and a firm belief in the interfusion of the human and
the divine ('The gods are with us and share our lives' [6.44];
'every man's mind is god' [12.26]).

For this translation I have used, with only a few minor vari-
ations, the text in A. S. L. Farquharson's two-volume edition
(Oxford, 1944). I have also followed Farquharson's division of
chapters into sub-sections, except in 6.16, 6.30, and 11.18.
The sub-sections are marked in the text of the translation by
marginal numbers in italics.

   Readers may wish to use the notes selectively, consecutively,
or of course not at all (much of Marcus is immediately accessible
without need of annotation). The notes are intended to give
detail and/or explanation where that might be helpful, and to
provide a 'road map' for the *Meditations*, so that at and from
any point the reader may find either discussion or directions to
discussion elsewhere: hence the welter of cross-references in the
notes, and a number of synoptic notes gathering together the
dispersed range of Marcus' thoughts on a particular topic (e.g.
Marcus on the gods, note on 6.44).

I have many debts of gratitude. To the Governors of Tonbridge
School for granting me a sabbatical term in Michaelmas 2002,
which accelerated what would otherwise have been the glacial
pace of progress in the writing of this book; to Peter Carson
and Lindeth Vasey of Penguin for encouragement, help, and
guidance; to Anna Rogers for her wonderfully calm and efficient
management of the conversion of my unevenly legible manuscript to printer's copy; to Professor Tony Long for much
detailed help and advice; to Andrew Crawshaw for giving us

the use of his delightful house on the island of Andros, where much of this book was written.

Above all, I am very grateful to Professor Diskin Clay of Duke University for kindly agreeing to write the Introduction to this book: he has also provided the suggestions for further reading.

Martin Hammond

Chronology

AD 121 26 April: Marcus born in Rome.

c.124 Death of Marcus' natural father, M. Annius Verus. Adopted by his grandfather.

138 Adopted (together with **Lucius** Ceionius Commodus) by his uncle **Antoninus**, who became emperor in succession to Hadrian on 10 July.

Betrothed to Antoninus' daughter **Faustina**.

140 Consul for the first time.

145 Married to Faustina.

147 Birth of first child.

between 155 and 161 Death of Marcus' mother, Domitia Lucilla.

161 7 March: Death of Antoninus Pius.

Succession of Marcus and Lucius as joint emperors.

31 August: Birth of son **Commodus** and twin brother.

166–7 Plague in Rome and throughout the empire.

168–80 Most of these years spent on campaign on the northern frontiers (in central and south-eastern Europe north of the Danube).

169 Death of Lucius.

175 Rebellion of Avidius Cassius, governor of Syria, in the east. Death of Faustina at Halala in Cappadocia.

177 Commodus (aged 15), Marcus' only surviving son, made joint emperor.

180 17 March: Died near Sirmium in Pannonia.

Succession of Commodus as sole emperor.

Introduction

Meditating on the *Meditations*

In his *Meditations*, Marcus Aurelius Antoninus describes himself as 'a male, mature in years, a statesman, a Roman, a ruler'.[1] When Marcus Aurelius wrote this simple description of himself, he was emperor. He was born in Rome as Marcus Annius Verus on 26 April AD 121 and died on the northern frontiers of the Roman empire (near Sirmium in Pannonia) on 17 March AD 180. Like his adoptive father and uncle by marriage, Titus Aurelius Antoninus, Marcus Annius Verus was not born to the purple. He was the last of the long series of 'adoptive' emperors that began with the accession of Nerva in AD 96 and ended when Marcus' natural son Lucius Aurelius Commodus became emperor in AD 180. This era of more than eighty years was recalled nostalgically by Edward Gibbon as a golden age for humankind: 'If a man were called to fix the period in the history of the world during which the human race was most happy and prosperous, he would, without hesitation, name that which elapsed from the death of Domitian to the accession of Commodus.'[2]

Marcus' father died when he was a boy and he was brought up in the home of his paternal grandfather, named, like his son and grandson, Marcus Annius Verus. The emperor Hadrian (ruled AD 117–38) came to know and admire Marcus when he was a young man of seventeen and liked to call him *verissimus* (most true and truthful), after his cognomen Verus (true). Marcus' names and titles (*nomina*) are an omen of his career as an emperor and a philosopher. His cognomen translates into Greek as *alethes*, and truthfulness, realism, and honesty, as we

will see, were the virtues Marcus admired most. In February of
AD 138, just months before his death, Hadrian adopted the man
who was to become Marcus' adoptive father, Titus Aurelius
Antoninus. In turn, Antoninus adopted Marcus that same year.
Marcus Annius Verus then took the name and title Marcus
Aurelius Antoninus. Antoninus Pius, as he came to be called,
ruled from 138 until his death in 161, when Marcus became
emperor in his turn.

Some of this history is evident in Book 1 of the *Meditations*
where Marcus speaks of his debts to those who had raised and
educated him and expresses his deep debt to the man who was
first his uncle by marriage and then his father. His progress
through the major offices of the Roman state (the *cursus
honorum*) was rapid. He was named Caesar (a cognomen recognizing him as a member of the imperial family) in 139 and he
served as consul (the highest office in Rome below the emperor)
in 140 and 145. He was serving as consul for the third time in
161, when at the death of Antoninus on 7 March he received
the titles Imperator Caesar Marcus Aurelius Antoninus Augustus, to which was added the title and office of Pontifex
Maximus, the highest religious office in Rome.

These were Marcus' titles when he became emperor. The
Romans made the distinction between service in Rome and
Italy and service abroad on military campaigns. The contrasting
terms they employed were *domi* and *militiae*, 'at home' and
'with the army on campaign'. Marcus' career as emperor is
distinguished in like manner between the eleven years he served
as emperor in Rome and the last stage of his life. On becoming
emperor, Marcus named Lucius Verus as co-emperor. Verus'
campaigns and fragile victories on the eastern frontiers of the
empire gained the emperor who remained in Rome the titles
Armenicus (164), Medicus, Parthicus Maximus, and Pater
Patriae (Father of the Fatherland) – all in 166. So far as we
know, Marcus did not leave Italy until 168, when he and Lucius
Verus headed north to command the legions on the northern
frontiers where tribes north of the Danube continued to break
into Italy, Pannonia, and Greece. In 169 Verus died suddenly
on the northern frontier, and it was left to Marcus, now sole

emperor, to continue the campaigns against the Quadi and Sarmatians and assume the additional titles Germanicus (172) and Sarmaticus (175).

All these weighty titles commemorated victories that did not last beyond the reign of Marcus Aurelius. His son Commodus soon abandoned the defence of the northern frontier. During Marcus' reign there were natural disasters at home: the flooding of the Tiber, the famine that inaugurated his rule, and the plague that reached Rome with the return of some of Lucius Verus' eastern armies (breaking out in AD 166/7 and continuing for years after). There was the very human threat to Marcus' authority that developed suddenly in the east when Marcus' general, Avidius Cassius, who had accompanied Lucius Verus on the Parthian campaign, announced in Antioch that the emperor had died and proclaimed himself emperor (175). All this is external history, commemorated by the triumph celebrated in 176, a victory column and arch erected in Rome, and on coins, but barely visible in the secret history of the emperor's *Meditations*.

There is another feature of Marcus' reign forgotten by the historian of his life in the *Historia Augusta* (identified as 'Julius Capitolinus'), who gives him the title Philosophus. This was the persecution of the Christians. The Christian, Justin Martyr, wrote an 'apology' for Christianity in a letter directed to Antoninus Pius but also meant for his co-religionists; in it he described Antoninus' son as *verissimus* and a philosopher. This letter, written after AD 155, constitutes Justin's first 'apology' for Christianity. Justin was condemned to death (in AD 165) by Quintus Junius Rusticus, the prefect of Rome and the Stoic who influenced Marcus in his early years (1.7). Justin thus earned the title Martyr. Then there were the persecutions of the Christians in Lyon and Vienne in Gaul and Smyrna in Asia Minor. These were important events during his rule and long remembered by the Christians after his death, but Marcus glances at the Christians in his *Meditations* only once (11.3), and his glance is one of scorn for their 'theatrics'.[3]

Marcus spent most of his life as emperor (AD 161–80) responding to the urgent solicitations of letters and petitions.

Yet he also maintained a very private life. Somehow in the last twenty years of this life of external pressures from every side he found – or made – the time to address himself. The writings now known as his *Meditations* are not so much silent dialogues with a divided self as admonitions and reflections the emperor addressed to himself and to which he seldom replies. Marcus wrote in Greek. In Greek these admonitions came to be entitled *ta eis heauton* – 'addresses to himself'. In these aphorisms, pithy definitions, reflections, reminders, and exhortations, Marcus occasionally urges himself to give up books and reading in favour of the more serious enterprise of self-mastery and self-improvement.[4] This admonition is one of the many that direct the emperor inward. Yet we possess a book that preserves a record of his thoughts as he withdraws from the external pressures and burdens of rule and warfare into himself in order to reassert his rule over himself. This inner retreat is his fortress (as he calls it in 8.48). His *Meditations* are our portal into that *acropolis*.[5]

In one entry of his *Meditations*, he is more explicit about the books he would give up. These were written by the emperor himself: 'No more wandering. You are not likely to read your own jottings, your histories of the ancient Greeks and Romans, your extracts from their literature laid up for your old age' (3.14). Nor, did he think, would others. We know from the first book of the *Meditations* that he had written dialogues as a boy (1.6), but by 'jottings' (the diminutive *hypomnematia*) he might refer to the instalments that now make up the twelve 'books' of his *Meditations*. Some readers have thought so. Marcus uses the word *hypomnemata* to describe the records of Epictetus' lectures (1.7). The more accurate description of the *Meditations* comes from an oration of the contemporary of Julian the 'Apostate' (emperor 361–3), Themistius. As we shall see when we turn to the fame of the *Meditations*, the word 'exhortations' (*parangelmata*) is the first description in later antiquity of the character of the *Meditations*. It is accurate, except it must be added that these exhortations are not to an army but the allocution of the emperor to himself.

The emperor never abandoned his *Meditations*, and the notebooks or scrolls out of which they developed somehow survived his death, unknown, it seems, even to his son and successors. Marcus might have never seriously contemplated publishing his *Meditations*. All that he says about the insubstantiality of fame persuades us that he did not. But he was mistaken about his own fame. We now remember him more as a philosopher than as an emperor and more for his *Meditations* than for his place in history and in the imperial lives of the *Historia Augusta*. But for his contemporaries and for posterity the monuments of his fame were ever present in Rome. He lived on in the imposing images of the emperor depicted on the monumental victory column in Rome that has given its name to the Piazza Colonna.[6] The spiral narrative of this column commemorates the northern campaigns of AD 169–76. On an arch (now destroyed) built to commemorate his victories of 176 he is shown in his campaign on the Danubian frontier mounted on a horse and greeted in awe and reverence by subdued Germans and Sarmatians. (The eight panels from this arch were inserted into the attic of the arch of Constantine.) The most memorable of the images of him as emperor is the mounted equestrian statue that once stood on the Lateran Hill. It was transported to the Capitoline in 1538, where it now attracts crowds of tourists. (The original regilded bronze is housed in the Portico of the Capitoline Museum.) Henry James said of it: 'I doubt if any statue of King or captain in the public places of the World has more to commend it to the general heart.' The emperor grips the bridle in his firm left hand, reminding us that 'the left hand is awkward for most tasks, but has a stronger grip on the bridle than the right' (12.6).

These prominent monuments in Rome project the emperor's public image. It is an image of power and submission to power. There are scenes in the column which show the emperor addressing his troops in a formal *adlocutio*. His *Meditations* too are devoted to power and submission to power: the power of what he calls the 'directing mind' (*to hegemonikon*) over impressions, impulses, desires, and passions. For all the very private entries in the *Meditations* that rudely dismiss the importance of fame, his *Meditations* have best preserved his fame and they have proved useful to those dedicated to his own sustained project of self-improvement and self-mastery, day by day. This inner life is best revealed not on a victory column or the equestrian statue in Rome but by the bust of Marcus that was once displayed in Athens, then still the epicentre of Greek philosophy and a city he visited in AD 178. It is likely that this bust was displayed with the bust of Herodes Atticus, the Athenian who instructed Marcus in Greek rhetoric and who was deeply and dangerously involved in Roman affairs. Of all the portraits of Roman emperors before him that advertised their power, this imperial image is the most introspective. It was broadcast in some 120 copies. It announces a new age of spirituality.

The Literary Character of the Meditations

There is no work quite like the *Meditations* in Greek or Roman philosophical literature. The *Meditations* are unique in three senses of this much abused word. First and foremost is the fact that Marcus silently addresses *himself*. Second, the author of these meditations was the Roman emperor and the emperor wrote in Greek. Most Roman philosophers wrote in Latin. Third, Marcus never seems to have intended for publication the long series of meditations he entered into his journal, although the refined rhetoric of some entries and the ordering of entries within a book often suggest that he had a larger audience in mind. Certainly they attest to his training in Greek rhetoric.

One looks for parallels to the *Meditations* in Greek literature and fails to discover them. Marcus was much impressed by Heraclitus of Ephesus, who, although he speaks of his inner search for himself, does not address himself. Nor are there any exact equivalents to be found in the writings of the French *moralistes*, who sometimes remind their reader of the *Meditations*. François, duc de La Rochefoucauld's *Maximes* are brief, well polished, and very public reflections; Blaise Pascal does not address himself in his *Pensées* (published posthumously in 1670), nor does Nietzsche, the master of aphorism – but not of meditation. The *Meditations* of Marcus Aurelius address a 'self' that has retreated from public view; they are a 'dialogue' in the sense envisaged by Socrates in Plato's *Theae-tetus*, that is, the inner conversation of the soul as it speaks to itself (*Theaetetus* 189E–190A). Impressively, Marcus addresses his soul in *Meditations* 10.1. It is clear from many of the admonitions that this self is divided and that the higher rational 'self' confronts a weaker self that has slipped into attitudes that are unphilosophical and threaten his pursuit of virtue (8.40):

> If you remove your judgement of anything that seems painful, you yourself stand quite immune to pain. 'What self?' Reason. 'But I am not just reason.' Granted. So let your reason cause itself no pain, and if some other part of you is in trouble, it can form its own judgement for itself.

A symptom of the shifting location of the 'self' of the *Meditations* can be found in the inconsistency in Marcus' Greek between the reflexive pronoun 'yourself' and 'himself'. In a remarkable entry Marcus uses the second person plural to describe the effect of tragedy upon the soul; thereby he becomes a part of the audience (11.6.1). The self of the *Meditations* is not entirely enclosed within the book itself. Most often we hear Marcus addressing his weaker nature, but on occasion we can hear the voices of others, the idle prayers to the gods he corrects in 9.40 and the vain lamentations of mourners in 10.36. Occasionally, he addresses an imaginary interlocutor, sometimes rudely (as in 11.15). In Book 11 we can overhear Epictetus (34) and Socrates (39) in brief exchanges with anonymous interlocutors. The emperor even dismisses another voice from without – the spectre of his sense impressions (*phantasiai*) as it breaks in on his solitude (7.17). This is a voice he would silence.

The most rhetorically impressive of his admonitions to himself is the address to his soul that opens Book 10. I give only its beginning (10.1):

> My soul, will you ever be good, simple, individual, bare, brighter than the body that covers you? Will you ever taste the disposition to love and affection? Will you ever be complete and free of need,

missing nothing, desiring nothing live or lifeless for the enjoyment of pleasure?

The chastised soul does not respond.

There is much more than inner dialogue – or soliloquy – to be found in the *Meditations*. There are long reflections on duty, virtue, the place of human rationality in the scheme of the universe, the kinship of all mankind that has its source in human rationality, the cities humans inhabit and the *polis* or 'higher city' or the 'other world' of the universe, the god within and the gods without, the purposefulness and cohesiveness of the universe, Providence, the nature of anger, death, and regret, and epigrams, aphorisms, and quotations that seem to come from a book of commonplaces.[7]

The reader will encounter a great deal of repetition in the *Meditations*. This might strike the reader as a stylistic flaw, but for a philosopher seeking to guide himself repetition is a philosophical virtue. Repetition is a form of spiritual exercise designed to reinforce the main principles of Marcus' philosophy; its purpose is to effect a 'dyeing of the soul' (5.16). Three of the most common imperatives Marcus addresses to himself are: 'Remember', 'Keep in mind', 'Do not forget.'

Readers who come to this book expecting the hardness and austerity of a Stoic will not be disappointed, but they will be surprised by prose that often reads like modern poetry and startled by the vivid illustrations that reveal Marcus' deep appreciation of the beauty and purposefulness of Nature (a word that is properly capitalized). I draw attention to three passages that reveal the poetry and philosophy to be found in the *Meditations*. The first is an excerpt (3.2.1 and 3):

We should also attend to things like these, observing that even the incidental effects of the processes of Nature have their own charm and attraction. Take the baking of bread. The loaf splits open here and there, and those very cracks, in one way a failure of the baker's profession, somehow catch the eye and give particular stimulus to our appetite. Figs likewise burst open at full maturity: and in olives ripened on the tree the very proximity of decay lends a special

beauty to the fruit . . . So any man with a feeling and deeper insight
for the workings of the Whole will find some pleasure in almost
every aspect of their disposition , . he will see a kind of bloom
and fresh beauty in an old woman or an old man . . .

Second (8.51):

'They kill, they cut in pieces, they hunt with curses.' What relevance
has this to keeping your mind pure, sane, sober, just? As if a man
were to come up to a spring of clear, sweet water and curse it – it
would still continue to bubble up water good to drink. He could
throw in mud or dung: in no time the spring will break it down,
wash it away, and take no colour from it. How then can you secure
an everlasting spring and not a cistern? By keeping yourself at all
times intent on freedom – and staying kind, simple, and decent.

Last (8.57):

The sun appears to pour itself down, and indeed its light pours in
all directions, but the stream does not run out. This pouring is
linear extension: that is why its beams are called rays, because they
radiate in extended lines. You can see what a ray is if you observe
the sun's light entering a dark room through a narrow opening. It
extends in a straight line and impacts, so to speak, on any solid
body in its path which blocks passage through the air on the other
side: it settles there and does not slip off or fall.

The reader who has meditated on Marcus Aurelius' *Meditations* will come to appreciate the philosophy expressed in
these seemingly poetic passages. In the first, a deep and hard-
won acceptance of the cycle of birth, growth, and decay reveals
the beauty of every natural stage of life, the rising and baking
of bread, the over-ripeness of a fig or olive, the natural beauty
of an old woman or an old man. Looking to escape from the
brutality of life and the desperate cries of other voices in the
Meditations, 'They kill, they cut in pieces', Marcus retreats
inward to a pure spring that wells up within. Unlike a cistern
that is filled by rain falling from above, a spring takes its source

in the divine rationality that permeates the world.[8] The complex description of the sun's light radiating into a darkened room is clarified in the conclusion of this meditation (continuing 8.57):

> Something similar will be true of the flow and diffusion of the universal mind – not an exhaustible stream but rather a constant radiation. And there will be nothing forceful or violent in its impact on the obstacles it meets: it will not fall off, but will settle there and illuminate what receives it. Anything unreflective will deprive itself of that light.

Perhaps the most sustained analogy to be encountered in the *Meditations* is that made possible by the discovery of the intimate and indissoluble connection between the macrocosm and the microcosm, between the providence, rationality, and benevolence of the Whole and the transitory part of it that we know as Marcus Aurelius.

The Book of Marcus' Meditations

The emperor, who was trained in Greek from his early years, wrote his *Meditations* in Greek. Greek was the language in which philosophy was taught and it was a language that Marcus preferred to Latin for the purpose of withdrawing inwards, meditating and clearing his mind. He might have preferred Greek for his *Meditations* as a means of alienating himself from Latin rhetoric and things Roman. Most of the entries in the *Meditations* were probably written far from Rome, the centre of the universe, in regions where Latin was barely understood and the Latin rhetoric exemplified by Marcus' tutor, Fronto, meant nothing.

We know very little about the dates of composition of the *Meditations*. Occasionally, Marcus expresses his belief that the end of his life is near (2.2, 10.15, 10.36) and he twice states that an intelligent man who has lived to the age of forty can fully comprehend the pattern and monotony of human life (7.49, 11.1.2). This suggests that the *Meditations* were written after he became emperor at the age of thirty-nine. We know from the titles to Books 2 and 3 that some of the entries were written in the northern campaigns of the early 170s on the frontiers of the Roman empire.[9]

In the letter to Lucius Gellius to whom he conveyed his records of Epictetus' lectures (*diatribai*), the historian Arrian of Nicomedia made a distinction between his transcription of the lectures of Epictetus at which he was present and which he preserved in something close to stenographic accuracy and the 'compositions' of other authors. Like the Roman Stoic, Musonius Rufus, and like Socrates, Epictetus did not commit his philosophy to writing. The same cannot be said of the *Meditations* of Marcus Aurelius. The long series of admonitions, aphorisms, and reflections that now make up the twelve 'books' of the *Meditations* were entered into a journal as the emperor made the time to set them down. They are so personal and inwardly directed – and at times incomprehensible – that it is difficult to imagine that he dictated them to his Greek secretary, Apollonius. An example of their dense privacy is the entry: 'A black character, an effeminate, unbending character, the character of a brute or dumb animal: infantile, stupid, fraudulent, coarse, mercenary, despotic' (4.28). We do not know who the emperor is describing.

As they have come down to us, the *Meditations* are not a mere transcript of the entries from Marcus' journals. Like his own life, these entries show signs of careful composition as they are redacted as his *Meditations*.[10] The first book of the *Meditations* is unlike any of the eleven books that follow. It is the carefully considered statement of the emperor's last will and testament. It constitutes the final testimonial of his gratitude to those who had directed, influenced, and improved his life. The beginning of the *Meditations* is the fitting conclusion of Marcus' life, not as an emperor but as a philosopher. He begins by recording his gratitude to his grandfather, Marcus Annius Verus, to his natural father (of the same name), and to his mother, Domitia Lucilla. He concludes by expressing his gratitude to and admiration for his adoptive father and uncle, Antoninus Pius, and finally his gratitude towards the gods.[11] There are many signs of arrangement or composition in the twelve books of the *Meditations*, especially in the first and last books. But the impression given by the manuscripts and printed editions of the *Meditations* now displayed in twelve books and divided into 488 'chapters' (some long; some of a single sentence) is misleading. 'Chapters' are better thought of as journal entries. 'Journal' is an accurate term to describe books or entries written 'at break of day' (5.1) or 'first thing in the morning' (2.1).

The pleasure of meditating on the *Meditations* resembles the challenge and austere pleasure of reading the epigrams and pronouncements that survive from the book of Heraclitus. There are 127 of these.[12] The challenge of reading them is like the challenge – and pleasure – of reading the *Meditations* of Marcus Aurelius. This can be expressed in the words E. M. Forster chose as the epigraph for his *Howards End*: 'Only connect . . .' Connecting was the project of the emperor, and it is now the challenge of his reader.

Marcus the Emperor of the Meditations

In the private entries of his *Meditations*, Marcus Aurelius Antoninus does not conceal from himself the fact that he is the Roman emperor and one in a long line of emperors. His insistent demand for rational analysis and stripping his human and material environment down to its essentials reveals an essential part of his character. Scattered through his *Meditations* we encounter reflections on his duty to serve, as 'a male, mature in years, a statesman, a Roman, a ruler' (3.5). This 'service' is subsumed under his more fundamental duty as a rational human being to benefit and tolerate – perhaps the more difficult task – his fellow human beings. He never reflects on the many difficult questions of policy that confronted him during his nearly twenty years as emperor. He never names any of the contemporaries who played important roles in his armies or administration;[13] nor does he allude to the serious threats posed by the revolt of his general Avidius Cassius in 175, whose head was brought to him as proof of his defeat. There is only the

most oblique recognition of his campaigns on the northern
frontiers begun in AD 169.

Typical of his philosophical attitude towards his military
career is the analogy: 'A spider is proud to trap a fly. Men are
proud of their own hunting – a hare, a sprat in the net, boars,
bears, Sarmatian prisoners. If you examine their motives, are
they all not bandits?' (10.10). Another more trenchant analogy
is set down in 8.34: 'If you have ever seen a severed hand or
foot, or a head cut off and lying some way away from the rest
of the body – analogous is what someone does to himself, as
far as he can, when he will not accept his lot and severs himself
from society or does some unsocial act.' As emperor, Marcus,
soon to be recognized as Germanicus, witnessed the beheading
of captive Germans. The two panels (LXI and LXVI) showing
this punishment are the grimmest scenes on his column in
Rome. What is most impressive about the emperor as philosopher are the analogies or images (*eikones*) his own brutal
experience as *imperator* (or military commander) suggested to
him.[14] The emperor who bore this heavy weight of honorific
titles was well aware of his predecessors and of Julius Caesar,
whose cognomen, Caesar, became the equivalent of emperor.
Marcus Aurelius mentions most of the emperors from Augustus
to Antoninus Pius, whom he admired more than any of his
predecessors.[15] But it was not from Rome or the military camp
that he looked at the empire and the court of the emperor. It
was from within the heights of his inner fortress.

Marcus also reflects on his own role as emperor. A deep
contempt for the recipients of his benefactions is tersely
expressed in one of the epigrams he quotes (itself a quotation)
in Book 7: 'A king's lot: to do good and be damned' (36). And
yet the emperor cautions himself not to complain of life in the
palace. It is no obstacle to his own virtue.[16] He reminds himself of the dangers of his station by inventing a new Greek
verb: 'Take care not to be Caesarified, or dyed in purple' (6.30).
As for the purple dye that distinguished his senatorial order, he
reduces it to 'the hair of a sheep soaked in shell-fish blood'
(6.13; cf. 9.36). In his meditations on the brevity and

insignificance of human life, he often turns to the 'great men' of the past. Once he looks back on the court of Augustus: 'wife, daughter, grandsons, step-sons, sister, Agrippa, relatives, household, friends, . . . doctors, diviners: an entire court dead' (8.31). In a similar exercise he imagines the contemporary equivalents of known but vanished figures of the past: 'when you see Severus, picture Crito or Xenophon; and when you look at yourself, picture one of the Caesars' (10.31). We do not know which of the fourteen Caesars who had preceded him he would have chosen, but the one that comes immediately to mind is his adoptive father, Antoninus Pius.

As seen from this perspective, the imperial court appears as an absurd and repetitive pageant, the same scene, the same play, 'just a different cast' (10.27). Of all the titles he had gained as emperor, those that meant most to him he lists as: 'good, decent, truthful; in mind clear, cooperative, and independent' (10.8). These titles do not match the four canonical virtues of Greek thought (to which we will turn), nor are they the virtues advertised by the Roman emperors. Only once does Marcus mention the city of Rome (6.44). In the entry that concludes his *Meditations*, he begins: 'Mortal man, you have lived as a citizen in this great city' (12.36). The city of Marcus' meditations was his provident Stoic universe, not the city and empire he prudently ruled over for what was, in his view, a brief moment in time.

The Stoic Emperor

The word 'Stoic' has two meanings: it describes both a member of the school of philosophy Zeno founded in the Painted Stoa at the approach to the ancient Agora of Athens and a person who represses his emotions and desires, is indifferent to pleasure or pain, and is enduring. Marcus Aurelius was trained by Stoics in his early years. As a boy of twelve he adopted the 'Greek way of life' and wore a thick cloak and slept on the floor. For his Greek training Marcus had Tandasis and Marcianus to thank (1.6). By 'Greek training' he means wearing a rough cloak and sleeping on the ground, something from which his mother had to dissuade him,[17] This is 'philosophical' training, not that of a university. His adoptive father, Antoninus Pius, was a stoic in this sense; Marcus Aurelius was both a Stoic and stoic.

He gained the title of Philosopher after his death. But how could the reader of his *Meditations* tell that he was a Stoic?[18] Throughout its long history in the ancient world, Stoicism was recognized not by the title 'Stoic' or by a strict allegiance to one of the four principal schools of philosophy, but by a kind of toughness and austerity, not to say an inhuman coldness and indifference to what other humans valued most: family, wealth, reputation, power, and even health. What attracted Zeno of Citium from Cyprus to Athens (in about 313 BC) was not its reputation at the end of the fourth century as the home of Platonists and Aristotelians; it was the example of Socrates, who had been executed by Athens in 399 BC. When Zeno arrived in Athens he made contact with Polemo, then head of Plato's Academy – of whom it was said that he never altered the set expression of his face – and, more importantly, with the Cynic Crates of Thebes, who himself emulated Socrates. Crates' master, Diogenes of Sinope, the originator of the Cynic movement, was styled 'Socrates gone mad' (*Sokrates maino-menos*).

Throughout the history of the Stoa the emulation of Socrates generated the moral impetus to the way of thought and action distinctive of the Stoa. We find it in Epictetus (*c.* AD 55–133) and in Marcus Aurelius in the last century of its prominence. Socrates was held up as the Stoic ideal of the sage (*sophos*). His unflinching commitment to the virtues subsumed under the word *arete* – courage, justice, prudent self-control, and practical intelligence (and an unusual kind of piety) – provided a stimulus to a rigorous reflection on human nature, the soul, impulses, passions, judgement and rationality, and the intelligible and thus the intelligent ordering of the world (*kosmos*) in which men lived. Zeno's sense of the indissoluble connection between the order of the human microcosm with a provident and con-trolling macrocosm led him to divide and unite the scope of philosophical inquiry into the concentric spheres of physics, ethics, and logic.[19] These divisions are united in a single enterprise.

The Stoics themselves were not united on every matter of doctrine, but they were one in their conception of divine Providence and a divinely established hierarchy: the great ladder that reached from the inanimate to the animate, from the animal to the human and rational, and, finally, from the human to the supreme rationality of the divine. The human soul too exhibited like gradations. As does any animal, the human animal as it develops gains a sense of itself (*oikeiosis* or, in the first sense of this term, 'proprioception'), that is, a manifestation of its instinct for self-preservation. In time this sense of the self extends to others, as it reaches beyond the herd instinct to an awareness that all human beings are kindred in their rationality. This rationality is the connection between what is divine within the individual human being and the divine fire without, that transforms this unique world of ours into a unified Whole in which everything has its appropriate role and fulfils its duty, and nothing happens by accident or is wasted.

The relation between human rationality and the 'directing principle' of reason is tight. As humans, we are presented with the raw data of sense impressions that come from objects without or from within our bodies (*phantasiai* and *hormai*). Some impressions are 'clear and distinct'. They are capable of moving us to pursuit or avoidance and they stir our passions in all of their variety. Our capacity to reason allows us to form judgements concerning these impressions and either to assent to them or to reject them. In this process of constant evaluation there is only one standard of good and evil: virtue and vice. One of the most important injunctions for a Stoic was to 'live in *agreement* with Nature'. The phase 'in agreement with' (*homologoumenos*) is significant; by Nature the Stoics meant the highest form of human nature – Reason (*Logos*). By 'agreement' they meant a participation in and conformity with a higher principle of rationality.

Falling beneath the high standard of the Stoic 'sage' in the gradation of values are the objects most humans either value and embrace or shun and despise: the indifferents (*adiaphora*).

But for some Stoics these 'indifferents' could be ranked, as the Stoics stepped down from the high pedestal of absolute and uncompromising virtue. Although health is not necessary to virtue, it is preferable to illness. It often seems that two of the Socratic 'paradoxes' are given new life by the Stoics. The first of these paradoxes is that virtue is knowledge; the second is its corollary: that no human being errs willingly, that is, knowingly. To know is to will. If the agent knows, there can be no weakness of will (*akrasia*).

There is much on which the Stoics disagreed, or on which they placed differing values. But in the third generation of the school in Athens, Stoic doctrine began to take a fixed form in the writings of Chrysippus. It was said that 'if there were no Chrysippus, there would have been no Stoa.'[20] Following on the beginnings established by Zeno (335–263 BC) and Cleanthes (c.331–232 BC), his follower and successor as head of his school, Chrysippus (c.280–207 BC) was credited with establishing an all-encompassing Stoic orthodoxy. That Zeno's follower Ariston of Chios embraced a strict conception of virtue and rejected the gradation of indifferents as 'preferred' or 'not preferred' does not mean that he created a schism in Stoic philosophy. Not every Stoic could commit to Zeno's theory that during regular intervals this world would be consumed by fire, the doctrine of *ekpyrosis*. Not every Stoic was as interested in language and the forms of propositional logic as was Chrysippus, and no Stoic wrote as many books as he did (the total of his books is given as 705). Indeed, to qualify as a Stoic an adherent of the school did not have to write a single line of philosophy. Nor was Stoicism confined to Athens. Like Epicureanism, it moved west.

This was true of the first phase of Stoic philosophy in Rome. In the late Republic two powerful figures were known as Stoics: Cato of Utica, who committed suicide in 48 BC rather than yield to Caesar, and Brutus (the 'tyrannicide') who committed suicide after the defeat of his army at Philippi in 42. Brutus is known to have written ethical treatises, but his wife, Porcia, might have been the more devout Stoic.[21] The Stoic tradition continues in Cicero, who was murdered by Mark Antony in late

43. Although he listed towards Academic philosophy, Cicero espoused Stoic doctrines in his *On the Nature of the Gods* (in Book 2 the spokesman for the Stoics is Balbus) and in the moral guide he wrote for his son, Marcus, *On Duties*, which owes a great deal to the Stoic philosopher Panaetius. He also made Cato spokesman for the conception of the highest good in his *De Finibus* ('On Ends'). Cicero's correspondent Posidonius of Apamea in Syria (*c.*135–51 BC) was the greatest Stoic of his age and one whose cosmological thought is most congenial to the outlook of the *Meditations*. Seneca of the *Letters to Lucilius* and the so-called Dialogues (*Dialogi*) and Lucan of the epic on the civil war between Caesar and Pompey (the *Pharsalia*) follow. They were both forced to commit suicide in 65 by Nero after he had discovered the conspiracy of Piso. Musonius Rufus, Thrasea Paetus, Helvidius Priscus and Dio of Prusa (whose Cynicism combined with Stoicism) were later Stoics.

Marcus Aurelius the Philosopher

Marcus was recognized as a philosopher by his contemporaries and later generations, but his *Meditations* do not read like a work of 'philosophy'. In them he does not recognize the tripartite division of philosophical inquiry into physics, logic, and ethics, and logic is almost entirely absent from the *Meditations* as a subject of reflection. Because he addresses himself, Marcus does not feel compelled to set out arguments to confute, convince, or convert others. Rather, in addressing himself, he seeks to review and confirm his fundamental beliefs about Providence, virtue, and duty. His response to his inner dialogues is not to prolong the conversation in quibbles or debate. His goal is not victory in debate with himself, but a reformed and confirmed attitude directing action. And action or *praxis* is one of the most important meanings of *philosophia* in Greek (2.17.2).

Marcus is unmistakably a Stoic, yet he never proclaims his allegiance to Stoicism, nor does he depend on the authority of the founders of his school to support his convictions. As emperor, Marcus concerned himself with the four philosophical

schools in Athens (the Academics, Peripatetics, Epicureans, and
Stoics) and treated and funded them all on an equal footing.[22]
His philosophy was never sectarian. On one occasion, he even
speaks of the Stoics as if he were not a Stoic himself (5.10).[23]
He invokes doctrines already established by Stoic philosophers
(and by Socrates), which he had long accepted as valid (4.3).
Never does he appeal to the authority of another philosopher
to support his fundamental beliefs. His beliefs (*dogmata*) are
ready at hand to effect an inward therapy and to confront an
emergency, like the ready instruments of the surgeon (3.13).
Remarkably, when he does refer to philosophers, he names
Plato, the founder of what was in his day the Academy, but not
Zeno, who founded the Stoa when he moved from Cyprus to
Athens in 313 BC, or Zeno's successor, Cleanthes (head of
the school in Athens from 263–232 BC). He twice refers to
Chrysippus, the Stoic who did most to develop and fix the
essential doctrines of the school, but not for any philosophical
doctrine.[24] The philosopher he was taught to admire by Rusticus
was Epictetus, a Greek slave who lived in exile from Rome and
taught in the small town of Nicopolis in Epirus. Epictetus was
a Stoic, but perhaps deeper down he was a Socratic. It is clear
that, on occasion, when Marcus refers to Socrates, his Socrates
was Epictetus' Socrates.[25]

Another philosopher who influenced him decisively was
Severus, who had the reputation of belonging to the school of
Aristotle. We have met him as the contemporary counterpart
to Crito or Xenophon. He is remembered gratefully by the
emperor, who learned much from him: 'love of family, love of
truth, love of justice; to have come by his help to understand
Thrasea, Helvidius, Cato, Dio, Brutus; to have conceived the
idea of a balanced constitution, a commonwealth based on
equality and freedom of speech, and of a monarchy which
values above all the liberty of the subject' (1.14.1). It is remarkable that the young Marcus was brought to admire figures who
were devoted to the Roman Republic and who emerged as fierce
opponents of Julius Caesar and the imperial order Marcus was
destined to maintain. Cato and Brutus were both regarded by
their contemporaries as philosophers: Cato a Stoic and Brutus a

philosopher attracted to the Academy of Antiochus of Ascalon. Thrasea Paetus was the admirer of Cato and, when he was condemned by Nero in AD 66, he too committed suicide. Helvidius Priscus was his son-in-law. His opposition to the emperor Vespasian brought about his exile and execution, perhaps in AD 75. Dio is not, I think, Dio of Syracuse, the associate of Plato, but Dio Chrysostom, the philosopher and orator, who was exiled from Rome in the reign of Domitian (emperor AD 81–96).

One of the remarkable things about Marcus is his generosity as a philosopher. Unlike Lucretius at the end of the Republic and unlike Marcus' contemporary, the Epicurean Diogenes of Oenoanda (the mountaintop city in Lycia), the emperor did not engage in corrosive polemic with rival philosophical views of the world, although, as we shall see, he was well aware of the philosophical divide that separated Stoics and Epicureans. Of the philosophers with whom he displays a deep affinity, the first and foremost is the slave and exile Epictetus. Then there is Socrates, who stood out for the Stoics as their most ready example of the sage (*sapiens*) and who had already been assimilated into the philosophical personality of Epictetus, just as he would become assimilated in the *Meditations* into the personality of the emperor.[26] And, surprisingly perhaps, there are many striking indications of the influence of Heraclitus, whom Marcus absorbed into his own Stoic view of the world (4.46), as had other Stoics before him:

> Always remember Heraclitus: 'The death of earth is the birth of water; the death of water is the birth of air; the death of air is fire, and back again.' Remember too his image of the man who forgets his way home; his saying that men are at odds with their most constant companion, the Reason which governs all things; that their everyday experience takes them by surprise; that we must not act or speak as if asleep, and sleep brings the illusion of speech and action; and that we should not be like children with their parents, simply accepting what we are told.[27]

Given Marcus' avowed tendency to assimilate and make a part of his character whatever fosters his rationality and self-control, we cannot be at all sure that he is reproducing the actual language of Heraclitus. But a number of things in the thought and art of Heraclitus appealed to him: Heraclitus' conception of a universal rationality embodied in the *Logos* of the universe and the rationality of human beings; his awareness of a cyclical pattern discernible within change; the river of change that seems to carry everything before it, but is in fact a part of the orderly transformations of the universe;[28] the unnatural estrangement of the individual from what all men share in common; and the aphoristic style that gave Heraclitus the nickname 'the dark'. At times Marcus can be dark himself (as in 4.28).

As was the Stoic Seneca before him, Marcus was generous to Epicurus, and he had so deeply absorbed Epicurus' heroic attitude towards death that he can quote one of his letters from memory – inaccurately to the letter, but faithfully to his message. Indeed, he owes a debt to Epicurus for his injunction to withdraw into himself.[29] The philosophical generosity of Marcus Aurelius is exactly parallel to his tolerance and openness to his fellow men. Its explanation is to be discovered in his sense that all human beings share in a common rationality and that this rationality establishes the human community he describes as 'the city of Zeus' (4.23). This community is not divided into philosophical sects.

Microcosm and Macrocosm

Yet Marcus remains firmly a Stoic in one fundamental conviction. He occupied one side of the great philosophical divide of his age. He tersely expresses the alternatives facing him: 'Revisit the alternatives – providence or atoms – and the many indications that the universe is a kind of community' (4.3.2). He returns to these alternative views time and time again. These alternatives pit the Epicureans against the Stoics, as well as the Academic and Peripatetic philosophers who were united in their commitment to teleology. Against the materialist view that this world and all other aggregates of matter are the product of an infinite number of atoms moving blindly in infinite space the Stoics held a conviction that everything that happens in this universe with its single inhabited world is coherent, providential, and serves some purpose in Nature's grand design: 'Either an ordered universe, or a stew of mixed ingredients, yet still coherent order. Otherwise how could a sort of private order subsist within you, if there is disorder in the Whole?' (4.27). 'Stew' (*kukeon*) is a word we find in a philosopher whose thought and aphoristic style impressed Marcus deeply, and he seems to have appreciated the underlying implication of cosmological order in a saying of Heraclitus. Marcus adapts it to describe the cosmic 'stew' produced by the transient and fortuitous combination of atoms. The word the Stoics used to describe their unique world was the Whole (*Holon*) or the Universe (*Kosmos*), that is, the order implied by the word *kosmos* in Greek. By polemical contrast, the Epicurean Lucretius described this world as 'this heap of matter' (*On the Nature of Things*, 5.416).

Marcus' outer world was made up of four elements: earth, water, air, and fire. His human constitution was made up of earth, water, air, and fire; his soul of air and his mind of fire. This fire which can transform into its own element anything it encounters is vividly evoked in the first entry of Book 4. It is both internal and external. The inner fire of the mind connects with the intelligent fire of the world that can design and has created a scale of being rising from the inanimate to the animate and from animal impulse and instinct to human rationality. What is truly divine about a human being in the great scale of nature is what he sometimes likes to refer to as 'the very god (*daimon*) that is seated in you' (3.6.2). Human rationality, or the controlling principle he refers to as the 'directing mind' (*to hegemonikon*), is a part of the directing mind of the *kosmos* that brings elements together and dissolves them again. At times, Marcus contemplates without commitment the possibility that the world will be consumed in this divine fire (the process of *ekpyrosis*).[30]

The other metaphor that reveals the connection between the individual and the universe of which he is a member is that of the city. This metaphor projects the ideal unity and organization of human cities onto the universe in which men are citizens of the 'city of Zeus'. Zeus, or the Roman Jupiter, favoured the pious emperor and Rome. One of the most providential events of his campaign against the Quadi on the Danube was Jupiter's answer to the Athenian prayer he refers to in *Meditations* ('Rain, dear Zeus', 5.7). It is depicted on his victory column (panel XVI) and shows Jupiter (or the Mysterious Rain God) who, in answer to his prayer, is sending the torrential rains that overwhelm the enemy forces. The city of Zeus makes its last appearance in the *Meditations* as Marcus takes leave of his journals and, it seems, his life (12.36).

The city of Zeus is the expression of an optimism not always present in the *Meditations*. There are passages that come close to articulating the belief that 'all is for the best in this the best of all possible worlds' (e.g. 12.5). Voltaire attempted to satirize this Stoic (and Catholic) optimism in his caustic poem on the Lisbon earthquake (1756) and *Candide* (1757). The Stoic ideal of the City is a construct that Lucretius and Diogenes of Oenoanda were bent on demolishing by showing how improvident Nature was in her provisions for human beings. Lucretius' condemnation of Nature's providence – *tanta stat praedita culpa* ('she stands convicted of so great a fault', *On the Nature of Things*, 2.181) – was Voltaire's favourite phrase from Latin poetry. But, as we shall now witness, this apparent optimism can give way to a disgust for the world.

Stripping down

For Marcus philosophy was the therapy of the soul and he practises a variety of therapies on his soul. In this sense, his *Meditations* are his medications. One of these therapies is described by the technical term *merismos* (2.12). The word means a breaking into parts or dissection. Parts (*mere*) and limbs (*mele*) are very much on Marcus' mind (as in 7.13). Like Plato before him, Marcus is convinced that one of the projects

of philosophy is to analyse the world of men and matter into
its parts; and then to reach a conception of the Whole of which
they are parts – or members. At times, this exercise can have
the effect of alienating us from the things we value most as
humans. We have already glimpsed it at work (6.13):

> How good it is, when you have roast meat or suchlike foods before
> you, to impress on your mind that this is the dead body of a fish,
> this the dead body of a bird or pig; and again, that the Falernian
> wine is the mere juice of grapes, and your purple-edged robe simply
> the hair of a sheep soaked in shell-fish blood! And in sexual inter-
> course that it is no more than the friction of a membrane and a
> spurt of mucus ejected.

In a similar entry he exploits his conception that we can only
live in (if not for) the present moment by analysing the pleasure
of watching a dance by breaking it down into movements that
become jerks as they are arrested frame by frame and music as
it is frozen note by note (11.2). A string of such reflections can
be threaded by the reader of the *Meditations*. As we come to
Marcus' therapy for the 'frenzy of renown',[31] we shall see how
he attempts to make the Roman desire for eternal renown seem
Lilliputian.

There are other therapies in Marcus' repertoire of spiritual
exercises that are not as difficult to accept as his radical dis-
secting and 'denuding' of human experience. One is the analysis
of experience into what is material and what is causal, a distinction that goes back to Aristotle's theory of four-fold causality
stated most fully in *Metaphysics* A. By its concentration on
causality and matter and of the active and the passive, it is an
analysis that encourages us to look into the mind and motivation of other active agents.[32]

The most important of the therapies of the *Meditations* is the
project of withdrawing into the self or, in our sense of the
word, 'meditation'. Seneca's words for this were 'withdraw into
yourself' (*secede in te ipsum, Letters to Lucilius*, 25.6). Marcus'
first full expression of this comes in the entry 4.3:[33]

Men seek retreats for themselves – in the country, by the sea, in the hills – and you yourself are particularly prone to this yearning. But all this is quite unphilosophic, when it is open to you, at any time you want, to retreat into yourself. No retreat offers someone more quiet and relaxation than that into his own mind, especially if he can dip into thoughts there which put him at immediate and complete ease: and by ease I simply mean a well-ordered life. So constantly give yourself this retreat, and renew yourself. The doctrines you will visit there should be few and fundamental, sufficient at one meeting to wash away all your pain and send you back free of resentment at what you must rejoin.

This is, I think, the most impressive of all the entries of the *Meditations*. But it has many rivals. It opens to us the 'inner citadel' into which Marcus retreated during his northern campaigns beyond the Danube, and it encourages us to find such a retreat within ourselves.

The Struggle for Virtue

For Plato and the Greek philosophers who followed him there were four cardinal virtues. We have noticed them in passing. They are: prudent self-control (*sophrosune*), practical intelligence (*phronesis*), courage (*andreia*), and justice (*dikaiosune*). Marcus embraced and exhibited all of these, but only once does he list these four virtues as a tetrad. The virtues to which he aspired were more numerous than these. He lists some of these in the address to his soul that opens Book 10. He wanted to be: 'good, simple, individual, bare, brighter than the body that covers you . . . [disposed to] love and affection . . . free of need, missing nothing, desiring nothing' (10.1). The virtue of honesty, truthfulness, and a courageous recognition of reality (*aletheia*) combine into one of the most important of the virtues of the *Meditations*, integrity. These virtues connect with Marcus' deep sense of responsibility to and tolerance for his fellow human beings. Some of these and many another[34] would strike the public who handled the coins proclaiming the manifold virtues of Marcus' rule as surpassing strange. Set against the public pronouncements of the virtues of Marcus' reign, ruled by Divine Providence (*Providentia Deorum*) and the blessings of Generosity (*Liberalitas*), Fairness (*Aequitas*), Integrity (*Fides*), Justice (*Justitia*), Safety and Security (*Salus* and *Securitas*) are the virtues Marcus aspired to as a philosopher. These private virtues might have seemed as strange to the public through whose hands his coinage passed as the virtues of Christ's Sermon on the Mount (Matthew 5:1–10) would have seemed foreign to Aristotle.

Marcus represents attainment of these virtues as a contest (*agon*), like a wrestling or a boxing match.[35] But his opponents are not external to him. In his conception of his inner soul he recognized a struggle between reason and the raw images (*phantasiai*), appetites, passions, impulses, and ambitions of his other 'self'. It was up to him and his 'directing mind' to weigh them and to assent to them and pursue them, or to reject and avoid them. The desire for sleep (but not for sex), the temptations of anger, the attractions of repute and fame are all threatening rivals to his victory over himself. And in these meditations, the self gains an absolute autonomy as Marcus asserts that 'all is as thinking makes it so' (most forcefully in 12.8 and 12.26). That is, it is not the world of matter or our bodies and their desires and pleasures or their pains and griefs or the opinion of others that control us; it is reason that by its careful judgement creates an autonomy of the rational self.

The Stoics held up a paradigm or ideal of the philosopher in complete, autonomous, and godlike control of himself. This was the sage (*sophos* in Greek, *sapiens* in Latin). This sage makes no appearance in the journals of Marcus Aurelius. The closest we come to discovering him (and he is always a male) is in the tenth book of the *Meditations*, when the emperor contemplates the death of others and obliquely his own death (10.36):

> No one is so fortunate as not to have standing round his death-bed some people who welcome the fate coming on him. Was he the earnest sage? Then maybe there will be someone at his final moment saying to himself: 'We can breathe again now, rid of this

schoolmaster. He was not hard on any one of us, but I could feel his silent criticism of us all'

Marcus does not identify himself with the famous sage. But his words 'the earnest sage' are ironic, precisely because they represent the judgement of others. No man can pass such judgement on himself.

Fame

There are two subjects of admonition that are recurrent in the *Meditations*: anger and the desire for fame. They connect in as much as both anger and fame surrender an individual's autonomy to the offence or judgement of others. Anger represents an 'involuntary spasm' and a momentary lapse of reason (2.10). It severs the rational bond that unites all human beings (2.1 and 16). Fame, of course, should mean nothing to the philosopher who focuses his attention on the present. For Marcus, it is only the present moment distinct from the 'abyss' of the past and future that should concern us. The past and future lie beyond our control. But there is an unsettling contrast in Marcus' meditations between his concentration on the present moment (*to akeriaion*) and his larger conception of his life as a path on which his reason, the gods, and those who influenced him in early life directed him. It is also discordant with his frequent presentation of his life as a play scripted by Providence.[36] His disdain for fame does not sit comfortably with his attachment to the past. All the actors in the play of history have, of course, disappeared, but in his *Meditations* Marcus constantly brings them back to the stage on which they had acted. They are mere 'names' and 'legends' (*mythoi* in Greek): 'All things fade and quickly turn to myth: quickly too utter oblivion drowns them' (4.33). But he keeps them alive. He even memorializes the names of slaves who would have remained unknown to us were it not for his mention of them.

One of the exercises that served Marcus as an antidote against the frenzy for renown, both among one's fellows and in future generations, is to take a distant view of our small,

inconsequential world. It is an exercise that we find in its most
dramatic form in the conclusion of Cicero's *Republic* (written
in 51 BC). Cicero has one of the speakers of this dialogue,
Publius Cornelius Aemilianus Africanus, describe a dream in
which his grandfather appeared to him. From the distant Milky
Way the great Africanus pointed his grandson to the tiny and
spotted globe of the earth. From this vantage the centre stage
of the world seems very small, and human fame a passing
shadow (*Republic*, Book 6). At times Marcus exhorts himself
to look down on human life from a height; at times he urges
himself to look up at the stars or sun, and once he speaks of
his kinship with the stars.[37] Looking down, the earth appears
as 'a mere point in space' (8.21).

The history of the preservation, publication and fame of
Marcus Aurelius' *Meditations* goes beyond the scope of this
Introduction, but something needs to be said of the fame the
emperor despised. The fitting conclusion of any treatment of
the *Meditations* can only be a repeated reading of the *Meditations*. One of his Greek readers (perhaps Simokattes Theo-
phylaktos in the early seventh century) wrote as a codicil to the
noble conclusion of Book 12 an eight-line poem that summar-
izes his reading of the book (in the Vatican codex and also in
the Palatine Anthology, 15.23):

> If you want to gain control of pain,
> open up this blessed book
> and enter deep within it.
> Its wealth of philosophy will bring you
> to see with ease all the future,
> the present, and the past,
> and you will see that joy and distress
> have no more power than smoke.

Smoke reflects one of the last entries of Book 12 (33).

Although Marcus' subjects bestowed upon him the title
'philosopher', the emperor's fame as a philosopher hung on the
survival of a set of meditations of which none of his subjects could have been aware. Julian the 'Apostate' (emperor

AD 361–3) recalls the emperor favourably in his satire, *The Caesars*. He might actually reflect the language of *Meditations* 10.1 in his description of Marcus, but he makes no mention of the *Meditations*. It was in a speech of the orator Themistius, Julian's contemporary and fervent supporter in his doomed attempt to restore his empire to paganism, that we find the first clear reference to the *Meditations*. In an address of 364 to the eastern emperor Valens, Themistius speaks of them as Marcus' 'exhortations' (*parangelmata*). From then on and for more than a millennium, the western emperor who wrote in Greek and died on the Danube was remembered only in the Greek east. Arethas, Deacon of Patras and then Archbishop of Caesarea (c.AD 850–935), writes to a colleague that he owned a tattered copy of the *Meditations*. Arethas preserved the emperor's fame as a philosopher by having the book copied, not for his correspondent, Demetrios of Herakleia, but for himself. A selfish and wise decision. The *Meditations* were known and cited by the commentators on Lucian, Marcus' brilliant contemporary, who refers to Marcus as 'the god' after his death. In his marginal comments we find Arethas engaged in vitriolic observations on his author. Then the Byzantine dictionary known as the Suda (of the late tenth century) contains entries taken from the *Meditations*.[38]

Providentially, a copy of the *Meditations* reached the west with the flood of learned refugees forced to leave Constantinople by the pressure of the Ottoman Turks. This manuscript seems to have been destroyed after it served as the basis for the first printed edition of the *Meditations* (Zurich, 1559). It was conveyed from Heidelberg to Zurich and the printing firm of Andreas Gesner by a Greek, Michael Toxites. The only nearly full manuscript of the *Meditations* that survives is that in the Vatican Library. Here in Rome, surviving but diminished in a corrupt manuscript, the emperor who was Pontifex Maximus has returned to his capital.

Men of power have naturally identified with the emperor and sought inner strength by withdrawing into the inner citadel of his *Meditations*. Frederick the Great, Cecil Rhodes, and William Jefferson Clinton (himself a Rhodes scholar) are three

of these. Marcus Aurelius also exerted a powerful spell over
two Christian intellectuals of the nineteenth century, Matthew
Arnold and Ernest Renan. Both were powerfully attracted by
the deep religious sentiment they detected in the *Meditations*.
Renan's *Marcus Aurelius and the End of the Ancient World*
(Paris, 1882) came as the last of the seven books he wrote on
the early history of the Christian Church. At the end of this
history, he composed an epitaph for the pagan world and the
emperor who died on 17 March AD 180: 'This day, as sorrowful
as it was for philosophy and civilization, was a bright day for
Christianity.' Arnold, who, like Renan, was much absorbed
by the Christian martyrs of Marcus' reign, detected an affinity
between the persecutor and the Christians he or his magistrates
persecuted. In the last glimpse of him that Arnold allows us,
we see Marcus at the end of his life 'stretching out his arms for
something beyond – *tendentem manus ripae ulterioris amore*'
('out of love for the further shore'). This is a quotation from
Virgil, *Aeneid* 6.314, but the further shore Arnold had in mind
is not the shore across the infernal river of Acheron but the
shore of the light of Christianity. It is appropriate that, since
the restorations effected by the architect Domenico Fontana in
1589, the apostle Paul should stand on the summit of the
Aurelian column in Rome, replacing Marcus and his wife
Faustina.

Marcus has been of compelling interest to writers too.
Anthony, the third Earl of Shaftesbury, cites (in Greek) Marcus'
own reflections on the moral effect of comedy (11.6) in his
advice to an author in *Characteristics of Men, Manners,
Opinions, Times* published in 1732; he calls him 'one of the
wisest, and most serious of antient authors' (I, ix). Goethe
mentions him in his correspondence; Water Pater involves him
prominently in his *Marius the Epicurean* (1882), as Marius
serves as secretary to the Stoic emperor; and Marguerite
Yourcenar makes him the addressee of the letter that develops
into her *Memoirs of Hadrian* (1951). As for others who read
the *Meditations* in time of war, and especially the young men
who fought World War I, we have no census of how many
retreated into Marcus' inner citadel in the trenches. There were

surely some, and it is perhaps to them that Marcus spoke most movingly as he addressed himself on campaign on the northern frontiers of the empire and withdrew into his inner fortress.

Diskin Clay

NOTES

1   This is his description of himself in 3.5. Compare the entry in 7.7, with the additional characterization of Marcus as a soldier assigned to his post. The reader looking to connect the themes of the entries that make up the *Meditations* should first consult Martin Hammond's very helpful notes to this excellent translation. Of this translation I can say, with Matthew Arnold (speaking of Jeremy Collier's translation): 'the acquaintance with a man like Marcus Aurelius is such an imperishable benefit, that one can never lose a peculiar sense of obligation to the man who confers it.'

2   *The Decline and Fall of the Roman Empire*, ed. J. B. Bury (London, 1909), 1.85–6. In Bury's edition the map on the inside front cover shows the extent of the Roman empire at the date of Marcus Aurelius' death.

3   For Marcus and the Christians, see the translator's note to 11.3 and A. R. Birley, *Marcus Aurelius: A Biography*, revised edition (New Haven and London, 2000), 152–5, 202–4, and Appendix IV.

4   As in 2.2 and 8.8. We know how important books were to him earlier in his career from his correspondence with Marcus Cornelius Fronto (whom he thanks in 1.11), and most vividly from Fronto's report that as a young man Marcus would read in the theatre and at banquets: C. R. Haines: *The Correspondence of Marcus Cornelius Fronto* (Cambridge, Mass. and London: Harvard University Press, 1962) 1.207.

5   The metaphor of the citadel of philosophy is found in Lucretius, *On the Nature of Things*, 2.7–13 and other sources. The *inner* fortress of the emperor is well reconnoitred by Pierre Hadot, *The Inner Citadel: The Meditations of Marcus Aurelius*, trans. Michael Chase (Cambridge, Mass. and London, 1998), ch. 6.

6   The best introduction to these is that of Penelope J. E. Davies, *Death and the Emperor: Roman Imperial Funerary Monuments from Augustus to Marcus Aurelius* (Cambridge, 2000).

7   We find a string of quotations and commonplaces in 7.35–52 and 11.22–39.

8   Compare 4.3.1 and 7.59. The outer world is not as pure as the inner world, as is painfully made clear from Marcus' comparison of the filth of bathwater to the filth of life: 'Just as you see your bath – all soap, sweat, grime, greasy water, the whole thing disgusting – so is every part of life and every object in it' (8.24).

9   Book 2, 'Written among the Quadi on the River Gran' (Hron in modern Hungary); Book 3, 'Written in Carnuntum' (Hainburg in Austria). These titles from the manuscript of the first printed edition of the Meditations (P, published by Xylander in 1559) would date the composition of Book 2 to 173, when the Roman army was active at Mitrovitz on the Save, and of Book 3 to the early 170s when Marcus' armies were active at Carnuntum. To help place the Meditations into an historical context the reader will want to consult Anthony Birley's Marcus Aurelius, chs 8 and 9 (with the map on pages 166–7), and P. A. Brunt, 'Marcus Aurelius in his Meditations', Journal of Roman Studies 64 (1974), 1–20.

10   The term 'compose' (suntithenai) is used by Marcus to describe his programme of 'composing' his own life, 8.32. Arrian's term for composition was suggraphein, to compose in writing.

11   1.16–17. The impression Antoninus, whose name he adopted, made upon him is evident in the tribute he pays to him in 6.30.2.

12   With the exception of the first two 'fragments', these are presented alphabetically by the name of the author who cites them in Hermann Diels and Walther Kranz, Die Fragmente der Vorsokratiker, sixth edition (Berlin, 1951), 1.150–79. Their B fragments represent textual citations. The most accessible presentation of the 'fragments' of Heraclitus is that of Charles H. Kahn, The Art and Thought of Heraclitus: An Edition of the Fragments with Translation and Commentary (Cambridge, 1979).

13   The apparent exception is his reflections on the death and burial of his imperial colleague Lucius Aurelius Verus (who died in 169) in 8.37. Verus was dead when Marcus wrote these entries.

14   These analogies or images (eikones) were part of the philosophical education offered by Fronto's teacher, Athenodorus, as is evident from his letter to Marcus (cited in note 4 above) 1.205. Similar is the image of the branch cut from the tree in 11.8.

15   In his treatment of his predecessors the emperor stresses the imperial courts that had been swept away by the tide of mortality:

those of Augustus (8.31), Vespasian, Hadrian, and finally that of his adoptive father, Antoninus Pius (4.32 and 33). He recalls the mortality of individual emperors: Hadrian (8.25), and Augustus, Hadrian, and Antoninus (4.33). His references to Caesar (3.3), Tiberius (12.27), and Nero (3.16) are all damning. He never mentions his son, Lucius Aelius Aurelius Commodus.

16   8.9 and the notes to 5.16.

17   *Historia Augusta*, Marcus Aurelius Antoninus 2.6–7.

18   This natural question is asked by John Rist in 'Are you a Stoic? The Case of Marcus Aurelius', in B. F. Meyer and E. P. Sanders (eds), *Jewish and Christian Self-Definition; Self-Definition in the Greco-Roman World*, vol. 3 (London: 1982), pp. 23–45.

19   A scheme best represented by the Stoic Seneca in his Letter to Lucilius (*Epistulae Morales* 118).

20   Diogenes Laertius, *Lives of the Philosophers*, 7.183.

21   The standard treatment of Stoicism translated to Rome remains that of E. Vernon Arnold, *Roman Stoicism* (Cambridge, 1911).

22   Cassius Dio, *History of Rome*, 72.5.

23   It is hardly surprising that only three short excerpts from the *Meditations* figure in the testimonia in A. A. Long and D. N. Sedley, *The Hellenistic Philosophers* (Cambridge, 1987). These are 52H, 61P, and 63K. (By contrast there are fourteen citations from Epictetus.) Marcus had so absorbed and applied his Stoicism that it is difficult to discover dogmatic statements of it in his *Meditations*.

24   In 7.19 he is a famous and dead philosopher; in 6.42 he is cited for his quotation of a poet.

25   This is clear from 3.6.2 where Marcus cites Socrates ('as Socrates used to say'). His Socrates comes from Epictetus' *Discourses* (3.12.15) and more remotely from Plato's *The Apology of Socrates* 38A.

26   The best treatment of the assimilation of Epictetus to Socrates is that of A. A. Long, *Epictetus: A Stoic and Socratic Guide to Life* (Oxford, 2002), ch. 3.

27   The quotations yield B 'fragments' 71–6 in Diels–Kranz. For a list of the allusions to Heraclitus, see the Index of Quotations.

28   'There is a river of creation, and time is a violent stream' (4.43). The image recurs in 5.10 and 5.23, and is Marcus' adaptation of the river fragments of Heraclitus (B 12 and 91) as he applies the image to universal change.

29   See 9.41 yielding fr. 191 in Hermann Usener's *Epicurea* (Leipzig, 1887). The exercise of withdrawal into one's self first stated

forcefully in 4.3 is attributed to Epicurus by Seneca in one of his letters to Lucilius, 25.6.

30 In 3.3 he comments wryly on the death by dropsy of Heraclitus, whom he took to be the advocate of periodic cosmic conflagration.

31 To borrow the title of Leo Braudy's *The Frenzy of Renown: Fame and its History* (New York and Oxford, 1986).

32 The relevant entries for the distinction between material and causal are 5.13 and 9.37; the implications of understanding the causal and material in terms of human character and motivation are brought out in 6.53, 7.30, 8.46 and 61, and 9.27.

33 Comparable examples of this exercise come in 7.28 and 8.48.

34 It is only in 5.12 that he lists the canonical tetrad of virtues. In 3.6, truth replaces practical intelligence. He names the virtues instilled in him in Book 1. He lists other virtues in 3.11; he lists the titles to virtue (*onomata*) in 10.8.

35 The metaphor of the athletic struggle for virtue occurs in 3.4.3, 7.61, 11.38 and 12.9.

36 The conceit of imperial life as a play echoes what are supposed to be Augustus' last words (in Greek) asking for applause for the role he had played in the comedy of his life (Suetonius, *Life of Augustus*, 99.1). The metaphor of the emperor's life as a play is most evident in the last entry of the *Meditations* (12.36, prepared for by 12.2). It is also evident in 10.27 and 11.1.

37 The higher view is the aspiration of the entries 9.30 and 12.24; looking up is the direction of 11.27 and 12.30. To contemplate the stars is to cleanse the soul, 7.47.

38 A fuller version of this brief history of the survival and fame of the *Meditations* can be found in A. S. L. Farquharson, *The Meditations of the Emperor Marcus Antoninus* (Oxford, 1944), vol. 1, pp. xiii–xxviii.

Further Reading

Arnold, E. V., *Roman Stoicism: Being Lectures on the History of the Stoic Philosophy with Special Reference to its Development within the Roman Empire* (Cambridge, 1911).

Arnold, M., 'Marcus Aurelius' (1865) in *Lectures and Essays in Criticism*, ed. R. H. Super, *The Complete Prose Works of Matthew Arnold* (Ann Arbor, Mich., 1962), pp. 133–57.

Birley, A. R., *Marcus Aurelius: A Biography*, revised edition (New Haven, Conn. and London, 1987; reprinted 2000).

Brunschwig, J., 'Stoicism', in *Greek Thought: A Guide to Classical Knowledge*, ed. Jacques Brunschwig and Geoffrey E. R. Lloyd, translated under the direction of Catherine Porter (Cambridge, Mass. and London, 2000), pp. 977–96.

Brunt, P. A., 'Marcus Aurelius in his *Meditations*', *Journal of Roman Studies* 64 (1974), 1–20.

Colish, M., *The Stoic Tradition from Antiquity to the Early Middle Ages*, 2 vols (Leiden and New York, 1990).

Davies, P. J. E., *Death and the Emperor: Roman Imperial Funerary Monuments from Augustus to Marcus Aurelius* (Cambridge, 2000).

Hadot, P., *The Inner Citadel: The Meditations of Marcus Aurelius*, trans. Paul Chase (Cambridge, Mass., 2001).

Long, A. A., *Hellenistic Philosophy*, second edition (Berkeley and Los Angeles, 1986).

—, *Epictetus: A Stoic and Socratic Guide to Life* (Oxford, 2002).

—, 'Heraclitus and Stoicism', *Philosophia* 5–6 (1975–6), 132–55.

— and D. N. Sedley, *The Hellenistic Philosophers*, 2 vols (Cambridge, 1987).

Rist, J. M., 'Are you a Stoic? The Case of Marcus Aurelius', in
   B. F. Meyer and E. P. Sanders (eds), *Jewish and Christian
   Self-Definition: Self-Definition in the Greco-Roman World*,
   vol. 3 (London, 1982), pp. 23–45.
—, *Stoic Philosophy* (Cambridge, 1969).
Rutherford, R. B., *The Meditations of Marcus Aurelius Anton-
   inus* (Oxford, 1997).
Sandbach, F. H., *The Stoics*, second edition (London and
   Indianapolis/Cambridge, 1989).
Schofield, M., *The Stoic Idea of the City* (Cambridge, 1988).
Sellars, J., *The Art of Living: The Stoics on the Nature of
   Philosophy* (Aldershot, 2003).
Stockdale, J. B., *Courage under Fire: Testing Epictetus' Doc-
   trines in a Laboratory of Human Behavior* (Stanford, Cal.,
   1993).

Meditations

BOOK 1

From my grandfather Verus: decency and a mild temper.　1

From what they say and I remember of my natural father:　2
integrity and manliness.

From my mother: piety, generosity, the avoidance of wrong-　3
doing and even the thought of it; also simplicity of living, well
clear of the habits of the rich.

From my great-grandfather: not to have attended schools for　4
the public; to have had good teachers at home, and to realize
that this is the sort of thing on which one should spend lavishly.

From my tutor: not to become a Green or Blue supporter at the　5
races, or side with the Lights or Heavies in the amphitheatre;
to tolerate pain and feel few needs; to work with my own hands
and mind my own business; to be deaf to malicious gossip.

From Diognetus: to avoid empty enthusiasms; to disbelieve all　6
that is talked by miracle-mongers and quacks about incanta-
tions, exorcism of demons, and the like; not to hold quail-fights
or be excited by such sports; to tolerate plain speaking; to have
an affinity for philosophy, and to attend the lectures first of
Baccheius, then of Tandasis and Marcianus; to write essays
from a young age; to love the camp-bed, the hide blanket, and
all else involved in the Greek training.

From Rusticus: to grasp the idea of wanting correction and　7

treatment for my character; not to be diverted into a taste for
rhetoric, so not writing up my own speculations, delivering my
own little moral sermons, or presenting a glorified picture of
2   the ascetic or the philanthropist; to keep clear of speechifying,
versifying, and pretentious language; not to walk around at
home in ceremonial dress, or do anything else like that; to write
letters in an unaffected style, like his own letter written to my
3   mother from Sinuessa; to be readily recalled to conciliation
with those who have taken or given offence, just as soon as
they themselves are willing to turn back; to read carefully, not
satisfied with my own superficial thoughts or quick to accept
the facile views of others; to have encountered the *Discourses*
of Epictetus, to which he introduced me with his own copy.

8   From Apollonius: moral freedom, the certainty to ignore the
dice of fortune, and have no other perspective, even for a
moment, than that of reason alone; to be always the same man,
unchanged in sudden pain, in the loss of a child, in lingering
sickness; to see clearly in his living example that a man can
2   combine intensity and relaxation; not to be impatient in explanation; the observance of a man who clearly regarded as the
least of his gifts his experience and skill in communicating
his philosophical insights; the lesson of how to take apparent
favours from one's friends, neither compromised by them nor
insensitive in their rejection.

9   From Sextus: a kindly disposition, and the pattern of a household governed by the paterfamilias; the concept of life lived
according to nature; an unaffected dignity; intuitive concern
for his friends; tolerance both of ordinary people and of the
2   emptily opinionated; an agreeable manner with all, so that the
pleasure of his conversation was greater than any flattery, and
his very presence brought him the highest respect from all the
company; certainty of grasp and method in the discovery and
3   organization of the essential principles of life; never to give
the impression of anger or any other passion, but to combine
complete freedom from passion with the greatest human affection; to praise without fanfare, and to wear great learning lightly.

From Alexander the grammarian: not to leap on mistakes, or   10
captiously interrupt when anyone makes an error of vocabu-
lary, syntax, or pronunciation, but neatly to introduce the
correct form of that particular expression by way of answer,
confirmation, or discussion of the matter itself rather than its
phrasing – or by some other such felicitous prompting.

From Fronto: to understand the effect of suspicion, caprice,   11
and hypocrisy in the exercise of absolute rule; and that for the
most part these people we call 'Patricians' are somewhat short
of human affection.

From Alexander the Platonist: rarely, and never without essen-   12
tial cause, to say or write to anyone that 'I am too busy'; nor
to use a similar excuse, advancing 'pressure of circumstances',
in constant avoidance of the proprieties inherent in our relations
to our fellows and contemporaries.

From Catulus: not to spurn a friend's criticism, even if it may   13
be an unreasonable complaint, but to try to restore his usual
feelings; to speak of one's teachers with wholehearted gratitude,
as is recorded of Domitius and Athenodotus; and a genuine
love for children.

From Severus: love of family, love of truth, love of justice; to   14
have come by his help to understand Thrasea, Helvidius, Cato,
Dio, Brutus; to have conceived the idea of a balanced constitution, a commonwealth based on equality and freedom of
speech, and of a monarchy which values above all the liberty
of the subject; from him, too, a constant and vigorous respect   2
for philosophy; beneficence, unstinting generosity, optimism;
his confidence in the affection of his friends, his frankness with
those who met with his censure, and open likes and dislikes, so
that his friends did not need to guess at his wishes.

From Maximus: self-mastery, immune to any passing whim;   15
good cheer in all circumstances, including illness; a nice balance
of character, both gentle and dignified; an uncomplaining

2 energy for what needs to be done; the trust he inspired in everyone that he meant what he said and was well-intentioned in all that he did; proof against surprise or panic; in nothing either hurried or hesitant, never short of resource, never downcast or cringing, or on the other hand angry or suspicious; 3 generosity in good works, and a forgiving and truthful nature; the impression he gave of undeviating rectitude as a path chosen rather than enforced; the fact that no one would ever have thought himself belittled by him, or presumed to consider himself superior to him; and a pleasant humour.

16 From my [adoptive] father: gentleness, and an immovable adherence to decisions made after full consideration; no vain taste for so-called honours; stamina and perseverance; a ready ear for anyone with any proposal for the common good; to reward impartially, giving everyone their due; experience of 2 where to tighten, where to relax; putting a stop to homosexual love of young men; a common courtesy, excusing his court from constant attendance at dinner with him and the obligation to accompany him out of town, and those kept away by some other commitment always found him no different towards them; focused and persistent in deliberation in council, never satisfied with first impressions and leaving a question prematurely; the concern to keep his friends, with no extremes of surfeit or favouritism; his own master in all things, and serene 3 with it; foresight for the longer issues and unfussy control of the least detail; the check he put in his reign on acclamations and all forms of flattery; his constant watch on the needs of the empire, his stewardship of its resources, and his tolerance of some people's criticism in this area; no superstitious fear of the gods, nor with men any populism or obsequious courting of the mob, but a sober steadfastness in all things, and nowhere any vulgar or newfangled taste.

4 In those things which conduce to the comfort of life – and here fortune gave him plenty – to enjoy them without pride or apology either, so no routine acceptance of their presence or regret in their absence; the fact that no one would ever describe him as a fraud or an impostor or a pedant, but rather as a man

of mellow wisdom and mature experience, beyond flattery, able
to take charge of his own and others' affairs.

Further, his high regard for genuine philosophers – for the ⁵
other sort he had no hard words, but easily saw through them;
sociability, too, and a sense of humour, not taken to excess;
sensible care of his own body, neither vain nor valetudinarian,
but not neglectful either, so that his own attention to himself
left very little need for doctors, doses, or applications.

Most importantly, his readiness to defer ungrudgingly to ⁶
those with some special ability – it might be in literary expression, or the study of laws or customs or any other subject –
and to give them his own active support to reach acknowledged
eminence in their own specialities. Acting always in accordance
with tradition, yet not making the preservation of tradition an
overt aim; further, no liking for change and chance, but a settled ⁷
habit in the same places and the same practices; to resume
instantly after attacks of migraine, fresh again and vigorous for
his usual work; not to keep many matters secret to himself,
only a very few exceptional cases and those solely of state
concern; sense and moderation in such things as the provision
of shows, contracting of public works, doles and distributions
– the acts of a man with an eye for precisely what needs to be
done, not the glory of its doing.

He was not one to bathe at all hours; he had no urge to build ⁸
houses; he was not particular about food, the material and
colour of his clothes, or youthful beauty in his slaves; the fact
that his dress came from Lorium, sent up from his country
house there; the many details of his way of life at Lanuvium;
how he handled the apologetic customs officer in Tusculum,
and all such modes of behaviour.

Nothing about him was harsh, relentless, or impetuous, and ⁹
you would never say of him that he 'broke out a sweat': but
everything was allotted its own time and thought, as by a
man of leisure – his way was unhurried, organized, vigorous,
consistent in all. What is recorded of Socrates would apply to
him too: that he could regulate abstinence and enjoyment where
many people are too weak-willed to abstain or enjoy too indul-
gently.

10   Strength of character – and endurance or sobriety as the case may be – signifies the man of full and indomitable spirit, as was shown by Maximus in his illness.

17 From the gods: to have had good grandparents, good parents, a good sister, good teachers, good family, relatives, and friends – almost everything; and that I did not blunder into offending any of them, even though I had the sort of disposition which might indeed have resulted in some such offence, given the occasion – it was the grace of the gods that no set of circum-
2 stances likely to show me up ever arose. That I was not brought up any longer than I was with my grandfather's mistress, and that I kept my innocence, leaving sexual experience to the
3 proper time and indeed somewhat beyond it. That I came under a ruler and a father who was to strip me of all conceit and bring me to realize that it is possible to live in a palace without feeling the need for bodyguards or fancy uniforms, candelabra, statues, or the other trappings of suchlike pomp, but that one can reduce oneself very close to the station of a private citizen and not thereby lose any dignity or vigour in the conduct of a ruler's responsibility for the common good.

4   That I was blessed with a brother whose character could spur me to care for myself, and whose respect and affection were likewise a source of joy to me. That my children were not born short of intelligence or physically deformed. That I did not make further progress in rhetoric, poetry, and the other pursuits in which I could well have been absorbed, if I had felt this my
5 right path. That I was quick to raise my tutors to the public office which I thought they desired and did not put them off, in view of their youth, with promises for the future. That I came to know Apollonius, Rusticus, Maximus.

6   That I acquired a clear and constant picture of what is meant by the life according to nature, so that, with regard to the gods, their communications from that world, their help and their inspiration, nothing now prevents me living the life of nature: my falling somewhat short, still, is due to my own fault and my failure to observe the promptings, not to say the instructions, of the gods.

That my body has held out so far in a life such as mine. 7
That I never touched Benedicta or Theodotus, and that later
experience of sexual passion left me cured. That, though I was
often angry with Rusticus, my behaviour ncver went to the
point of regret. That my mother, fated to die young, nevertheless lived her last years with me.

That whenever I wanted to help someone in poverty or some 8
other need I was never told that there was no source of afford-
able money: and that I myself never fell into similar want of
financial assistance from another. That my wife is as she is, so
submissive, loving, and unaffected: and that I found no lack of
suitable tutors for my children.

That I was given help through dreams, especially how to 9
avoid spitting blood and bouts of dizziness: and the response
of the oracle at Caieta, 'Just as you use yourself'. That, for all
my love of philosophy, I did not fall in with any sophist, or
devote my time to the analysis of literature or logic, or busy
myself with cosmic speculation. All these things need 'the help
of gods and Fortune's favour'.

BOOK 2

Written among the Quadi on the River Gran

1 Say to yourself first thing in the morning: today I shall meet people who are meddling, ungrateful, aggressive, treacherous, malicious, unsocial. All this has afflicted them through their ignorance of true good and evil. But I have seen that the nature of good is what is right, and the nature of evil what is wrong; and I have reflected that the nature of the offender himself is akin to my own – not a kinship of blood or seed, but a sharing in the same mind, the same fragment of divinity. Therefore I cannot be harmed by any of them, as none will infect me with their wrong. Nor can I be angry with my kinsman or hate him. We were born for cooperation, like feet, like hands, like eyelids, like the rows of upper and lower teeth. So to work in opposition to one another is against nature: and anger or rejection is opposition.

2 Whatever it is, this being of mine is made up of flesh, breath, and directing mind. Now the flesh you should disdain – blood, bones, a mere fabric and network of nerves, veins, and arteries. Consider too what breath is: wind – and not even a constant, but all the time being disgorged and sucked in again. That leaves the third part, the directing mind. Quit your books – no more hankering: this is not your gift. No, think like this, as if you were on the point of death: 'you are old; don't then let this directing mind of yours be enslaved any longer – no more jerking to the strings of selfish impulse, no more disquiet at your present or suspicion of your future fate.'

The works of the gods are full of providence. The works of 3
Fortune are not independent of Nature or the spinning and
weaving together of the threads governed by Providence. All
things flow from that world: and further factors are necessity
and the benefit of the whole universe, of which you are a part.
Now every part of nature benefits from that which is brought
by the nature of the Whole and all which preserves that nature:
and the order of the universe is preserved equally by the changes
in the elements and the changes in their compounds. Let this
be enough for you, and your constant doctrine. And give up
your thirst for books, so that you do not die a grouch, but in
true grace and heartfelt gratitude to the gods.

Remember how long you have been putting this off, how many 4
times you have been given a period of grace by the gods and
not used it. It is high time now for you to understand the
universe of which you are a part, and the governor of that
universe of whom you constitute an emanation: and that there
is a limit circumscribed to your time – if you do not use it to
clear away your clouds, it will be gone, and you will be gone,
and the opportunity will not return.

Every hour of the day give vigorous attention, as a Roman and 5
as a man, to the performance of the task in hand with precise
analysis, with unaffected dignity, with human sympathy, with
dispassionate justice – and to vacating your mind from all its
other thoughts. And you will achieve this vacation if you perform each action as if it were the last of your life: freed, that is,
from all lack of aim, from all passion-led deviation from the
ordinance of reason, from pretence, from love of self, from
dissatisfaction with what fate has dealt you. You see how few
things a man needs to master for the settled flow of a god-
fearing life. The gods themselves ask nothing more of one who
keeps these observances.

Self-harm, my soul, you are doing self-harm: and you will have 6
no more opportunity for self-respect. Life for each of us is a
mere moment, and this life of yours is nearly over, while you

still show yourself no honour, but let your own welfare depend on other people's souls.

7 Do externals tend to distract you? Then give yourself the space to learn some further good lesson, and stop your wandering. That done, you must guard against the other sort of drift. Those who are dead to life and have no aim for the direction of every impulse and, more widely, every thought are drivellers in deed as well as word.

8 Failure to read what is happening in another's soul is not easily seen as a cause of unhappiness: but those who fail to attend to the motions of their own soul are necessarily unhappy.

9 Always remember these things: what the nature of the Whole is, what my own nature is, the relation of this nature to that, what kind of part it is of what kind of Whole; and that there is no one who can prevent you keeping all that you say and do in accordance with that nature, of which you are a part.

10 In his comparative ranking of sins, applying philosophy to the common man's distinctions, Theophrastus says that offences of lust are graver than those of anger: because it is clearly some sort of pain and involuntary spasm which drives the angry man to abandon reason, whereas the lust-led offender has given in to pleasure and seems somehow more abandoned and less manly in his wrongdoing. Rightly, then, and like a true philosopher, Theophrastus said that greater censure attaches to an offence committed under the influence of pleasure than to one under the influence of pain. And in general the one is more like an injured party, forced to anger by the pain of provocation: whereas the other is his own source of the impulse to wrong, driven to what he does by lust.

11 You may leave this life at any moment: have this possibility in your mind in all that you do or say or think. Now departure from the world of men is nothing to fear, if gods exist: because they would not involve you in any harm. If they do not exist,

or if they have no care for humankind, then what is life to me in a world devoid of gods, or devoid of providence? But they do exist, and they do care for humankind: and they have put it absolutely in man's power to avoid falling into the true kinds of harm. If there were anything harmful in the rest of experience, they would have provided for that too, to make it in everyone's power to avoid falling into it; and if something cannot make a human being worse, how could it make his life a worse life?

The nature of the Whole would not have been blind to this, either through ignorance or with knowledge unaccompanied by the power to prevent and put right. Nor would it have made so great an error, through lack of power or skill, as to have good and bad falling indiscriminately, on good and bad people alike. Yes, death and life, fame and ignominy, pain and pleasure, wealth and poverty – all these come to good and bad alike, but they are not in themselves either right or wrong: neither then are they inherent good or evil.

How all things quickly vanish, our bodies themselves lost in the physical world, the memories of them lost in time; the nature of all objects of the senses – especially those which allure us with pleasure, frighten us with pain, or enjoy the applause of vanity – how cheap they are, how contemptible, shoddy, perishable, and dead: these are matters for our intellectual faculty to consider. And further considerations. What are they, these people whose judgements and voices confer or deny esteem? What is death? Someone looking at death *per se*, and applying the analytical power of his mind to divest death of its associated images, will conclude then that it is nothing more than a function of nature – and if anyone is frightened of a function of nature, he is a mere child. And death is not only a function of nature, but also to her benefit.

Further. How does man touch god, with what part of his being, and when that part of him is in what sort of disposition?

Nothing is more miserable than one who is always out and about, running round everything in circles – in Pindar's words 'delving deep in the bowels of the earth' – and looking for signs and symptoms to divine his neighbours' minds. He does not realize that it is sufficient to concentrate solely on the divinity within himself and to give it true service. That service is to keep it uncontaminated by passion, triviality, or discontent at what is dealt by gods or men. What comes from the gods demands reverence for their goodness. What comes from men is welcome for our kinship's sake, but sometimes pitiable also, in a way, because of their ignorance of good and evil: and this is no less a disability than that which removes the distinction of light and dark.

14 Even if you were destined to live three thousand years, or ten times that long, nevertheless remember that no one loses any life other than the one he lives, or lives any life other than the one he loses. It follows that the longest and the shortest lives are brought to the same state. The present moment is equal for all; so what is passing is equal also; the loss therefore turns out to be the merest fragment of time. No one can lose either the past or the future – how could anyone be deprived of what he does not possess?

2   So always remember these two things. First, that all things have been of the same kind from everlasting, coming round and round again, and it makes no difference whether one will see the same things for a hundred years, or two hundred years, or for an infinity of time. Second, that both the longest-lived and the earliest to die suffer the same loss. It is only the present moment of which either stands to be deprived: and if indeed this is all he has, he cannot lose what he does not have.

15 'All is as thinking makes it so.' The retort made to Monimus the Cynic is clear enough: but clear too is the value of his saying, if one takes the kernel of it, as far as it is true.

16 The soul of a man harms itself, first and foremost, when it becomes (as far as it can) a separate growth, a sort of tumour on the universe: because to resent anything that happens is to separate oneself in revolt from Nature, which holds in collective

embrace the particular natures of all other things. Secondly, when it turns away from another human being, or is even carried so far in opposition as to intend him harm – such is the case in the souls of those gripped by anger. A soul harms itself, thirdly, when it gives in to pleasure or pain. Fourthly, whenever it dissimulates, doing or saying anything feigned or false. Fifthly, whenever it fails to direct any of its own actions or impulses to a goal, but acts at random, without conscious attention – whereas even the most trivial action should be undertaken in reference to the end. And the end for rational creatures is to follow the reason and the rule of that most venerable archetype of a governing state – the Universe.

In man's life his time is a mere instant, his existence a flux, his   17
perception fogged, his whole bodily composition rotting, his mind a whirligig, his fortune unpredictable, his fame unclear. To put it shortly: all things of the body stream away like a river, all things of the mind are dreams and delusion; life is warfare, and a visit in a strange land; the only lasting fame is oblivion.

What then can escort us on our way? One thing, and one   2
thing only: philosophy. This consists in keeping the divinity within us inviolate and free from harm, master of pleasure and pain, doing nothing without aim, truth, or integrity, and independent of others' action or failure to act. Further, accepting all that happens and is allotted to it as coming from that other source which is its own origin: and at all times awaiting death with the glad confidence that it is nothing more than the dissolution of the elements of which every living creature is composed. Now if there is nothing fearful for the elements themselves in their constant changing of each into another, why should one look anxiously in prospect at the change and dissolution of them all? This is in accordance with nature: and nothing harmful is in accordance with nature.

BOOK 3

Written in Carnuntum

1 We must take into our reckoning not only that life is expended day by day and the remaining balance diminishes, but also this further consideration: if we live longer, there is no guarantee that our mind will likewise retain that power to comprehend and study the world which contributes to our experience of things divine and human. If dementia sets in, there will be no failure of such faculties as breathing, feeding, imagination, desire: before these go, the earlier extinction is of one's proper use of oneself, one's accurate assessment of the gradations of duty, one's ability to analyse impressions, one's understanding of whether the time has come to leave this life – these and all other matters which wholly depend on trained calculation. So we must have a sense of urgency, not only for the ever closer approach of death, but also because our comprehension of the world and our ability to pay proper attention will fade before we do.

2 We should also attend to things like these, observing that even the incidental effects of the processes of Nature have their own charm and attraction. Take the baking of bread. The loaf splits open here and there, and those very cracks, in one way a failure of the baker's profession, somehow catch the eye and give
2 particular stimulus to our appetite. Figs likewise burst open at full maturity: and in olives ripened on the tree the very proximity of decay lends a special beauty to the fruit. Similarly the ears of corn nodding down to the ground, the lion's puckered brow, the foam gushing from the boar's mouth, and much else besides – looked at in isolation these things are far from lovely, but

their consequence on the processes of Nature enhances them
and gives them attraction. So any man with a feeling and deeper 3
insight for the workings of the Whole will find some pleasure in
almost every aspect of their disposition, including the incidental
consequences. Such a man will take no less delight in the living
snarl of wild animals than in all the imitative representations
of painters and sculptors; he will see a kind of bloom and fresh
beauty in an old woman or an old man; and he will be able to
look with sober eyes on the seductive charm of his own slave
boys. Not all can share this conviction – only one who has
developed a genuine affinity for Nature and her works. For him
there will be many such perceptions.

Hippocrates cured many diseases then died of disease himself. 3
The Chaldean astrologers foretold the deaths of many people,
then their own fated day claimed them. Alexander, Pompey,
Julius Caesar annihilated whole cities time after time, and
slaughtered tens of thousands of horse and foot in the field of
battle, and yet the moment came for them too to depart this
life. Heraclitus speculated long on the conflagration of the
universe, but the water of dropsy filled his guts and he died
caked in a poultice of cow-dung. Vermin were the death of
Democritus, and vermin of another sort killed Socrates. What
of it, then? You embarked, you set sail, you made port. Go
ashore now. If it is to another life, nothing is empty of the gods,
even on that shore: and if to insensibility, you will cease to
suffer pains and pleasures, no longer in thrall to a bodily vessel
which is a master as far inferior as its servant is superior. One
is mind and divinity: the other a clay of dust and blood.

Do not waste the remaining part of your life in thoughts about 4
other people, when you are not thinking with reference to some
aspect of the common good. Why deprive yourself of the time
for some other task? I mean, thinking about what so-and-so is
doing, and why, what he is saying or contemplating or plotting,
and all that line of thought, makes you stray from the close
watch on your own directing mind.
    No, in the sequence of your thoughts you must avoid all that 2

is casual or aimless, and most particularly anything prying or malicious. Train yourself to think only those thoughts such that in answer to the sudden question 'What is in your mind now?' you could say with immediate frankness whatever it is, this or that: and so your answer can give direct evidence that all your thoughts are straightforward and kindly, the thoughts of a social being who has no regard for the fancies of pleasure or wider indulgence, for rivalry, malice, suspicion, or anything else that one would blush to admit was in one's mind.

3   A man such as this, if he postpones no longer his ready place among the best, is in some way a priest and minister of the gods. He responds to the divinity seated within him, and this renders the man unsullied by pleasures, unscathed by any pain, untouched by any wrong, unconscious of any wickedness; a wrestler for the greatest prize of all, to avoid being thrown by any passion; dyed to the core with justice; embracing with his whole heart all the experience allotted to him; rarely, and only when there is great need for the common good, wondering what others may be saying or doing or thinking. He has only his own work to bring to fulfilment, and only his own fated allocation from the Whole to claim his constant attention. As for his work, he makes it excellent: as for his lot, he is convinced it is good. And each person's appointed lot is both his fellow-passenger and his driver.

4   He bears in mind too the kinship of all rational beings, and that caring for all men is in accordance with man's nature: but that nevertheless he should not hold to the opinions of all, but only of those who live their lives in agreement with nature. He will constantly remind himself what sort of people they are who do not lead such lives – what they are like both at home and abroad, by night and by day, they and the polluting company they keep. So he disregards even the praise of such men – these are people who are not even satisfied with themselves.

5   You should take no action unwillingly, selfishly, uncritically, or with conflicting motives. Do not dress up your thoughts in smart finery: do not be a gabbler or a meddler. Further, let the god that is within you be the champion of the being you are –

a male, mature in years, a statesman, a Roman, a ruler: one
who has taken his post like a soldier waiting for the Retreat
from life to sound, and ready to depart, past the need for any
loyal oath or human witness. And see that you keep a cheerful
demeanour, and retain your independence of outside help and
the peace which others can give. Your duty is to stand straight
– not held straight.

If you discover in human life something better than justice, 6
truth, self-control, courage – in short, something better than
the self-sufficiency of your own mind which keeps you acting
in accord with true reason and accepts your inheritance of fate
in all outside your choice: if, as I say, you can see something
better than this, then turn to it with all your heart and enjoy
this prime good you have found. But if nothing is shown to be 2
better than the very god that is seated in you, which has brought
all your own impulses under its control, which scrutinizes your
thoughts, which has withdrawn itself, as Socrates used to say,
from all inducements of the senses, which has subordinated
itself to the gods and takes care for men – if you find all else by
comparison with this small and paltry, then give no room to
anything else: once turned and inclined to any alternative, you
will struggle thereafter to restore the primacy of that good
which is yours and yours alone. Because it is not right that the 3
rational and social good should be rivalled by anything of a
different order, for example the praise of the many, or power,
or wealth, or the enjoyment of pleasure. All these things may
seem to suit for a little while, but they can suddenly take control
and carry you away. So you, I repeat, must simply and freely
choose the better and hold to it. 'But better is what benefits.' If
to your benefit as a rational being, adopt it: but if simply to
your benefit as an animal, reject it, and stick to your judgement
without fanfare. Only make sure that your scrutiny is sound.

Never regard as a benefit to yourself anything which will force 7
you at some point to break your faith, to leave integrity behind,
to hate, suspect, or curse another, to dissemble, to covet anything needing the secrecy of walls and drapes. A man who has

put first his own mind and divinity, and worships the supremacy
of the god within him, makes no drama of his life, no hand-
wringing, no craving for solitude or crowds: most of all, his
will be a life of neither pursuit nor avoidance, and it is of no
remote concern to him whether he will retain the bodily envelope of his soul for a longer or a shorter time. Even if release
must come here and now, he will depart as easily as he would
perform any other act that admits of integrity and decency.
Throughout all his life his one precaution is that his mind
should not shift to a state without affinity to a rational and
social being.

8   In the mind of one who is chastened and cleansed you will find
no suppuration, no simmering ulcer, no sore festering under
the skin. Fate does not catch him with his life unfulfilled, as
one might speak of an actor leaving the stage before his part is
finished and the play is over. Moreover you will find nothing
servile or pretentious, no dependence or alienation, nothing to
answer for, no lurking fault.

9   Revere your power of judgement. All rests on this to make sure
that your directing mind no longer entertains any judgement
which fails to agree with the nature or the constitution of a
rational being. And this state guarantees deliberate thought,
affinity with other men, and obedience to the gods.

10   So discard all else and secure these few things only. Remind
yourself too that each of us lives only in the present moment, a
mere fragment of time: the rest is life past or uncertain future.
Sure, life is a small thing, and small the cranny of the earth in
which we live it: small too even the longest fame thereafter,
which is itself subject to a succession of little men who will
quickly die, and have no knowledge even of themselves, let
alone of those long dead.

11   One addition to the precepts already mentioned. Always make
a definition or sketch of what presents itself to your mind, so
you can see it stripped bare to its essential nature and identify

it clearly, in whole and in all its parts, and can tell yourself its proper name and the names of those elements of which it is compounded and into which it will be dissolved.

Nothing is so conducive to greatness of mind as the ability   2
to subject each element of our experience in life to methodical and truthful examination, always at the same time using this scrutiny as a means to reflect on the nature of the universe, the contribution any given action or event makes to that nature, the value this has for the Whole, and the value it has for man – and man is an inhabitant of this highest City, of which all other cities are mere households.

Ask then, what is this which is now making its impression on me? What is it composed of? How long in the nature of things will it last? What virtue is needed to meet it – gentleness, for example, or courage, truthfulness, loyalty, simplicity, self-sufficiency, and so on? So in each case we must say: This has   3
come from god; this is due to a juncture of fate, the mesh of destiny, or some similar coincidence of chance; and this is from my fellow man, my kinsman and colleague, though one who does not know what accords with his own nature. But I do know: and so I treat him kindly and fairly, following the natural law of our fellowship, but at the same time I aim to give him his proper desert in matters which are morally neutral.

If you set yourself to your present task along the path of true   12
reason, with all determination, vigour, and good will: if you admit no distraction, but keep your own divinity pure and standing strong, as if you had to surrender it right now; if you grapple this to you, expecting nothing, shirking nothing, but self-content with each present action taken in accordance with nature and a heroic truthfulness in all that you say and mean – then you will lead a good life. And nobody is able to stop you.

Just as doctors always have their instruments and knives at   13
hand for any emergency treatment, so you should have your doctrines ready for the recognition of the divine and the human, and the performance of every action, even the smallest, in consciousness of the bond which unites the two. No action in

the human context will succeed without reference to the divine, nor vice versa.

14 No more wandering. You are not likely to read your own jottings, your histories of the ancient Greeks and Romans, your extracts from their literature laid up for your old age. Hurry then to the end, abandon vain hopes, rescue yourself, if you have any care for yourself, while the opportunity is still there.

15 They do not know all the meanings of theft, of sowing, of buying, of keeping at rest, of seeing what needs to be done – this is not for the eye, but for a different sort of vision.

16 Body, soul, mind. To the body belong sense perceptions, to the soul impulses, to the mind judgements. The receipt of sense impressions is shared with cattle; response to the puppet-strings of impulse is shared with wild beasts, with catamites, with a Phalaris or a Nero; having the mind as guide to what appears appropriate action is shared with those who do not believe in the gods, those who betray their country, those who get up to anything behind closed doors.

2   So if all else is held in common with the categories mentioned above, it follows that the defining characteristic of the good person is to love and embrace whatever happens to him along his thread of fate; and not to pollute the divinity which is seated within his breast, or trouble it with a welter of confused impressions, but to preserve its constant favour, in proper allegiance to god, saying only what is true, doing only what is just.

And if all people mistrust him, for living a simple, decent, and cheerful life, he has no quarrel with any of them, and no diversion from the road which leads to the final goal of his life: to this he must come pure, at peace, ready to depart, in unforced harmony with his fate.

BOOK 4

Wherever it is in agreement with nature, the ruling power within 1 us takes a flexible approach to circumstances, always adapting itself easily to both practicality and the given event. It has no favoured material for its work, but sets out on its objects in a conditional way, turning any obstacle into material for its own use. It is like a fire mastering whatever falls into it. A small flame would be extinguished, but a bright fire rapidly claims as its own all that is heaped on it, devours it all, and leaps up yet higher in consequence.

No action should be undertaken without aim, or other than in 2 conformity with a principle affirming the art of life.

Men seek retreats for themselves – in the country, by the sea, 3 in the hills – and you yourself are particularly prone to this yearning. But all this is quite unphilosophic, when it is open to you, at any time you want, to retreat into yourself. No retreat offers someone more quiet and relaxation than that into his own mind, especially if he can dip into thoughts there which put him at immediate and complete ease: and by ease I simply mean a well-ordered life. So constantly give yourself this retreat, and renew yourself. The doctrines you will visit there should be few and fundamental, sufficient at one meeting to wash away all your pain and send you back free of resentment at what you must rejoin.

And what is it you will resent? Human wickedness? Recall 2 the conclusion that rational creatures are born for each other's sake, that tolerance is a part of justice, that wrongdoing is not deliberate. Consider the number of people who spent their lives in enmity, suspicion, hatred, outright war, and were then laid out for burial or reduced to ashes. Stop, then. Or will you fret at your allocation from the Whole? Revisit the alternatives – providence or atoms – and the many indications that the universe is a kind of community. But will matters of the flesh still have their hold on you? Consider that the mind, once it has abstracted itself and come to know its own defining power, has no contact with the movement of the bodily spirit, be that smooth or troubled: and finally remember all that you have heard and agreed about pain and pleasure.

3   Well then, will a little fame distract you? Look at the speed of universal oblivion, the gulf of immeasurable time both before and after, the vacuity of applause, the indiscriminate fickleness of your apparent supporters, the tiny room in which all this is confined. The whole earth is a mere point in space: what a minute cranny within this is your own habitation, and how many and what sort will sing your praises here!

4   Finally, then, remember this retreat into your own little territory within yourself. Above all, no agonies, no tensions. Be your own master, and look at things as a man, as a human being, as a citizen, as a mortal creature. And here are two of the most immediately useful thoughts you will dip into. First that *things* cannot touch the mind: they are external and inert; anxieties can only come from your internal judgement. Second, that all these things you see will change almost as you look at them, and then will be no more. Constantly bring to mind all that you yourself have already seen changed. The universe is change: life is judgement.

4   If mind is common to us all, then we have reason also in common – that which makes us rational beings. If so, then common too is the reason which dictates what we should or should not do. If so, then law too is common to us all. If so, then we are citizens. If so, we share in a constitution. If so, the universe is a kind of community. In what else could one say that the whole human race shares a common constitution?

From there, then, this common city, we take our very mind, our reason, our law – from where else? Just as the earthy part of me has been derived from some earth, the watery from the next element, the air of my breath from some other source, the hot and fiery from its own origin (for nothing comes from nothing, nor returns to nothing) – so the mind also has its source.

Death, just like birth, is a mystery of nature: first a combination, 5 then a dissolution, of the same elements. Certainly no cause for shame: because nothing out of the order for an intelligent being or contrary to the principle of his constitution.

With such people such an outcome is both natural and inevit- 6 able – if you wish it otherwise you are hoping that figs will no longer produce their rennet. In any case remember that in a very brief time both you and he will be dead, and shortly after not even your names will be left.

Remove the judgement, and you have removed the thought 'I 7 am hurt': remove the thought 'I am hurt', and the hurt itself is removed.

What does not make a human being worse in himself cannot 8 make his life worse either: it cannot harm him from outside or inside.

The nature of the beneficial was bound to act thus. 9

'All's right that happens in the world.' Examine this saying 10 carefully, and you will find it true. I do not mean 'right' simply in the context of cause and effect, but in the sense of 'just' – as if some adjudicator were assigning dues. So keep on observing this, as you have started, and in all that you do combine doing it with being a good man, in the specific conception of 'good man'. Preserve this in every sphere of action.

When someone does you wrong, do not judge things as he 11

interprets them or would like *you* to interpret them. Just see them as they are, in plain truth.

12   Always have these two principles in readiness. First, to do only what the reason inherent in kingly and judicial power prescribes for the benefit of mankind. Second, to change your ground, if in fact there is someone to correct and guide you away from some notion. But this transference must always spring from a conviction of justice or the common good: and your preferred course must be likewise, not simply for apparent pleasure or popularity.

13   'Do you possess reason?' 'I do.' 'Why not use it then? With reason doing its job, what else do you want?'

14   You have subsisted as a part of the Whole. You will vanish into that which gave you birth: or rather you will be changed, taken up into the generative principle of the universe.

15   Many grains of incense on the same altar. One falls to ash first, another later: no difference.

16   Within ten days you will be regarded as a god by those very people who now see you as beast or baboon – if you return to your principles and the worship of Reason.

17   No, you do not have thousands of years to live. Urgency is on you. While you live, while you can, become good.

18   What ease of mind you gain from not looking at what your neighbour has said or done or thought, but only at your own actions, to make them just, reverential, imbued with good! So do not glance at the black characters either side, but run right on to the line: straight, not straggly.

19   One who is all in a flutter over his subsequent fame fails to imagine that all those who remember him will very soon be dead – and he too. Then the same will be true of all successors,

until the whole memory of him will be extinguished in a
sequence of lamps lit and snuffed out. But suppose immortality
in those who will remember you, and everlasting memory. Even
so, what is that to you? And I do not simply mean that this is
nothing to the dead, but to the living also what is the point of
praise, other than for some practical aspect of management?
As it is, you are losing the opportunity of that gift of nature
which does not depend on another's word. So . . .

Everything in any way beautiful has its beauty of itself, inherent   20
and self-sufficient: praise is no part of it. At any rate, praise
does not make anything better or worse. This applies even to
the popular conception of beauty, as in material things or works
or art. So does the truly beautiful need anything beyond itself?
No more than law, no more than truth, no more than kindness
or integrity. Which of these things derives its beauty from
praise, or withers under criticism? Does an emerald lose its
quality if it is not praised? And what of gold, ivory, purple, a
lyre, a dagger, a flower, a bush?

You may ask how, if souls live on, the air can accommodate   21
them all from the beginning of time. Well, how does the earth
accommodate all those bodies buried in it over the same eternity? Just as here on earth, once bodies have kept their residence
for whatever time, their change and decomposition makes room
for other bodies, so it is with souls migrated to the air. They
continue for a time, then change, dissolve, and take fire as they
are assumed into the generative principle of the Whole: in this
way they make room for successive residents. Such would be
one's answer on the assumption that souls do live on.

We should consider, though, not only the multitude of bodies   2
thus buried, but also the number of animals eaten every day by
us and other creatures – a huge quantity consumed and in a
sense buried in the bodies of those who feed on them. And yet
there is room for them, because they are reduced to blood and
changed into the elements of air and fire.

How to investigate the truth of this? By distinguishing the
material and the causal.

22 No wandering. In every impulse, give what is right: in every thought, stick to what is certain.

23 Universe, your harmony is my harmony: nothing in your good time is too early or too late for me. Nature, all that your seasons bring is fruit to me: all comes from you, exists in you, returns to you. The poet says, 'Dear city of Cecrops': will you not say, 'Dear city of Zeus'?

24 'If you want to be happy', says Democritus, 'do little.' May it not be better to do what is necessary, what the reason of a naturally social being demands, and the way reason demands it done? This brings the happiness both of right action and of little action. Most of what we say and do is unnecessary: remove the superfluity, and you will have more time and less bother. So in every case one should prompt oneself: 'Is this, or is it not, something necessary?' And the removal of the unnecessary should apply not only to actions but to thoughts also: then no redundant actions either will follow.

25 Try out too how the life of the good man goes for you – the man content with his dispensation from the Whole, and satisfied in his own just action and kind disposition.

26 You have seen that: now look at this. Do not trouble yourself, keep yourself simple. Someone does wrong? He does wrong to himself. Has something happened to you? Fine. All that happens has been fated by the Whole from the beginning and spun for your own destiny. In sum, life is short: make your gain from the present moment with right reason and justice. Keep sober and relaxed.

27 Either an ordered universe, or a stew of mixed ingredients, yet still coherent order. Otherwise how could a sort of private order subsist within you, if there is disorder in the Whole? Especially given that all things, distinct as they are, nevertheless permeate and respond to each other.

A black character, an effeminate, unbending character, the   28
character of a brute or dumb animal: infantile, stupid, fraudulent, coarse, mercenary, despotic.

If one who does not recognize the contents of the universe is a   29
stranger in it, no less a stranger is the one who fails to recognize
what happens in it. He is a fugitive if he runs away from social
principle; blind, if he shuts the eye of the mind; a beggar, if he
depends on others and does not possess within him all he
needs for life; a tumour on the universe, if he stands aside and
separates himself from the principle of our common nature in
disaffection with his lot (for it is nature which brings this about,
just as it brought you about too); a social splinter, if he splits
his own soul away from the soul of all rational beings, which
is a unity.

One philosopher has no shirt, one has no book. Here is another   30
half-naked: 'I have no bread', he says, 'but I am faithful to
Reason.' But I for my part have all the food of learning, and
yet I am not faithful.

Love the art which you have learnt, and take comfort in it. Go   31
through the remainder of your life in sincere commitment of all
your being to the gods, and never making yourself tyrant or
slave to any man.

Consider, for example, the time of Vespasian. You will see   32
everything the same. People marrying, having children, falling
ill, dying, fighting, feasting, trading, farming, flattering, push-
ing, suspecting, plotting, praying for the death of others, grumbling at their lot, falling in love, storing up wealth, longing for
consulships and kingships. And now that life of theirs is gone,
vanished.

Pass on again to the time of Trajan. Again, everything the   2
same. That life too is dead.

Similarly, look at the histories of other eras and indeed whole
nations, and see how many lives of striving met with a quick
fall and resolution into the elements. Above all, review in your

mind those you have seen yourself in empty struggles, refusing to act in accord with their own natural constitution, to hold tight to it and find it sufficient. And in this context you must remember that there is proportionate value in our attention to each action – so you will not lose heart if you devote no more time than they warrant to matters of less importance.

33 Words in common use long ago are obsolete now. So too the names of those once famed are in a sense obsolete – Camillus, Caeso, Volesus, Dentatus; a little later Scipio and Cato, then Augustus too, then Hadrian and Antoninus. All things fade and quickly turn to myth: quickly too utter oblivion drowns them. And I am talking of those who shone with some wonderful brilliance: the rest, once they have breathed their last, are immediately 'beyond sight, beyond knowledge'. But what in any case is everlasting memory? Utter emptiness.

So where should a man direct his endeavour? Here only – a right mind, action for the common good, speech incapable of lies, a disposition to welcome all that happens as necessary, intelligible, flowing from an equally intelligible spring of origin.

34 Gladly surrender yourself to Clotho: let her spin your thread into whatever web she wills.

35 All is ephemeral, both memory and the object of memory.

36 Constantly observe all that comes about through change, and habituate yourself to the thought that the nature of the Whole loves nothing so much as to change one form of existence into another, similar but new. All that exists is in a sense the seed of its successor: but your concept of 'seed' is simply what is put into the earth or the womb – that is very unphilosophic thinking.

37 Your death will soon be on you: and you are not yet clear-minded, or untroubled, or free from the fear of external harm, or kindly to all people, or convinced that justice of action is the only wisdom.

Look into their directing minds: observe what even the wise 38
will avoid or pursue.

Harm to you cannot subsist in another's directing mind, nor 39
indeed in any turn or change of circumstance. Where, then? In
that part of you which judges harm. So no such judgement, and
all is well. Even if what is closest to it, your own body, is
subjected to knife or cautery, or left to suppurate or mortify,
even so that faculty in you which judges these things should
stay untroubled. That is, it should assess nothing either bad or
good which can happen equally to the bad man or the good:
because what can happen to a man irrespective of his life's
conformity to nature is not of itself either in accordance with
nature or contrary to it.

Think always of the universe as one living creature, comprising 40
one substance and one soul: how all is absorbed into this one
consciousness; how a single impulse governs all its actions; how
all things collaborate in all that happens; the very web and
mesh of it all.

You are a soul carrying a corpse, as Epictetus used to say.   41

Change: nothing inherently bad in the process, nothing 42
inherently good in the result.

There is a river of creation, and time is a violent stream. As 43
soon as one thing comes into sight, it is swept past and another
is carried down: it too will be taken on its way.

All that happens is as habitual and familiar as roses in spring 44
and fruit in the summer. True too of disease, death, defamation,
and conspiracy – and all that delights or gives pain to fools.

What comes after is always in affinity to what went before. Not 45
some simple enumeration of disparate things and a merely
necessary sequence, but a rational connection: and just as existing things are harmoniously interconnected, so the processes of

becoming exhibit no mere succession, but a wonderfully inherent affinity.

46 Always remember Heraclitus: 'The death of earth is the birth of water; the death of water is the birth of air; the death of air is fire, and back again.' Remember too his image of the man who forgets his way home; his saying that men are at odds with their most constant companion, the Reason which governs all things; that their everyday experience takes them by surprise; that we must not act or speak as if asleep, and sleep brings the illusion of speech and action; and that we should not be like children with their parents, simply accepting what we are told.

47 Just as if a god told you that you would die tomorrow or at least the day after tomorrow, you would attach no importance to the difference of one day, unless you are a complete coward (such is the tiny gap of time): so you should think there no great difference between life to the umpteenth year and life to tomorrow.

48 Think constantly how many doctors have died, after knitting their brows over their own patients; how many astrologers, after predicting the deaths of others, as if death were something important; how many philosophers, after endless deliberation on death or immortality; how many heroes, after the many others they killed; how many tyrants, after using their power over men's lives with monstrous insolence, as if they themselves were immortal. Think too how many whole cities have 'died' –
2 Helice, Pompeii, Herculaneum, innumerable others. Go over now all those you have known yourself, one after the other: one man follows a friend's funeral and is then laid out himself, then another follows him – and all in a brief space of time. The conclusion of this? You should always look on human life as short and cheap. Yesterday sperm: tomorrow a mummy or ashes.

So one should pass through this tiny fragment of time in tune with nature, and leave it gladly, as an olive might fall when

ripe, blessing the earth which bore it and grateful to the tree
which gave it growth.

Be like the rocky headland on which the waves constantly   49
break. It stands firm, and round it the seething waters are laid
to rest.

'It is my bad luck that this has happened to me.' No, you
should rather say: 'It is my good luck that, although this has
happened to me, I can bear it without pain, neither crushed by
the present nor fearful of the future.' Because such a thing could
have happened to any man, but not every man could have borne
it without pain. So why see more misfortune in the event than
good fortune in your ability to bear it? Or in general would
you call anything a misfortune for a man which is not a deviation from man's nature? Or anything a deviation from man's
nature which is not contrary to the purpose of his nature?
Well, then. You have learnt what that purpose is. Can there be   2
anything, then, in this happening which prevents you being
just, high-minded, self-controlled, intelligent, judicious, truthful, honourable and free – or any other of those attributes
whose combination is the fulfilment of man's proper nature?
So in all future events which might induce sadness remember
to call on this principle: 'this is no misfortune, but to bear it
true to yourself is good fortune.'

An unphilosophic but nonetheless effective help to putting   50
death in its place is to run over the list of those who have clung
long to life. What did they gain over the untimely dead? At any
rate they are all in their graves by now – Caedicianus, Fabius,
Julianus, Lepidus, and all others like them who took part in
many funerals and then their own. In truth, the distance we
have to travel is small: and we drag it out with such labour, in
such poor company, in such a feeble body. No great thing,
then. Look behind you at the huge gulf of time, and another
infinity ahead. In this perspective what is the difference between
an infant of three days and a Nestor of three generations?

Always run on the short road: and nature's road is short. Go   51

then for the healthiest in all you say and do. Such a purpose
releases a man from the labours of service, from all need to
manage or impress.

BOOK 5

At break of day, when you are reluctant to get up, have this ₁
thought ready to mind: 'I am getting up for a man's work. Do
I still then resent it, if I am going out to do what I was born
for, the purpose for which I was brought into the world? Or
was I created to wrap myself in blankets and keep warm?' 'But
this is more pleasant.' Were you then born for pleasure – all for
feeling, not for action? Can you not see plants, birds, ants,
spiders, bees all doing their own work, each helping in their
own way to order the world? And then you do not want to do
the work of a human being – you do not hurry to the demands
of your own nature. 'But one needs rest too.' One does indeed: ₂
I agree. But nature has set limits to this too, just as it has to
eating and drinking, and yet you go beyond these limits, beyond
what you need. Not in your actions, though, not any longer:
here you stay below your capability.

The point is that you do not love yourself – otherwise you ₃
would love both your own nature and her purpose for you.
Other men love their own pursuit and absorb themselves in its
performance to the exclusion of bath and food: but you have
less regard for your own nature than the smith has for his
metal-work, the dancer for his dancing, the money-grubber for
his money, the exhibitionist for his little moment of fame. Yet
these people, when impassioned, give up food and sleep for the
promotion of their pursuits: and you think social action less
important, less worthy of effort?

How easy it is to drive away or obliterate from one's mind ₂ every impression which is troublesome or alien, and then to be immediately in perfect calm.

3 Judge yourself entitled to any word or action which is in accord with nature, and do not let any subsequent criticism or persuasion from anyone talk you out of it. No, if it was a good thing to do or say, do not revoke your entitlement. Those others are guided by their own minds and pursue their own impulses. Do not be distracted by any of this, but continue straight ahead, following your own nature and universal nature: these two have one and the same path.

4 I travel on by nature's path until I fall and find rest, breathing my last into that air from which I draw my daily breath, and falling on that earth which gave my father his seed, my mother her blood, my nurse her milk; the earth which for so many years has fed and watered me day by day; the earth which bears my tread and all the ways in which I abuse her.

5 They cannot admire you for intellect. Granted – but there are many other qualities of which you cannot say, 'but that is not the way I am made'. So display those virtues which are wholly in your own power – integrity, dignity, hard work, self-denial, contentment, frugality, kindness, independence, simplicity, discretion, magnanimity. Do you not see how many virtues you can already display without any excuse of lack of talent or aptitude? And yet you are still content to lag behind. Or does the fact that you have no inborn talent oblige you to grumble, to scrimp, to toady, to blame your poor body, to suck up, to brag, to have your mind in such turmoil? No, by heaven, it does not! You could have got rid of all this long ago, and only be charged – if charge there is – with being rather slow and dull of comprehension. And yet even this can be worked on – unless you ignore or welcome your stupidity.

6 One sort of person, when he has done a kindness to another, is quick also to chalk up the return due to him. A second is not so quick in that way, but even so he privately thinks of the

other as his debtor, and is well aware of what he has done. A
third sort is in a way not even conscious of his action, but is
like the vine which has produced grapes and looks for nothing
else once it has borne its own fruit. A horse that has raced, a   2
dog that has tracked, a bee that has made honey, and a man
that has done good – none of these knows what they have done,
but they pass on to the next action, just as the vine passes on
to bear grapes again in due season. So you ought to be one of
those who, in a sense, are unconscious of the good they do.
'Yes', he says, 'but this is precisely what one should be conscious
of: because it defines the social being to be aware of his social
action, and indeed to want his fellow to be aware of it also.'
'True, but you misunderstand the point I am now making: and
for that reason you will fall into one of the first categories I
mentioned. They too are misled by some sort of plausible logic.
But if you want to follow my meaning, don't fear that this will
lead you to any deficiency of social action.'

A prayer of the Athenian people: 7

> Rain, rain, dear Zeus:
> rain on the cornfields
> and the plains of Athens.

Prayer should be thus simple and open, or not at all.

Just as it is commonly said that Asclepius has prescribed some-   8
one horse-riding, or cold baths, or walking barefoot, so we
could say that the nature of the Whole has prescribed him
disease, disablement, loss, or any other such affliction. In the
first case 'prescribed' means something like this: 'ordered this
course for this person as conducive to his health'. In the second
the meaning is that what happens to each individual is somehow
arranged to conduce to his destiny. We speak of the fitness of   2
these happenings as masons speak of the 'fit' of squared stones
in walls or pyramids, when they join each other in a defined
relation.
    In the whole of things there is one harmony: and just as

all material bodies combine to make the world one body, a harmonious whole, so all causes combine to make Destiny one

3 harmonious cause. Even quite unsophisticated people intuit what I mean. They say: 'Fate brought this on him.' Now if 'brought', also 'prescribed'. So let us accept these prescriptions just as we accept those of Asclepius – many of them too are harsh, but we welcome them in the hope of health.

4   You should take the same view of the process and completion of the design of universal nature as you do of your own health: and so welcome all that happens to you, even if it seems rather cruel, because its purpose leads to the health of the universe and the prosperity and success of Zeus. He would not bring this on anyone, if it did not also bring advantage to the Whole: no more than any given natural principle brings anything inappropriate to what it governs.

5   So there are two reasons why you should be content with your experience. One is that this has happened to you, was prescribed for you, and is related to you, a thread of destiny spun for you from the first by the most ancient causes. The second is that what comes to each individual is a determining part of the welfare, the perfection, and indeed the very coherence of that which governs the Whole. Because the complete Whole is maimed if you sever even the tiniest fraction of its connection and continuity: this is true of its constituent parts, and true likewise of its causes. And you do sever something, to the extent that you can, whenever you fret at your lot: this is, in a sense, a destruction.

9 Do not give up in disgust or impatience if you do not find action on the right principles consolidated into a habit in all that you do. No: if you have taken a fall, come back again, and be glad if most of your actions are on the right side of humanity. And love what you return to. Do not come back to philosophy as schoolboy to tutor, but rather as a man with ophthalmia returns to his sponge and salve, or another to his poultice or lotion. In this way you will prove that obedience to reason is no great burden, but a source of relief. Remember too that philosophy wants only what your nature wants: whereas you were wanting

something unnatural to you. Now what could be more agreeable than the needs of your own nature? This is the same way
that pleasure trips us: but look and see whether there is not
something more agreeable in magnanimity, generosity, simplicity, consideration, piety. And what is more agreeable than
wisdom itself, when you reflect on the sure and constant flow
of our faculty for application and understanding?

Realities are wrapped in such a veil (as it were) that several 10
philosophers of distinction have thought them altogether
beyond comprehension, while even the Stoics think them hard
to comprehend. And every assent we may give to our perceptions is fallible: the infallible man does not exist. Pass, then, to
the very objects of our experience – how short-lived they are,
how shoddy: a catamite, a whore, a thief could own them. Go
on now to the characters of your fellows: it is hard to tolerate
even the best of them, not to speak of one's difficulty in enduring
even oneself.

   In all this murk and dirt, in all this flux of being, time,   2
movement, things moved, I cannot begin to see what on earth
there is to value or even to aim for. Rather the opposite: one
should console oneself with the anticipation of natural release,
not impatient of its delay, but taking comfort in just these two
thoughts. One, that nothing will happen to me which is not in
accordance with the nature of the Whole: the other, that it is
in my control to do nothing contrary to my god and the divinity
within me – no one can force me to this offence.

To what use, then, am I now putting my soul? Ask yourself this 11
question on every occasion. Examine yourself. 'What do I now
have in this part of me called the directing mind? What sort of
soul do I have after all? Is it that of a child? A boy? A woman?
A despot? A beast of the field? A wild animal?'

Here is a way to understand what sort of things the majority 12
take to be 'goods'. If you think of the true goods there are –
wisdom, for example, self-control, justice, courage – with these
in your mind you could not give any credence to the popular

saying of 'too many goods to make room', because it will not apply. But bearing in mind what the majority see as goods you will hear and readily accept what the comic poet says as a fair comment. Even the majority can intuit this difference. Otherwise this saying would not both cause offence and rejection, while at the same time we take it as a telling and witty comment on wealth and the privileges of luxury and fame. Go on, then, and ask whether we should value and judge as goods those things which, when we have thought of them, would properly apply to their owner the saying, 'He is so rich, he has no room to shit.'

13 I am made up of the causal and the material. Neither of these will disappear into nothing, just as neither came to be out of nothing. So every part of me will be assigned its changed place in some part of the universe, and that will change again into another part of the universe, and so on to infinity. A similar sequence of change brought me into existence, and my parents before me, and so back in another infinity of regression. Nothing forbids this assertion, even if the universe is subject to the completion of cycles.

14 Reason and the art of reasoning are faculties self-determined by their own nature and their own products. They start from the relevant premise and follow the path to the proposed end. That is why acts of reason are called 'right' acts, signifying the rightness of the path thus followed.

15 One should pay no attention to any of those things which do not belong to man's portion incumbent on him as a human being. They are not demanded of a man; man's nature does not proclaim them; they are not consummations of that nature. Therefore they do not constitute man's end either, nor yet any means to that end – that is, good. Further, if any of these things were incumbent on a man, then it would not have been incumbent on him to disdain or resist them; we would not commend the man who shows himself free from need of them; if these things were truly 'goods', a man who fails to press for

his full share of any of them could not be a good man. But in fact the more a man deprives himself of these or suchlike, or tolerates others depriving him, the better a man he is.

Your mind will take on the character of your most frequent thoughts: souls are dyed by thoughts. So dye your own with a succession of thoughts like these. For example: where life can be lived, so can a good life; but life can be lived in a palace; therefore a good life can be lived in a palace. Again: each creature is made in the interest of another; its course is directed to that for which it was made; its end lies in that to which its course is directed; and where its end is, there also for each is its benefit and its good. It follows that the good of a rational creature is community. It has long been shown that we are born for community – or was it not clear that inferior creatures are made in the interest of the superior, and the superior in the interest of each other? But animate is superior to inanimate, and rational to the merely animate. 16

To pursue the impossible is madness: and it is impossible for bad men not to act in character. 17

Nothing happens to any creature beyond its own natural endurance. Another has the same experience as you: either through failure to recognize what has happened to him, or in a display of courage, he remains calm and untroubled. Strange, then, that ignorance and pretension should be stronger than wisdom. 18

Things of themselves cannot touch the soul at all. They have no entry to the soul, and cannot turn or move it. The soul alone turns and moves itself, making all externals presented to it cohere with the judgements it thinks worthy of itself. 19

In one respect man is something with the closest affinity to us, in that it is our duty to do good to men and tolerate them. But in so far as some are obstacles to my proper work, man joins the category of things indifferent to me – no less than the sun, the wind, a wild animal. These can impede some activity, yes, 20 but they form no impediments to my impulse or my disposition, because here there is conditional commitment and the power of adaptation. The mind adapts and turns round any obstacle to action to serve its objective: a hindrance to a given work is turned to its furtherance, an obstacle in a given path becomes an advance.

21 Revere the ultimate power in the universe: this is what makes use of all things and directs all things. But similarly revere the ultimate power in yourself: this is akin to that other power. In you too this is what makes use of all else, and your life is governed by it.

22 What is not harmful to the city does not harm the citizen either. Whenever you imagine you have been harmed, apply this criterion: if the city is not harmed by this, then I have not been harmed either. If on the other hand harm is done to the city, you should not be angry, but demonstrate to the doer of this harm what he has failed to see himself.

23 Reflect often on the speed with which all things in being, or coming into being, are carried past and swept away. Existence is like a river in ceaseless flow, its actions a constant succession of change, its causes innumerable in their variety: scarcely anything stands still, even what is most immediate. Reflect too on the yawning gulf of past and future time, in which all things vanish. So in all this it must be folly for anyone to be puffed with ambition, racked in struggle, or indignant at his lot – as if this was anything lasting or likely to trouble him for long.

24 Think of the whole of existence, of which you are the tiniest part; think of the whole of time, in which you have been assigned a brief and fleeting moment; think of destiny – what fraction of that are you?

25 Another does wrong. What is that to me? Let him see to it: he has his own disposition, his own action. I have now what

universal nature wishes me to have now, and I do what my own nature wishes me to do now.

The directing and sovereign part of your soul must stay immune 26 to any current in the flesh, either smooth or troubled, and keep its independence: it must define its own sphere and confine those affections to the parts they affect. When, though, as must happen in a composite unity, these affections are transmitted to the mind along the reverse route of sympathy, then you must not try to deny the perception of them: but your directing mind must not of itself add any judgement of good or bad.

'Live with the gods.' He lives with the gods who consistently 27 shows them his soul content with its lot, and performing the wishes of that divinity, that fragment of himself which Zeus has given each person to guard and guide him. In each of us this divinity is our mind and reason.

Are you angry with the man who smells like a goat, or the one 28 with foul breath? What will you have him do? That's the way his mouth is, that's the way his armpits are, so it is inevitable that they should give out odours to match. 'But the man is endowed with reason', you say, 'and if he puts his mind to it he can work out why he causes offence.' Well, good for you! So you too are no less endowed with reason: bring your rationality, then, to bear on his rationality – show him, tell him. If he listens, you will cure him, and no need for anger.

Neither hypocrite nor whore.

You can live here in this world just as you intend to live when 29 you have left it. But if this is not allowed you, then you should depart life itself – but not as if this were some misfortune. 'The fire smokes and I leave the house.' Why think this any big matter? But as long as no such thing drives me out, I remain a free man and no one will prevent me doing what I wish to do: and my wish is to follow the nature of a rational and social being.

30   The intelligence of the Whole is a social intelligence. Certainly it has made the lower for the sake of the higher, and set the higher in harmony with each other. You can see how it has subordinated some creatures, coordinated others, given each its proper place, and brought together the superior beings in unity of mind.

31   How have you behaved up to now towards gods, parents, brother, wife, children, teachers, tutors, friends, relations, servants? Has your principle up to now with all of these been 'say no evil, do no evil'? Remind yourself what you have been through and had the strength to endure; that the story of your life is fully told and your service completed; how often you have seen beauty, disregarded pleasure and pain, forgone glory, and been kind to the unkind.

32   Why do unskilled and ignorant minds confound the skilful and the wise? Well, what is the mind of true skill and wisdom? It is the mind which knows the beginning and the end, and knows the Reason which informs all of existence and governs the Whole in appointed cycles through all eternity.

33   In no time at all ashes or bare bones, a mere name or not even a name: and if a name, only sound and echo. The 'prizes' of life empty, rotten, puny: puppies snapping at each other, children squabbling, laughter turning straight to tears. And Faith, Honour, Justice and Truth 'fled up to Olympus from the wide-wayed earth'.
     So what is there left to keep us here, if the objects of sense are ever changeable and unstable, if our senses themselves are blurred and easily smudged like wax, if our very soul is a mere exhalation of blood, if success in such a world is vacuous? What, then? A calm wait for whatever it is, either extinction or translation. And until the time for that comes, what do we need? Only to worship and praise the gods, and to do good to men – to bear and forbear. And to remember that all that lies within the limits of our poor carcass and our little breath is neither yours nor in your power.

You can always ensure the right current to your life if you can   34
first follow the right path – if, that is, your judgements and
actions follow the path of reason. There are two things common
to the souls of all rational creatures, god or man: they are
immune to any external impediment, and the good they seek
resides in a just disposition and just action, with this the limit
of their desire.

If this is no wrongdoing of mine, nor the result of any wrong   35
done to me, and if the community is not harmed, then why do
I let it trouble me? And what is the harm that can be done to
the community?

Don't let the impression of other people's grief carry you away   36
indiscriminately. Help them, yes, as best you can and as the
case deserves, even if their grief is for the loss of something
indifferent: but do not imagine their loss as any real harm –
that is the wrong way of thinking. Rather, you should be like the
old man in the play who reclaimed at the end his foster-child's
favourite toy, never forgetting that it was only a toy. So there
you are, broadcasting your pity on the hustings – have you
forgotten, man, what these things are worth? 'Yes, but they are
important to these folk.' Is that any reason for you to join their
folly?

'There was a time when I met luck at every turn.' But luck is   37
the good fortune you determine for yourself: and good fortune
consists in good inclinations of the soul, good impulses, good
actions.

BOOK 6

1   The substance of the Whole is passive and malleable, and the reason directing this substance has no cause in itself to do wrong, as there is no wrong in it: nothing it creates is wrongly made, nothing harmed by it. All things have their beginning and their end in accordance with it.

2   If you are doing your proper duty let it not matter to you whether you are cold or warm, whether you are sleepy or well-slept, whether men speak badly or well of you, even whether you are on the point of death or doing something else: because even this, the act in which we die, is one of the acts of life, and so here too it suffices to 'make the best move you can'.

3   Look within: do not allow the special quality or worth of any thing to pass you by.

4   All that exists will soon change. Either it will be turned into vapour, if all matter is a unity, or it will be scattered in atoms.

5   The governing reason knows its own disposition, what it creates, and what is the material for its creation.

6   The best revenge is not to be like your enemy.

7   Let one thing be your joy and comfort: to move on from social act to social act, with your mind on god.

The directing mind is that which wakes itself, adapts itself, 8
makes itself of whatever nature it wishes, and makes all that
happens to it appear in the way it wants.

All things have their accomplishment in accordance with the 9
nature of the Whole: it could not be in accordance with any
other nature, either enclosing from without or enclosed within,
or any external influence.

Either a stew, an intricate web, and dispersal into atoms: or 10
unity, order, and providence. Now if the former, why do I even
wish to spend my time in a world compounded at random and
in like confusion? Why have any concern other than somehow,
some time, to become 'earth unto earth'? And why actually am
I troubled? Dispersal will come on me, whatever I do. But if
the latter is true, I revere it, I stand firm, I take courage in that
which directs all.

When circumstances force you to some sort of distress, quickly 11
return to yourself. Do not stay out of rhythm for longer than
you must: you will master the harmony the more by constantly
going back to it.

If you had a step-mother and a mother at the same time, you 12
would pay attention to your step-mother but nevertheless your
constant recourse would be to your mother. That is now how
it is with the Court and philosophy. So return to philosophy
again and again, and take your comfort in her: she will make
the other life seem bearable to you, and you bearable in it.

How good it is, when you have roast meat or suchlike foods 13
before you, to impress on your mind that this is the dead body
of a fish, this the dead body of a bird or pig; and again, that
the Falernian wine is the mere juice of grapes, and your purple-
edged robe simply the hair of a sheep soaked in shell-fish blood!
And in sexual intercourse that it is no more than the friction of
a membrane and a spurt of mucus ejected. How good these
perceptions are at getting to the heart of the real thing and

penetrating through it, so you can see it for what it is! This should be your practice throughout all your life: when things have such a plausible appearance, show them naked, see their shoddiness, strip away their own boastful account of themselves. Vanity is the greatest seducer of reason: when you are most convinced that your work is important, that is when you are most under its spell. See, for example, what Crates says even about Xenocrates.

14   Most of the things valued by the masses come under the categories of what is sustained by cohesion (minerals, timber) or natural growth (figs, vines, olives). What is valued by the slightly more advanced belongs to the class of things sustained by a principle of life, such as flocks and herds, or the bare ownership of a multitude of slaves. The things valued by yet more refined people are those sustained by the rational soul – not, however, reason as such, but reason expressed in craftsmanship or some other skill. But the man who fully esteems the soul as both rational and political no longer has any regard for those other things, but above all else keeps his own soul in a constant state of rational and social activity, and cooperates to that end with his like.

15   Some things are hurrying to come into being, others are hurrying to be gone, and part of that which is being born is already extinguished. Flows and changes are constantly renewing the world, just as the ceaseless passage of time makes eternity ever young. In this river, then, where there can be no foothold, what should anyone prize of all that races past him? It is as if he were to begin to fancy one of the little sparrows that fly past – but already it is gone from his sight. Indeed this is the nature of our very lives – as transient as the exhalation of vapour from the blood or a breath drawn from the air. No different from a single breath taken in and returned to the air, something which we do every moment, no different is the giving back of your whole power of breathing – acquired at your birth just yesterday or thereabouts – to that world from which you first drew it.

There is nothing to value in transpiring like plants or breathing   16
like cattle and wild creatures; nothing in taking the stamp of
sense impressions or jerking to the puppet-strings of impulse;
nothing in herding together or taking food – this last is no
better than voiding the wastes of that food. What, then, is to be
valued? Applause? No. Not therefore the applause of tongues
either: the praise of the masses is the mere rattle of tongues. So
you have jettisoned trivial glory too. What remains to be
valued? To my mind, it is to act or refrain from action according
to our own proper constitution, something to which skills and
crafts show the way. Every craft seeks to make its product suit
the purpose for which it is produced: this is the aim of the
gardener, the vine-dresser, the breaker of horses, the dog-
trainer. And what is the end to which the training of children
and their teaching strives?

So this is the true value: and if this is firmly held, you will   2
not be set on acquiring any of the other things for yourself.
Will you not then cease to value much else besides? Otherwise
you will not be free or self-sufficient or devoid of passion: you
will need to be envious and jealous, to suspect those who have
the power to deprive you of these things, and to intrigue against
people who possess what you value. In short, anyone who feels
the need of any of these things is necessarily sullied, and what
is more he will often be driven to blame the gods too. But
reverence of your own mind and the value you give to it will
make you acceptable to yourself, in harmony with your fellows,
and consonant with the gods – that is, praising all that they
assign and have disposed.

Up, down, round and round are the motions of the elements,   17
but the movement of active virtue follows none of these: it is
something more divine, and it journeys on to success along a
path hard to understand.

What a way to behave! They refuse to speak well of people   18
who live as their contemporaries and in their company, but
they set great store by their own good name among future
generations which they have never seen nor ever will see. Yet

this is brother to feeling vexed that your predecessors were not singing your praises.

19 Do not imagine that, if something is hard for you to achieve, it is therefore impossible for any man: but rather consider anything that is humanly possible and appropriate to lie within your own reach too.

20 In the field of play an opponent scratches us with his nails, say, or gives us a butting blow with his head: but we do not 'mark' him for that, or take offence, or suspect him afterwards of deliberate attack. True, we do keep clear of him: but this is good-natured avoidance, not suspicion or treating him as an enemy. Something similar should be the case in the other areas of life too: we have people who are our 'opponents in the game', and we should overlook much of what they do. We can avoid them, as I say, without suspicion or enmity.

21 If someone can prove me wrong and show me my mistake in any thought or action, I shall gladly change. I seek the truth, which never harmed anyone: the harm is to persist in one's own self-deception and ignorance.

22 I do my own duty: the other things do not distract me. They are either inanimate or irrational, or have lost the road and are ignorant of the true way.

23 Since you have reason and they do not, treat dumb animals and generally all things and objects with generosity and decency; treat men, because they do have reason, with social concern; and in all things call on the gods. And do not let it matter to you for how long you will be alive in this work: even three hours spent thus are sufficient.

24 Alexander of Macedon and his muleteer were levelled in death: either they were taken up into the same generative principles of the universe, or they were equally dispersed into atoms.

Reflect on how many separate events, both bodily and mental,   25
are taking place in each one of us in the same tiny fragment of
time: and then you will not be surprised if many more events,
indeed all that comes to pass, subsist together in the one and
the whole, which we call the Universe.

If someone puts to you the question 'How is the name Anton-   26
inus spelt?', will you shout your way through each of the syl-
lables? What then if they get angry? Will you lose your temper
too? Will you not rather calmly go through the sequence of
letters, telling each one in turn? So also in your life here remember that every duty is the completed sum of certain actions. You
must observe these, without being disconcerted or answering
others' resentment with your own, but following each purpose
methodically to its end.

How cruel it is not to allow people to strive for what seems to   27
them their interest and advantage! And yet in a way you are
forbidding them to do this, when you fuss that they are wrong:
they are surely drawn to their own interest and advantage. 'But
it is not actually so': well then, teach them, show them, do not
fuss.

Death is relief from reaction to the senses, from the puppet-   28
strings of impulse, from the analytical mind, and from service
to the flesh.

Disgraceful if, in this life where your body does not fail, your   29
soul should fail you first.

Take care not to be Caesarified, or dyed in purple: it happens.   30
So keep yourself simple, good, pure, serious, unpretentious, a
friend of justice, god-fearing, kind, full of affection, strong for
your proper work. Strive hard to remain the same man that
philosophy wished to make you. Revere the gods, look after
men. Life is short. The one harvest of existence on earth is a
godly habit of mind and social action.
    Always as a pupil of Antoninus: his energy for all that was   2

done according to reason, his constant equability, his piety, his serene expression, his gentleness, his lack of conceit, his drive to take a firm grasp of affairs. How he would never put anything at all aside without first looking closely into it and understanding it clearly; how he would tolerate those who unfairly blamed him without returning the blame; how he was never rushed in anything. He would not listen to malicious gossip; he was an accurate judge of men's character and actions; slow to criticize, immune to rumour and suspicion, devoid of pretence. How he was content with little by way of house, bed, dress, food, servants; his love of work, and his stamina.

He was a man to stay at the same task until evening, not even needing to relieve himself except at his usual hour, such was his frugal diet. Constant and fair in his friendships; tolerant of frank opposition to his own views, and delighted to be shown a better way; god-fearing, but not superstitious.

So may your own last hour find you with a conscience as clear as his.

31   Sober up, recall yourself, shake off sleep once more: realize they were mere dreams that troubled you, and now that you are awake again look on these things as you would have looked on a dream.

32   I am made of body and soul. Now to the poor body all things are indifferent, as it cannot even make any distinction. To the mind all that is not its own activity is indifferent: and its own activities are all in its control. But within these the mind is only concerned with the present: its activities in the future and in the past are also indifferent at any present moment.

33   The pain of labour for hand or foot is not contrary to nature, as long as the foot is doing the work of a foot and the hand the work of a hand. So likewise for a man, *qua* man, there is nothing contrary to nature in pain, as long as he is doing the work of a man: and if not contrary to nature for him, not an evil either.

As for pleasure, pirates, catamites, parricides, and tyrants have 34
enjoyed it to the full.

Do you not see how the working craftsman, while deferring to 35
the layman up to a point, nevertheless sticks to the principle of
his craft and will not bear to desert it? Is it not strange, then,
that the architect and the doctor will show greater respect for
the guiding principle of their craft than man will for his own
guiding principle, which he has in common with the gods?

Asia, Europe are mere nooks of the universe. Every ocean is a 36
drop in the universe: Mount Athos a spadeful of earth in the
universe. The whole of present time is a pin-prick of eternity.
All things are tiny, quickly changed, evanescent.

   All things come from that other world, taking their start from
that universal governing reason, or in consequence of it. So
even the lion's gaping jaws, poison, every kind of mischief are,
like thorns or bogs, consequential products of that which is
noble and lovely.

   So do not think them alien to what you worship, but reflect
rather on the fountain of all things.

He who sees the present has seen all things, both all that has 37
come to pass from everlasting and all that will be for eternity:
all things are related and the same.

You should meditate often on the connection of all things in 38
the universe and their relationship to each other. In a way all
things are interwoven and therefore have a family feeling for
each other: one thing follows another in due order through the
tension of movement, the common spirit inspiring them, and
the unity of all being.

Fit yourself for the matters which have fallen to your lot, and 39
love these people among whom destiny has cast you – but your
love must be genuine.

An instrument, a tool, a utensil – all these are fine if they 40 perform the function for which they were made. And yet in such cases the maker is external to the object made. In the case of things held together by organic nature, the power that made them is within, and immanent in them. You should therefore respect it the more, and believe that if you keep your being and your conduct in accordance with the will of this power, all then conforms to your mind. So it is in the Whole also: all that is in it conforms to the mind of the Whole.

41 If you set up as good or evil any of the things beyond your control, it necessarily follows that in the occurrence of that evil or the frustration of that good you blame the gods and hate the men who are the real or suspected causes of that occurrence or that frustration: and indeed we do much injustice through our concern for such things. But if we determine that only what lies in our own power is good or evil, there is no reason left us either to charge a god or to take a hostile stance to a man.

42 We all work together to the same end, some with conscious attention, others without knowing it – just as Heraclitus, I think, says that even people asleep are workers in the factory of all that happens in the world. One person contributes in this way, another in that: and there is room even for the critic who tries to oppose or destroy the production – the world had need for him too. So it remains for you to decide in which category you place yourself. Certainly He who governs the Whole will make good use of you and welcome you into some part of the joint workforce: but just make sure that your part is not that of the cheap and vulgar line in the comedy, as noted by Chrysippus.

43 Does the sun presume to do the work of the rain-god, or Asclepius that of the goddess of harvest? And what of each of the stars? Is it not that they are different, but work together to the same end?

44 Now if the gods took thought for me and for what must happen to me, they will have taken thought for my good. It is not easy

to conceive of a thoughtless god, and what possible reason could they have had to be bent on my harm? What advantage would there have been from that either for themselves or for the common good, which is the main concern of their providence? If they did not take individual thought for me, then certainly they took thought for the common good, and since what happens to me is a consequential part of that, I should accept and welcome it. But if after all they take thought for nothing (an ² impious thing to believe – otherwise let us abandon sacrifice, prayer to the gods, swearing by the gods, all the other things which we variously do on the assumption that the gods are with us and share our lives) – if, then, they take no thought for any of our concerns, it is open to me to take thought for myself: and my concern is for what is best. Best for each is what suits his own condition and nature: and my nature is both rational and social.

As Antoninus, my city and country is Rome: as a human being, it is the world. So what benefits these two cities is my only good.

All that happens to the individual is to the benefit of the Whole. 45 So far, so clear. But if you look more closely you will also see as a general rule that what benefits one person benefits other people too – though here 'benefit' should be taken in its popular application to things which are in fact indifferent.

Just as all the business of the amphitheatre and such places 46 offends you as always one and the same sight, and this monotony of the spectacle bores you, so it is too with your experience of life as a whole: everything, up or down, is the same, with the same causes. How much longer, then?

Think constantly of all the sorts of men, of various professions 47 and of all the nations on earth, who have died: and so bring your thought down to Philistion, Phoebus, and Origanion. Pass now to the other classes of men. We too are bound to change our abode to that other world, where there are so many skilled orators, so many distinguished philosophers – Heraclitus,

Pythagoras, Socrates – so many heroes of old, so many later commanders and kings.

Add Eudoxus, Hipparchus, Archimedes; add other men of penetrating intellect, men of great vision, men dedicated to their work; add rogues, bigots, and even satirists of this transient mortal life, like Menippus and his kind. Reflect of all of these that they are long dead and buried. So is this anything terrible for them – or indeed for men whose very names are lost? In this world there is only one thing of value, to live out your life in truth and justice, tolerant of those who are neither true nor just.

48 Whenever you want to cheer yourself, think of the qualities of your fellows – the energy of one, for example, the decency of another, the generosity of a third, some other merit in a fourth. There is nothing so cheering as the stamp of virtues manifest in the character of colleagues – and the greater the collective incidence, the better. So keep them ready to hand.

49 You do not resent your weight, do you – that you weigh only so many pounds and not three hundred? So why resent either a life-span of so many years and not more? Just as you are content with the amount of matter allocated to you, so you should be content with your allocation of time.

50 Try to persuade them, but act even if they are unpersuaded, whenever the principle of justice so directs. But if someone forcibly resists, change tack to an unhurt acceptance, so using the obstacle to bring forth a different virtue. And remember that you set out on a conditional course – you were not aiming at the impossible. So what were you aiming at? An impulse qualified by a condition. This you have achieved: what we proposed to ourselves has been accomplished.

51 How to understand your own good: the lover of glory takes it to be the reactions of others; the lover of pleasure takes it to be his own passive experience; the intelligent man sees it as his own action.

It is possible to have no understanding of this and not to be   52
troubled in mind: things of themselves have no inherent power
to form our judgements.

Accustom yourself not to be disregarding of what someone else   53
has to say: as far as possible enter into the mind of the speaker.

What does not benefit the hive does not benefit the bee either.   54

If sailors spoke ill of their captain or patients of their doctor,   55
who else would they listen to? Otherwise how would the captain achieve a safe voyage for his passengers or the doctor
health for those in his care?

How many with whom I came into the world have already left!   56

Appearances: to the jaundiced honey seems bitter, to those   57
bitten by rabid dogs water is a terror, to little boys a ball is joy.
Why then am I angry? Or do you think that false representation
has less effect than bile in the jaundiced or poison in the hydro-
phobic?

No one will prevent you living in accordance with the principle   58
of your own nature: nothing will happen to you contrary to the
principle of universal nature.

What sort of people they wish to please! And what kind of   59
actions are the means of their success! How quickly time will
cover everything – and how much is covered already.

BOOK 7

1   This is wickedness: this is what you have often seen. And you should have this thought ready to hand against any eventuality: 'I have seen this often before.' Generally wherever you look you will find the same things. The histories – ancient, more recent, and modern – are full of them: cities and households are full of them today. There is nothing new. All is familiar, and all short-lived.

2   Your principles are living things. How else could they be deadened, except by the extinction of the corresponding mental images? And the constant rekindling of these is up to you. 'I am able to form the judgement I should about this event. If able, why troubled? All that lies outside my own mind is nothing to it.' Learn this, and you stand upright. You can live once more. Look at things again as you used to look at them: in this is the resumption of life.

3   The empty pomp of a procession, plays on the stage, flocks and herds, jousting shows, a bone thrown to puppies, tit-bits into the fishponds, ants toiling and carrying, the scurries of frightened mice, puppets dancing on their strings. Well, amid all this you must keep yourself tolerant – do not snort at them. But bear in mind that a person's worth is measured by the worth of what he values.

4   In conversation one ought to follow closely what is said, in any impulse to follow closely what takes place. In the latter case, to

see immediately the intended object of reference: in the former, to watch carefully what is meant.

Is my mind sufficient for this task, or is it not? If it is, I use it   5
for the task as an instrument given me by the nature of the Whole. If it is not, I either cede the work (if it is otherwise my responsibility) to someone better able to accomplish it, or do it as best I can, calling in aid someone who, in cooperation with my own directing mind, can achieve what is at this particular time the need and benefit of the community. Whatever I do, either by myself or with another, should have this sole focus – the common benefit and harmony.

How many who once rose to fame are now consigned to obliv-   6
ion: and how many who sang their fame are long disappeared.

Do not be ashamed of help. It is your task to achieve your   7
assigned duty, like a soldier in a scaling-party. What, then, if you are lame and cannot climb the parapet by yourself, but this is made possible by another's help?

Do not let the future trouble you. You will come to it (if that is   8
what you must) possessed of the same reason that you apply now to the present.

All things are meshed together, and a sacred bond unites   9
them. Hardly a single thing is alien to the rest: ordered together in their places they together make up the one order of the universe. There is one universe out of all things, one god pervading all things, one substance, one law, one common reason in all intelligent beings, and one truth – if indeed there is also one perfection of all cognate beings sharing in the same reason.

Everything material rapidly disappears in the universal sub-   10
stance; every cause is rapidly taken up into the universal reason; and the memory of everything is rapidly buried in eternity.

11 For a rational being, to act in accordance with nature is also to
    act in accordance with reason.

12 Standing straight – or held straight.

13 Rational beings collectively have the same relation as the vari-
    ous limbs of an organic unity – they were created for a single
    cooperative purpose. The notion of this will strike you more
    forcefully if you keep on saying to yourself: 'I am a limb of the
    composite body of rational beings.' If, though, by the change
    of one letter from *l* to *r* [*melos* to *meros*], you call yourself
    simply a *part* rather than a *limb*, you do not yet love your
    fellow men from your heart: doing good does not yet delight
    you as an end in itself; you are still doing it as a mere duty, not
    yet as a kindness to yourself.

14 Let any external thing that so wishes happen to those parts of
    me which can be affected by its happening – and they, if they
    wish, can complain. I myself am not yet harmed, unless I judge
    this occurrence something bad: and I can refuse to do so.

15 Whatever anyone does or says, I must be a good man. It is as
    if an emerald, or gold or purple, were always saying: 'Whatever
    anyone does or says, I must be an emerald and keep my own
    colour.'

16 The directing mind does not disturb itself: for example, it does
    not frighten itself or lead itself to desire. If anyone else can
    frighten it or cause it pain, let him do so: of itself, of its own
    judgement, it will not deliberately turn to such modes. The
    body should take care, as far as it can, to avoid harm; the
    sensual soul, which feels fear or pain, should say if it does so;
    but that which makes general assessment of all these things will
    not suffer at all – it will not itself rush to any such judgement.
    Of itself the directing mind is without needs, unless it creates a
    need for itself: in the same way it is untroubled and unhindered,
    unless it troubles or hinders itself.

Happiness is a benign god or divine blessing. Why then, my   17
imagination, are you doing what you do? Go away, in the gods'
name, the way you came: I have no need of you. You have come
in your old habit. I am not angry with you. Only go away.

Is someone afraid of change? Well, what can ever come to be   18
without change? Or what is dearer or closer to the nature of
the Whole than change? Can you yourself take your bath, if
the wood that heats it is not changed? Can you be fed, unless
what you eat changes? Can any other of the benefits of life be
achieved without change? Do you not see then that for you to
be changed is equal, and equally necessary to the nature of the
Whole?

All our bodies (being of one nature with the Whole and   19
cooperating with it as our limbs do with each other) pass
through the universal substance as through a swirling stream.
How many a Chrysippus, a Socrates, an Epictetus has eternity
already swallowed! This same thought should strike you about
any man at all and any thing.

I have only one anxiety: that I myself should not do something   20
which the human constitution does not intend – or does not
intend in this way or at this time.

Soon you will have forgotten all things: soon all things will   21
have forgotten you.

It is human nature to love even those who trip and fall. This   22
follows if you reflect at the time that all men are brothers; that
they go wrong through ignorance, not intent; that in a short
while both you and they will be dead; and, above all, that the
man has not harmed you – he has not made your directing
mind worse than it was before.

Universal nature uses the substance of the universe like wax,   23
making now the model of a horse, then melting it down and
using its material for a tree; next for a man; next for something

else. Each one of these subsists for only the briefest time. It is no more hardship for a box to be broken up than to be put together.

24 A deep scowl on the face is contrary to nature, and when it becomes habitual expressiveness begins to die or is even finally extinguished beyond rekindling. Try to attend to this very point, that this is something against reason. In the field of moral behaviour, if even the consciousness of doing wrong is lost, what reason is there left for living?

25 All that you see will in a moment be changed by the nature which governs the Whole: it will create other things out of this material, and then again others out of that, so that the world is always young.

26 When someone does you some wrong, you should consider immediately what judgement of good or evil led him to wrong you. When you see this, you will pity him, and not feel surprise or anger. You yourself either still share his view of good, or something like it, in which case you should understand and forgive: if, on the other hand, you no longer judge such things as either good or evil, it will be the easier for you to be patient with the unsighted.

27 Do not dream of possession of what you do not have: rather reflect on the greatest blessings in what you do have, and on their account remind yourself how much they would have been missed if they were not there. But at the same time you must be careful not to let your pleasure in them habituate you to dependency, to avoid distress if they are sometimes absent.

28 Withdraw into yourself. It is in the nature of the rational directing mind to be self-content with acting rightly and the calm it thereby enjoys.

29 Erase the print of imagination. Stop the puppet-strings of impulse. Define the present moment of time. Recognize what

happens to you or to another. Analyse and divide the event into the causal and the material. Think of your final hour. Leave the wrong done by another where it started.

Stretch your thought to parallel what is being said. Let your 30
mind get inside what is happening and who is doing it.

Take your joy in simplicity, in integrity, in indifference to all 31
that lies between virtue and vice. Love mankind. Follow god.
Democritus says, 'All else is subject to the law of convention:
only the elements are absolute and real', but enough for you to
remember that *all* is subject to *law*. Precepts reduced to very
few.

On death. Either dispersal, if we are atoms: or, if we are a unity, 32
extinction or a change of home.

On pain. Unbearable pain carries us off: chronic pain can be 33
borne. The mind preserves its own serenity by withdrawal, and
the directing reason is not impaired by pain. It is for the parts
injured by the pain to protest if they can.

On fame. Look at their minds, the nature of their thought and 34
what they seek or avoid. And see how, just as drifting sands
constantly overlay the previous sand, so in our lives what we
once did is very quickly covered over by subsequent layers.

'So, to a man endowed with noble intelligence and a vision of 35
all time and all being, do you think that this human life will
seem of great importance? "Impossible," he said. So such a
man will not think there is anything fearful in death either?
"Certainly not".'

'A king's lot: to do good and be damned.' 36

It is shameful that the face should be so obedient, shaping and 37
ordering its expression as the mind dictates, when the mind
cannot impose its own shape and order on itself.

38   'Mere things, brute facts, should not provoke your rage:
            They have no mind to care.'

39   'May you give joy to the immortal gods, and joy to us.'

40   'Ripe ears of corn are reaped, and so are lives:
            One stands, another falls.'

41   'If I and my two sons are now no more
            The gods' concern, this too will have its cause.'

42   'For good and right stand on my side.'

43   'Don't join in mourning, or in ecstasy.'

44   'But I could give this man a proper answer. I would say: "You
     are mistaken, my friend, if you think that a man of any worth
     at all should take into account the risk of life or death, and not
     have as his sole consideration in any action whether he is doing
     right or wrong, the act of a good man or a bad".'

45   'The truth of the matter, my fellow Athenians, is this. Whatever
     position a man has taken up in his own best judgement, or is
     assigned by his commander, there, it seems to me, he should
     stay and face the danger, giving no thought to death or anything
     else before dishonour.'

46   'But, my dear fellow, consider it possible that nobility and
     virtue are something other than saving one's life or having it
     saved. Could it not be that anyone who is truly a man should
     dismiss any concern for a particular length of life, and not
     simply live for the sake of living? Rather he should leave all
     this to god and believe what the womenfolk say, that no one
     ever escapes the day of his fate: his thought should be on this
     further question, how best to live his life in the time he has to
     be alive.'

47   Observe the movement of the stars as if you were running their

courses with them, and let your mind constantly dwell on the changes of the elements into each other. Such imaginings wash away the filth of life on the ground.

Further, when your talk is about mankind, view earthly things 48 as if looking down on them from some point high above – flocks, armies, farms, weddings, divorces, births, deaths, the hubbub of the law-courts, desert places, various foreign nations, festivals, funerals, markets; all the medley of the world and the ordered conjunction of opposites.

Look back over the past – all those many changes of dynasties. 49 And you can foresee the future too: it will be completely alike, incapable of deviating from the rhythm of the present. So for the study of human life forty years are as good as ten thousand: what more will you see?

Again: 50

> 'What is born of earth goes back to earth:
> but the growth from heavenly seed
> returns whence it came, to heaven.'

Or else this: a dissolution of the nexus of atoms, and senseless molecules likewise dispersed.

Again: 51

> 'With special food or drink, or sorcery,
> Seeking a channel from the stream of death.'

>> 'The wind that blows from god
>> we must endure, and labour
>> uncomplaining.'

'Better at throwing his man': but not more public-spirited, or 52 more decent, or more disciplined to circumstance, or more tolerant of neighbours' faults.

53   Where a task can be accomplished in accordance with the reason which gods and men share, there is nothing to be afraid of: because where there is the possibility of benefit from an action which moves along the proper path, following our own human constitution, there should be no lurking fear of any harm.

54   Everywhere and all the time it is up to you to honour god in contentment with your present circumstance, to treat the men who are your present company with justice, and to lavish thought on every present impression in your mind, so that nothing slips in past your understanding.

55   Do not look around at the directing minds of other people, but keep looking straight ahead to where nature is leading you – both universal nature, in what happens to you, and your own nature, in what you must do yourself. Every creature must do what follows from its own constitution. The rest of creation is constituted to serve rational beings (just as in everything else the lower exists for the higher), but rational beings are here to serve each other. So the main principle in man's constitution is the social. The second is resistance to the promptings of the flesh. It is the specific property of rational and intelligent activity to isolate itself and never be influenced by the activity of the senses or impulses: both these are of the animal order, and it is the aim of intelligent activity to be sovereign over them and never yield them the mastery – and rightly so, as it is the very nature of intelligence to put all these things to its own use. The third element in a rational constitution is a judgement unhurried and undeceived. So let your directing mind hold fast to these principles and follow the straight road ahead: then it has what belongs to it.

56   Imagine you were now dead, or had not lived before this moment. Now view the rest of your life as a bonus, and live it as nature directs.

57   Love only what falls your way and is fated for you. What could suit you more than that?

In every contingency keep in your mind's eye those who had the   58
same experience before, and reacted with vexation, disbelief, or
complaint. So where are they now? Nowhere. Well then, do
you want to act like them? Why not leave the moods and
shifts of others to the shifting and the shifted, and for yourself
concentrate wholly on how to make use of these contingencies?
You will then use them well, and they will be raw material
in your hands. Only take care, and seek your own best good in
all that you do. Remember these two things: the action is
important, the context indifferent.

Dig inside yourself. Inside there is a spring of goodness ready   59
to gush at any moment, if you keep digging.

The body, too, should stay firmly composed, and not fling itself   60
about either in motion or at rest. Just as the mind displays
qualities in the face, keeping it intelligent and attractive, something similar should be required of the whole body. But all this
should be secured without making an obvious point of it.

The art of living is more like wrestling than dancing, in that   61
it stands ready for what comes and is not thrown by the
unforeseen.

All the time you should consider who are these people whose   62
endorsement you wish, and what are the minds that direct
them. When you look into the sources of their judgement and
impulse, you will not blame their unwitting error, nor will you
feel the need of their endorsement.

'No soul', says Plato, 'likes to be robbed of truth' – and the same   63
holds of justice, moderation, kindness, and all such virtues.
Essential that you should keep this constantly in your mind:
this will make you more gentle to all.

Whenever you suffer pain, have ready to hand the thought that   64
pain is not a moral evil and does not harm your governing
intelligence: pain can do no damage either to its rational or to

its social nature. In most cases of pain you should be helped too by the saying of Epicurus: 'Pain is neither unendurable nor unending, as long as you remember its limits and do not exaggerate it in your imagination.' Remember too that many things we find disagreeable are the unrecognized analogues of pain – drowsiness, for example, oppressive heat, loss of appetite. So when you find yourself complaining of any of these, say to yourself, 'You are giving in to pain.'

65   Take care that you never treat the misanthropic as they treat mankind.

66   How do we know that Telauges' character did not make him a better man than Socrates? It is not enough that Socrates died a more glorious death, that he argued more skilfully with the sophists, that he showed greater endurance in spending a whole night out in the frost, that he was braver in his decision to refuse the order to arrest Leon of Salamis, that he 'swaggered in the streets' (though one could well question if this last is true). No, what we need to investigate is the nature of Socrates' soul. We should ask whether he was able to be content with a life of justice shown to men and piety to the gods; neither condemning all vice wholesale nor yet toadying to anyone's ignorance; not regarding anything allotted to him by the Whole as misplaced in him or a crushing burden to endure; not lending his mind to share the poor passions of the flesh.

67   The way nature has blended you into the compound whole does not prevent you drawing a boundary around yourself and keeping what is your own in your own control. Always remember this: remember too that the happy life depends on very little. And do not think, just because you have given up hope of becoming a philosopher or a scientist, you should therefore despair of a free spirit, integrity, social conscience, obedience to god. It is wholly possible to become a 'divine man' without anybody's recognition.

68   Live through your life without pressure and in the utmost

contentment, even if all are clamouring what they will against you, even if wild beasts are tearing off the limbs of this poor lump of a body accreted round you. What in all this prevents the mind from preserving itself in tranquillity, in true judgement of circumstance and readiness to use any event submitted to it? So that Judgement says to Circumstance: 'This is what you really are, however different you may conventionally appear'; and Ready Use says to Event: 'I was looking for you. I always take the present moment as raw material for the exercise of rational and social virtue – in short, for the art of man or god.' Because a god or a man can assimilate anything that happens: it will not be new or hard to handle, but familiar and easy.

Perfection of character is this: to live each day as if it were your 69 last, without frenzy, without apathy, without pretence.

The gods, who are free from death, do not resent their need 70 throughout all the length of eternity to tolerate in such numbers such worthless creatures as men: what is more, they even care for them in all sorts of ways. And do you, with the merest time before your own exit, refuse to make the effort – and that when you are one of the worthless creatures yourself?

It is ridiculous not to escape from one's own vices, which is 71 possible, while trying to escape the vices of others, which is impossible.

Whatever the rational and social faculty finds neither intelligent 72 nor to the common good it judges, with good reason, beneath itself.

When you have done good and another has benefited, why do 73 you still look, as fools do, for a third thing besides – credit for good works, or a return?

No one tires of receiving benefit: and action in accordance with 74 nature is your own benefit. Do not then tire of benefit gained by benefit given.

75 The nature of the Whole set itself to create a universe. So now either everything that comes into being springs from that as logical consequence, or else even the primary aims to which the directing mind of the universe sets its own impulse are irrational. Reminding yourself of this will help you to face much with greater tranquillity.

BOOK 8

This too is a counter to pretension, that you have lost now the 1
chance to live your whole life, or at least your adult life, as
a philosopher: indeed it has become clear to many, yourself
included, that you are far from philosophy. You are tarnished,
then: difficult for you now to win the reputation of a philosopher, and besides your station in life is a contrary pull. So if
you have a true perception of how things lie, abandon any
concern for reputation, and be satisfied if you can just live the
rest of your life, whatever remains, in the way your nature
wishes. You must consider, then, what those wishes are, and
then let nothing else distract you. You know from experience
that in all your wanderings you have nowhere found the good
life – not in logic, not in wealth, not in glory, not in indulgence:
nowhere. Where then is it to be found? In doing what man's
nature requires. And how is he to do this? By having principles
to govern his impulses and actions. What are these principles?
Those of good and evil – the belief that nothing is good for a
human being which does not make him just, self-controlled,
brave, and free: and nothing evil which does not make him the
opposite of these.

Ask yourself this about each action: 'How does this sit with 2
me? Shall I regret it?' In a short while I am dead and all things
are gone. What more do I want, if this present work is that of
an intelligent and social being, sharing one law with god?

Alexander, Julius Caesar, Pompey – what are they to Diogenes, 3
Heraclitus, Socrates? These men saw into reality, its causes and

its material, and their directing minds were their own masters. As for the former, they were slaves to all their ambitions.

4   Even if you burst with indignation, they will still carry on regardless.

5   First, do not be upset: all things follow the nature of the Whole, and in a little while you will be no one and nowhere, as is true now even of Hadrian and Augustus. Next, concentrate on the matter in hand and see it for what it is. Remind yourself of your duty to be a good man and rehearse what man's nature demands: then do it straight and unswerving, or say what you best think right. Always, though, in kindness, integrity, and sincerity.

6   The work of universal nature is to translate this reality to another, to change things, to take them from here and carry them there. All things are mutations, but there is equality too in their distribution. All is familiar: no cause then for fear of anything new.

7   Every living organism is fulfilled when it follows the right path for its own nature. For a rational nature the right path is to withhold assent to anything false or obscure in the impressions made on its mind, to direct its impulses solely to social action, to reserve its desires and aversions to what lies in our power, and to welcome all that is assigned to it by universal nature. Because it is a part of universal nature just as the nature of the leaf is part of the plant's nature: except that in the case of the leaf its nature partakes of a nature which lacks perception or reason and is liable to impediment. Whereas man's nature is part of a nature which is unimpeded, intelligent, and just – in that to each creature it gives fair and appropriate allocations of duration, substance, cause, activity, and experience. But do not look to find a one-to-one correspondence in every case, but rather an overall equivalence – the totality of this to the aggregate of that.

Not possible to study. But possible to rein in arrogance; possible   8
to triumph over pleasures and pains; possible to rise above mere
glory; possible not to be angry with the unfeeling and the
ungrateful, and even, yes, to care for them.

Let nobody any more hear you blaming palace life: don't hear   9
yourself blaming it.

Regret is a censure of yourself for missing something beneficial.   10
The good must be something beneficial, and of concern to the
wholly good person. No wholly good person would regret
missing a pleasure. Therefore pleasure is neither beneficial nor
a good.

What is this thing in itself, in its own constitution? What are   11
its elements of substance and material, and of cause? What is
its function in the world? What is its duration?

When you are reluctant to get up from your sleep, remind   12
yourself that it is your constitution and man's nature to perform
social acts, whereas sleep is something you share with dumb
animals. Now what accords with the nature of each being is
thereby the more closely related to it, the more in its essence,
and indeed the more to its liking.

Constantly test your mental impressions – each one individu-   13
ally, if you can: investigate the cause, identify the emotion,
apply the analysis of logic.

Whenever you meet someone, ask yourself first this immediate   14
question: 'What beliefs does this person hold about the good
and bad in life?' Because if he believes this or that about pleasure
and pain and their constituents, about fame and obscurity,
death and life, then I shall not find it surprising or strange if he
acts in this or that way, and I shall remember that he has no
choice but to act as he does.

It would be absurd to be surprised at a fig-tree bearing figs.   15

Remember that there is as little cause for surprise if the world brings forth fruits such as these when the crop is there. Equally absurd for a doctor or ship's captain to be surprised at fever in a patient or a head-wind springing up.

16 Remember that to change course or accept correction leaves you just as free as you were. The action is your own, driven by your own impulse and judgement, indeed your own intelligence.

17 If the choice is yours, why do the thing? But if it is another's choice, what do you blame – atoms or gods? Either is madness. There is no blame. If you can, put him right: if you can't, at the least put the matter itself right. If that too is impossible, what further purpose does blame serve? Nothing should be done without purpose.

18 What dies does not pass out of the universe. If it remains here and is changed, then here too it is resolved into the everlasting constituents, which are the elements of the universe and of you yourself. These too change, and make no complaint of it.

19 Everything has come into being for a purpose – a horse, say, a vine. Does this surprise you? Even the sun will say, 'I came into being for a purpose': likewise the other gods. For what purpose, then, were you created? For your pleasure? Just see whether this idea can be entertained.

20 Nature's aim for everything includes its cessation just as much as its beginning and its duration – like someone throwing up a ball. How can it be good for the ball on the way up and bad on the way down, or even when it hits the ground? How can it be good for a bubble when it forms, and bad when it bursts? A candle is a similar example.

21 Turn it inside out and see what it is like, what it becomes in age, sickness, death.
    Life is short both for praiser and praised, for the remembering

and the remembered. And this, moreover, in just a cranny of one continent: even here not all are attuned to each other, or even an individual to himself. And the whole earth is a mere point in space.

Concentrate on the subject or the act in question, on principle   22
or meaning.

You deserve what you're going through. You would rather become good tomorrow than be good today.

Doing something? I do it with reference to the benefit of man-   23
kind. Something happening to me? I accept it in reference to the gods and the universal source from which all things spring interrelated.

Just as you see your bath – all soap, sweat, grime, greasy water,   24
the whole thing disgusting – so is every part of life and every object in it.

Lucilla buried Verus, then Lucilla was buried. Secunda buried   25
Maximus, then Secunda next. So with Epitynchanus and Diotimus, Antoninus and Faustina. The same story always. Celer saw Hadrian to his grave, then went to his own grave. Where are they now, those sharp minds, those prophets or prigs? Certainly Charax, Demetrius, Eudaemon, and others like them were sharp minds. But all creatures of a day, long dead. Some not remembered even briefly, some turned into legend, and some now vanishing even from legend.

So remember this, that either the poor compound of your body must be scattered, or your frail spirit must be extinguished, or else migrate and take its post elsewhere.

Man's joy is to do man's proper work. And work proper to   26
man is benevolence to his own kind, disdain for the stirrings of the senses, diagnosis of the impressions he can trust, contemplation of universal nature and all things thereby entailed.

Three relations. First, to your environment; second, to the   27 divine cause which is the source of all that happens to all men; third, to your fellows and contemporaries.

28 Pain is an evil either to the body – so let the body give its evidence – or to the soul. But the soul can preserve its own clear sky and calm voyage by not assessing pain as an evil. Every judgement, every impulse, desire and rejection is within the soul, where nothing evil can penetrate.

29 Erase the impressions on your mind by constantly saying to yourself: 'It is in my power now to keep this soul of mine free from any vice or passion, or any other disturbance at all: but seeing all things for what they are, I can treat them on their merits.' Remember this power which nature gives you.

30 When you speak in the senate or to any individual, be straightforward, not pedantic. Use language which rings true.

31 The court of Augustus – wife, daughter, grandsons, step-sons, sister, Agrippa, relatives, household, friends, Areius, Maecenas, doctors, diviners: an entire court dead. Go on now to other cases, where it is not the death of just one individual but of a whole family, like the Pompeys. And there is the inscription you see on tombstones: 'The last of his line'. Just think of all the anxiety of previous generations to leave behind an heir, and then one has to be the last. Here again the death of a whole family.

32 You must compose your life action by action, and be satisfied if each action achieves its own end as best can be: and no one can prevent you from that achievement. 'But there will be some external obstacle.' No obstacle, though, to justice, self-control, and reason. 'But perhaps some other source of action will be obstructed.' Well, gladly accept the obstruction as it is, make a judicious change to meet the given circumstance, and another action will immediately substitute and fit into the composition of your life as discussed.

Accept humbly: let go easily.   33

If you have ever seen a severed hand or foot, or a head cut off   34
and lying some way away from the rest of the body – analogous
is what someone does to himself, as far as he can, when he will
not accept his lot and severs himself from society or does some
unsocial act. Suppose you have made yourself an outcast from
the unity of nature – you were born a part of it, but now you
have cut yourself off. Yet here lies the paradox – that it is open
to you to rejoin that unity. No other part has this privilege
from god, to come together again once it has been separated
and cut away. Just consider the grace of god's favour to man.
He has put it in man's power not to be broken off from the
Whole in the first place, and also, if he has broken off, to return
and grow back again, resuming his role as a member.

Just as the nature of the Whole is the source of all other faculties 35
in every rational creature, so it has given us this power too. In
the same way that nature turns to its own purpose anything
obstructive or contrary, placing it in the fated scheme of things
and making it part of itself, so the rational being can also
convert every obstacle into material for his own use, and use it
to further whatever his original purpose was.

Do not let the panorama of your life oppress you, do not dwell   36
on all the various troubles which may have occurred in the past
or may occur in the future. Just ask yourself in each instance of
the present: 'What is there in this work which I cannot endure
or support?' You will be ashamed to make any such confession.
Then remind yourself that it is neither the future nor the past
which weighs on you, but always the present: and the present
burden reduces, if only you can isolate it and accuse your mind
of weakness if it cannot hold against something thus stripped
bare.

Is Panthea or Pergamus still sitting by the coffin of Verus? Or   37
Chabrias or Diotimus by Hadrian's? Ridiculous! And if they
were still sitting there, would the dead be aware? And if they

were aware, would they be pleased? And if they were pleased, would that make their mourners immortal? Was it not their fate also first to grow old – old women and old men like any others – and then to die? And with them dead, what would those they mourned do then? It is all stench and corruption in a bag of bones.

38   If you have sharp sight, use it: but, as the poet says, add wise judgement.

39   In the constitution of the rational being I can see no virtue that counters justice: but I do see the counter to pleasure – self-control.

40   If you remove your judgement of anything that seems painful, you yourself stand quite immune to pain. 'What self?' Reason. 'But I am not just reason.' Granted. So let your reason cause itself no pain, and if some other part of you is in trouble, it can form its own judgement for itself.

41   An obstacle to sense perception is harmful to animal nature. An obstacle to impulse is likewise harmful to animal nature. (Something else will be similarly obstructive and harmful to the constitution of plants.) It follows that an obstacle to the mind is harmful to intelligent nature.
     Now apply all this to yourself. Is pain or pleasure affecting you? That is for the senses. You have formed an impulse and then met some obstruction? If this was an unconditional aim, then, yes, the obstruction harms your rational nature: but if you accept what is common experience, no harm is yet done or hindrance caused. You see, no one else will impede the proper functions of the mind. The mind cannot be touched by fire, steel, tyranny, slander, or anything whatever, once it has become 'a perfect round in solitude'.

42   I have no cause to hurt myself: I have never consciously hurt anyone else.

Joy varies from person to person. My joy is if I keep my directing 43
mind pure, denying no human being or human circumstance,
but looking on all things with kindly eyes, giving welcome or
use to each as it deserves.

Look, make yourself a gift of this present time. Those who are 44
more inclined to pursue fame hereafter fail to reckon that the
next generation will have people just like those they dislike
now: and they too will die. What, anyway, is it to you if this is
the echo in future voices and this the judgement they make of
you?

Pick me up and throw me where you will. Wherever I land I 45
shall keep the god within me happy – satisfied, that is, if attitude
and action follow its own constitution.
     Is this present thing any good reason for my soul to be sick
and out of sorts – humbled, craving, shackled, shying? Will you
find any good reason for that?

Nothing can happen to any human being outside the experience 46
which is natural to humans – an ox too experiences nothing
foreign to the nature of oxen, a vine nothing foreign to the
nature of vines, a stone nothing outside the property of a stone.
So if each thing experiences what is usual and natural for it,
why should you complain? Universal nature has brought you
nothing you can't endure.

If your distress has some external cause, it is not the thing itself 47
that troubles you, but your own judgement of it – and you can
erase this immediately. If it is something in your own attitude
that distresses you, no one stops you correcting your view. So
too if you are distressed at not achieving some action you think
salutary, why not carry on rather than fret? 'But there's an
obstacle in the way too solid to move.' No cause for distress,
then, since the reason for failure does not lie with you. 'But life
is not worth living if I fail in this.' Well then, you must depart
this life, as gracious in death as one who does achieve his
purpose, and at peace, too, with those who stood in your way.

48 Remember that your directing mind becomes invincible when
    it withdraws into its own self-sufficiency, not doing anything it
    does not wish to do, even if its position is unreasonable. How
    much more, then, when the judgement it forms is reasoned and
    deliberate? That is why a mind free from passions is a fortress:
    people have no stronger place of retreat, and someone taking
    refuge here is then impregnable. Anyone who has not seen this
    is short of wisdom: anyone who has seen it and does not take
    refuge is short of fortune.

49 Do not elaborate to yourself beyond what your initial impres-
    sions report. You have been told that so-and-so is maligning
    you. That is the report: you have not been told that you are
    harmed. I see that my little boy is ill. That is what I see: I do
    not see that he is in danger. So always stay like this within your
    first impressions and do not add conclusions from your own
    thoughts – and then that is all. Or rather you can add the
    conclusion of one acquainted with all that happens in the world.

50 A bitter cucumber? Throw it away. Brambles in the path? Go
    round them. That is all you need, without going on to ask, 'So
    why are these things in the world anyway?' That question
    would be laughable to a student of nature, just as any carpenter
    or cobbler would laugh at you if you objected to the sight of
    shavings or off-cuts from their work on the shop floor. Yet they
    have somewhere to throw their rubbish, whereas the nature of
    the Whole has nothing outside itself. The marvel of its craft is
    that it sets its own confines and recycles into itself all within
    them which seems to be decaying, growing old, or losing its
    use: and then creates afresh from this same material. This way
    it requires no substance other than its own, and has no need
    for a rubbish-dump. So it is complete in its own space, its own
    material, and its own craftsmanship.

51 Do not be dilatory in action, muddled in communication, or
    vague in thought. Don't let your mind settle into depression or
    elation. Allow some leisure in your life.
        'They kill, they cut in pieces, they hunt with curses.' What

relevance has this to keeping your mind pure, sane, sober, just?
As if a man were to come up to a spring of clear, sweet water
and curse it – it would still continue to bubble up water good
to drink. He could throw in mud or dung: in no time the spring
will break it down, wash it away, and take no colour from it.
How then can you secure an everlasting spring and not a cistern? By keeping yourself at all times intent on freedom – and
staying kind, simple, and decent.

Someone who does not know that there is an ordered universe   52
does not know where he is. Someone who does not know the
natural purpose of the universe does not know who he is or
what the universe is. Someone who fails in any one of these
ways could not tell the purpose of his own existence either. So
what do you think of the man who fears or courts the applause
of an audience who have no idea where they are or who they
are?

aise of a man who curses himself three times   53
ant to please a man who can't please himself?
imself when he regrets almost everything he

your breath from the surrounding air, but   54
oo from the mind which embraces all things.
spreads everywhere and permeates no less
than the air: it is there for all who want to absorb it, just like
the air for those who can draw breath.

Wickedness overall does no harm to the universe. Individual   55
wickedness does no harm to the recipient: it is only harmful to
the perpetrator, and he has the option to be rid of it just as
soon as he himself decides.

To my determining will my neighbour's will is as indifferent as   56
his breath and his body. Sure, we are born above all for the
sake of each other: nevertheless the directing mind of each of us
has its own sovereignty. Otherwise my neighbour's wickedness

would be my own harm: and this was not god's intention, to leave my misfortune up to another.

57 The sun appears to pour itself down, and indeed its light pours in all directions, but the stream does not run out. This pouring is linear extension: that is why its beams are called rays, because they radiate in extended lines. You can see what a ray is if you observe the sun's light entering a dark room through a narrow opening. It extends in a straight line and impacts, so to speak, on any solid body in its path which blocks passage through the air on the other side: it settles there and does not slip off or fall.

Something similar will be true of the flow and diffusion of the universal mind – not an exhaustible stream but rather a constant radiation. And there will be nothing forceful or violent in its impact on the obstacles it meets: it will not fall off, but will settle there and illuminate what receives it. Anything unreflective will deprive itself of that light.

58 He who fears death fears either unconsciousness or another sort of consciousness. Now if you will no longer be conscious you will not be conscious either of anything bad. If you are to take on a different consciousness, you will be a different being and life will not cease.

59 Men are born for the sake of each other. So either teach or tolerate.

60 An arrow flies in one way, the mind in another. Yet even when it is keeping on the alert or circling round an inquiry, the mind moves no less directly, and straight to its target.

61 Enter into the directing mind of everyone, and let anyone else enter your own.

BOOK 9

Injustice is sin. When universal Nature has constituted rational 1
creatures for the sake of each other – to benefit one another as
deserved, but never to harm – anyone contravening her will is
clearly guilty of sin against the oldest of the gods: because
universal Nature is the nature of ultimate reality, to which all
present existence is related.

Lying, too, is a sin against the same goddess: her name is 2
Truth, and she is the original cause of all that is true. The
conscious liar sins to the extent that his deceit causes injustice:
the unconscious liar to the extent that he is out of tune with
the nature of the Whole and out of order with the nature of the
ordered universe against which he fights. And it *is* fighting when
he allows himself to be carried in opposition to the truth. He
has received the prompts from nature: by ignoring them he is
now incapable of distinguishing false from true.

Moreover, the pursuit of pleasure as a good and the avoid- 3
ance of pain as an evil constitutes sin. Someone like that must
inevitably and frequently blame universal Nature for unfair
distribution as between bad men and good, since bad men are
often deep in pleasures and the possessions which make for
pleasure, while the good often meet with pain and the circumstances which cause pain.

Further, anyone who fears pain will also at times be afraid 4
of some future event in the world, and that is immediate sin.
And a man who pursues pleasure will not hold back from
injustice – an obvious sin. Those who wish to follow Nature
and share her mind must themselves be indifferent to those
pairs of opposites to which universal Nature is indifferent – she

would not create these opposites if she were not indifferent either way. So anyone who is not himself indifferent to pain and pleasure, death and life, fame and obscurity – things which universal Nature treats indifferently – is clearly committing a sin.

5 By 'universal Nature treating these things indifferently' I mean that they happen impartially by cause and effect to all that comes into being and owes its being to the fulfilment of an original impulse of Providence. Under this impulse Providence set out from a first premise to establish the present order of the universe: she had conceived certain principles of what was to be, and determined generative powers to create substances, transformations, and successive regeneration.

2 A man of sense and sensitivity would depart the company of men without ever tasting falsehood, pretence of any kind, excess, or pomp. The next best course is at least to sicken of these things before your final breath. Or do you prefer to sit at table with wickedness? Has your experience not yet persuaded you to shun this plague? Because the corruption of the mind is much more a plague than any such contaminating change in the surrounding air we breathe. The latter infects animate creatures in their animate nature: the former infects human beings in their humanity.

3 Do not despise death: welcome it, rather, as one further part of nature's will. Our very dissolution is just like all the other natural processes which life's seasons bring – like youth and old age, growth and maturity, development of teeth and beard and grey hair, insemination, pregnancy, and childbirth. In the educated attitude to death, then, there is nothing superficial or demanding or disdainful: simply awaiting it as one of the functions of nature. And just as you may now be waiting for the child your wife carries to come out of the womb, so you should look forward to the time when your soul will slip this bodily sheath.

2 If you want another criterion – unscientific but emotionally effective – you will find it quite easy to face death if you stop

to consider the business you will be leaving and the sort of characters which will no longer contaminate your soul. You must not of course take offence at them, rather care for them and tolerate them kindly: but still remember that the deliverance death brings is not deliverance from the like-minded. This alone, if anything could, might pull you back and hold you to life – if you were allowed to live in the company of people who share your principles. But as things are you see how wearisome it is to live out of tune with your fellows, so that you say: 'Come quickly, death, or I too may forget myself.'

The sinner sins against himself: the wrongdoer wrongs himself, 4 by making himself morally bad.

There can often be wrongs of omission as well as commission. 5

These will suffice: the present certainty of judgement, the 6 present social action, the present disposition well content with any effect of an external cause.

Erase the print of imagination, stop impulse, quench desire: 7 keep your directing mind its own master.

Irrational creatures share in one animate soul, and rational 8 creatures partake in one intelligent soul: just as there is one earth for all the things of earth, and one light to see by, one air to breathe for all of us who have sight and life.

All things which share some common quality tend to their own 9 kind. Everything earthy inclines to earth. Everything watery flows together, and the same with air, so they need physical obstacles to force a separation. Fire rises upwards because of the elemental fire, but is nevertheless so eager to help the ignition of any fire here below that any material which is a little too dry is easily ignited, for the lack of ingredients which hinder combustion.
    So too everything which shares in a common intelligent

nature tends equally, or yet more so, to its own kind. Proportionate to its superiority over the rest, it is that much readier to mix and blend with its family.

2 So right from the beginning among the irrational creatures there could be seen hives, flocks, birds rearing their young, a sort of love: already there were animate souls at work there, and in the higher orders an increasingly strong collective bond which is not found in plants or stones or wood. And among the rational creatures there were civic communities, friendships, households, assemblies: and in war treaties and truces. Among yet higher things there exists a sort of unity even at a distance, as with the stars. Thus the upper reaches of the scale of being can effect fellow-feeling even when the members are far apart.

3 Look then at what is happening now. Only the intelligent creatures have now forgotten that urge to be unified with each other: only here will you see no confluence. They may run from it, but nevertheless they are overtaken: such is the power of nature. Look carefully and you will see what I mean. You are more likely to find earth not returning to earth than a man cut off from man.

10 Man, god, and the universe all bear fruit, each in its own due season. No matter if common use confines the strict sense of 'bearing fruit' to vines and the like. Reason too has its fruit, both universal and particular: other things grow from it which share its own nature.

11 If you can, show them the better way. If you cannot, remember that this is why you have the gift of kindness. The gods too are kind to such people, and in their benevolence even help them achieve some ends – health, wealth, fame. You can do it too. Or tell me – who is stopping you?

12 Work. Don't work as a miserable drudge, or in any expectation of pity or admiration. One aim only: action or inaction as civic cause demands.

13 Today I escaped from all bothering circumstances – or rather I

threw them out. They were nothing external, but inside me, just my own judgements.

All things are the same: familiar in experience, transient in time,   14
sordid in substance. Everything now is as it was in the days of those we have buried.

Mere things stand isolated outside our doors, with no know-   15
ledge or report of themselves. What then reports on them? Our directing mind.

Good or ill for the rational social being lies not in feeling but   16
in action: just as also his own virtue or vice shows not in what he feels, but in what he does.

A stone thrown in the air: nothing bad for it on the way down   17
or good for it on the way up.

Penetrate into their directing minds, and you will see what sort   18
of critics you fear – and what poor critics they are of themselves.

All things are in a process of change. You yourself are subject   19
to constant alteration and gradual decay. So too is the whole universe.

You should leave another's wrong where it lies.   20

The termination of an activity, the pause when an impulse or   21
judgement is finished – this is a sort of death, but no harm in it. Turn now to the stages of your life – childhood, say, adolescence, prime, old age. Here too each change a death: anything fearful there? Turn now to your life with your grandfather, then with your mother, then with your [adoptive] father. And as you find many other examples of dissolution, change, or termination, ask yourself: 'Was there anything to fear?' So too there is nothing to fear in the termination, the pause, and the change of your whole life.

22 Hurry to your own directing mind, to the mind of the Whole, and to the mind of this particular man. To your own mind, to make its understanding just; to the mind of the Whole, to recall what you are part of; to this man's mind, to see whether there is ignorance or design – and at the same time to reflect that his is a kindred mind.

23 Just as you yourself are a complementary part of a social system, so too your every action should complement a life of social principle. If any action of yours, then, does not have direct or indirect relation to the social end, it pulls your life apart and destroys its unity. It is a kind of sedition, like an individual in a democracy unilaterally resigning from the common harmony.

24 Children's tantrums and toys, 'tiny spirits carrying corpses' – the Underworld in the *Odyssey* strikes more real!

25 Go straight to the qualifying cause and examine it separately from the material element. Then establish the maximum time for which this individual thing thus qualified can by its nature subsist.

26 You have endured innumerable troubles by not leaving your directing mind to do the work it was made for. But enough.

27 When another blames you or hates you, or people voice similar criticisms, go to their souls, penetrate inside and see what sort of people they are. You will realize that there is no need to be racked with anxiety that they should hold any particular opinion about you. But you should still be kind to them. They are by nature your friends, and the gods too help them in various ways – dreams and divination – at least to the objects of their concern.

28 The recurrent cycles of the universe are the same, up and down, from eternity to eternity. And either the mind of the Whole has a specific impulse for each individual case – if so, you should welcome the result – or it had a single original impulse, from

which all else follows in consequence: and why should you be anxious about that? The Whole is either a god – then all is well: or if purposeless – some sort of random arrangement of atoms or molecules – you should not be without purpose yourself.

In a moment the earth will cover us all. Then the earth too will change, and then further successive changes to infinity. One reflecting on these waves of change and transformation, and the speed of their flow, will hold all mortal things in contempt.

The universal cause is a torrent, sweeping everything in its 29 stream. So, man, what does that mean for you? Do what nature requires at this moment. Start straight away, if that is in your power: don't look over your shoulder to see if people will know. Don't hope for Plato's utopian republic, but be content with the smallest step forward, and regard even that result as no mean achievement. How worthless are these little men in the public eye who think their actions have anything to do with philosophy! They are full of snot. And who will change their views? Without a change of view what alternative is there to slavery – men groaning and going through the motions of compliance? Go on, then, talk to me now of Alexander and Philip and Demetrius of Phalerum. I shall follow them, if they saw the will of universal nature and took themselves to her school. But if they simply strutted a dramatic role, no one has condemned me to imitate them. The work of philosophy is simple and modest. Do not seduce me to pompous pride.

Take a view from above – look at the thousands of flocks and 30 herds, the thousands of human ceremonies, every sort of voyage in storm or calm, the range of creation, combination, and extinction. Consider too the lives once lived by others long before you, the lives that will be lived after you, the lives lived now among foreign tribes; and how many have never even heard your name, how many will very soon forget it, how many may praise you now but quickly turn to blame. Reflect that neither memory nor fame, nor anything else at all, has any importance worth thinking of.

31   Calm acceptance of what comes from a cause outside yourself,
     and justice in all activity of your own causation. In other words,
     impulse and action fulfilled in that social conduct which is an
     expression of your own nature.

32   You can strip away many unnecessary troubles which lie wholly
     in your own judgement. And you will immediately make large
     and wide room for yourself by grasping the whole universe in
     your thought, contemplating the eternity of time, and reflecting
     on the rapid change of each thing in every part – how brief the
     gap from birth to dissolution, how vast the gulf of time before
     your birth, and an equal infinity after your dissolution.

33   All that you see will soon perish; those who witness this per-
     ishing will soon perish themselves. Die in extreme old age or
     die before your time – it will all be the same.

34   What are the directing minds of these people? What are they
     set on, what governs their likes and values? Train yourself to
     look at their souls naked. When they think that their blame will
     hurt or their praise advantage, what a conceit that is!

35   Loss is nothing more than change. Universal nature delights in
     change, and all that flows from nature happens for the good.
     Similar things have happened from time everlasting, and there
     will be more such to eternity. So why do you say that everything
     has always happened for the bad and always will, that all those
     gods between them have evidently never found any power to
     right this, so the world is condemned to the grip of perpetual
     misery?

36   The rotting of the base material of everything. Water, dust,
     bones, stench. Again: marble is a mere deposit in the earth,
     gold and silver mere sediments; your clothing is animal hair,
     your purple is fish blood; and so on with all else. And the vital
     spirit is just the same, changing from this to that.

37   Enough of this miserable way of life, enough of grumbling and

aping! Why are you troubled? What is new in this? What is it that drives you mad? The cause? Then face it. Or rather the material? Then face that. Apart from cause and material there is nothing. But you should even now, late though it is, see to your relation to the gods also: make yourself simpler, and better. Three years is as good as a hundred in this quest.

If he did wrong, the harm is to himself. But perhaps he did not   38
do wrong.

Either all things flow from one intelligent source and supervene   39
as in one coordinated body, so the part should not complain at what happens in the interest of the whole – or all is atoms, and nothing more than present stew and future dispersal. Why then are you troubled? Say to your directing mind: 'Are you dead, are you decayed, have you turned into an animal, are you pretending, are you herding with the rest and sharing their feed?'

Either the gods have power or they do not. Now, if they have   40
no power, why pray? If they do have power, why not pray for their gift of freedom from all worldly fear, desire, or regret, rather than for the presence or absence of this or that? Certainly, if the gods can cooperate with men, they can cooperate to these ends.

But you might say: 'The gods have put these things in my own power.' Is it not then better to use your own power in freedom rather than show a servile and supine concern for what you cannot control? And who told you that the gods do not help us even to the ends which lie within our own power? At any rate, pray about these things, and you will see. One man prays: 'How can I sleep with that woman?' Your prayer is: 'How can I lose the desire to sleep with her?' Another prays: 'How can I be rid of that man?' You pray: 'How can I stop wanting to be rid of him?' Another: 'How can I save my little child?' You: 'How can I learn not to fear his loss?' And so on. Give all your prayers this turn, and observe what happens.

41 Epicurus says: 'In my illness my conversations were not about
    the sufferings of my poor body, and I did not prattle on to my
    visitors in this vein, but I continued to discuss the cardinal
    principles of natural philosophy, with particular reference to
    this very point, how the mind shares in such disturbances of
    the flesh while still preserving its calm and pursuing its own
    good.' He goes on: 'I did not allow the doctors either to preen
    themselves on any great achievement, but my life continued fine
    and proper.' An example, then, for you in sickness, if you are
    sick, and in any other circumstance. All schools agree that you
    should not abandon philosophy in any eventualities of life, nor
    join the ignorant chatter of the uneducated layman. Concen-
    trate only on the work of the moment, and the instrument you
    use for its doing.

42 Whenever you are offended at someone's lack of shame, you
    should immediately ask yourself: 'So is it possible for there to
    be no shameless people in the world?' It is not possible. Do not
    then ask for the impossible. This person is just one of the
    shameless inevitably existing in the world. Have the same
    thought ready for the rogue, the traitor, every sort of offender.
    The recognition that this class of people must necessarily exist
    will immediately make you kinder to them as individuals.
 2 Another useful thought of direct application is the particular
    virtue nature has given us to counter a particular wrong. Gentle-
    ness is given as the antidote to cruelty, and other qualities to
    meet other offences. In general, you can always re-educate one
    who has lost his way: and anyone who does wrong has missed
    his proper aim and gone astray.
        And what harm have you suffered? You will find that none
    of these who excite your anger has done anything capable of
    affecting your mind for the worse: and it is only in your mind
    that damage or harm can be done to you – they have no other
    existence.
 3   Anyway, where is the harm or surprise in the ignorant behav-
    ing as the ignorant do? Think about it. Should you not rather
    blame yourself, for not anticipating that this man would make
    this error? Your reason gave you the resource to reckon this

mistake likely from this man, yet you forgot and are now surprised that he went wrong.

Above all, when you complain of disloyalty or ingratitude, turn inwards on yourself. The fault is clearly your own, if you trusted that a man of that character would keep his trust, or if you conferred a favour without making it an end in itself, your very action its own and complete reward. What more do you want, man, from a kind act? Is it not enough that you have done something consonant with your own nature – do you now put a price on it? As if the eye demanded a return for seeing, or the feet for walking. Just as these were made for a particular purpose, and fulfil their proper nature by acting in accordance with their own constitution, so man was made to do good: and whenever he does something good or otherwise contributory to the common interest, he has done what he was designed for, and inherits his own.

BOOK 10

1   My soul, will you ever be good, simple, individual, bare, brighter than the body that covers you? Will you ever taste the disposition to love and affection? Will you ever be complete and free of need, missing nothing, desiring nothing live or lifeless for the enjoyment of pleasure? Or time for longer enjoyment, or amenity of place, space, and climate? Or good company? No, will you not rather be satisfied with your present state and take pleasure in all that is presently yours? Will you not convince yourself that all your experience comes from the gods, that all is well and all will be well for you, all that the gods see fit to give you, now and hereafter, in the maintenance of that perfect Being which is good and just and beautiful, which generates all things, sustains and contains all things, embraces all things as they dissolve into the generation of others like them? Will you ever be such as to share the society of gods and men without any criticism of them or condemnation by them?

2   Observe what your physical nature requires, as one subject to the condition of mere life. Then do it and welcome it, as long as your nature as an animate being will not be impaired. Next, you should observe what your nature as an animate being requires: again, adopt all of this, as long as your nature as a rational being will not be impaired. And rational directly implies social. Follow these rules, and no further fuss.

3   All that happens is an event either within your natural ability to bear it, or not. So if it is an event within that ability, do not

complain, but bear it as you were born to. If outside that ability, do not complain either: it will take you away before you have the chance for complaint. Remember, though, that you are by nature born to bear all that your own judgement can decide bearable, or tolerate in action, if you represent it to yourself as benefit or duty.

If he is going wrong, teach him kindly and show him what he 4 has failed to see. If you can't do that, blame yourself – or perhaps not even yourself.

Whatever happens to you was being prepared for you from 5 everlasting, and the mesh of causes was ever spinning from eternity both your own existence and the incidence of this particular happening.

Whether atoms or a natural order, the first premise must be 6 that I am part of the Whole which is governed by nature: the second, that I have some close relationship with the other kindred parts. With these premises in mind, in so far as I am a part I shall not resent anything assigned by the Whole. Nothing which benefits the Whole can be harmful to the part, and the Whole contains nothing which is not to its benefit. All organic natures have this in common, but the nature of the universe has this additional attribute, that no external cause can force it to create anything harmful to itself.

So remembering that I am part of a Whole so constituted will 2 leave me happy with all that happens to me. And in so far as I have some close relationship with the other kindred parts, I shall do nothing unsocial, but rather look to the good of my kin and have every impulse directed to the common benefit and diverted from its opposite. All this in operation guarantees that life will flow well, just as you would judge a citizen's life in proper flow when he moves on through acts which benefit his fellow citizens, and welcomes all that his city assigns him.

The parts of the Whole, all that form the natural complement 7 of the universe, must necessarily perish – and 'perish' should be taken in the sense of 'change'. Now if nature made this 'perishing' of the parts detrimental to them as well as necessary, the Whole would be poorly maintained when its parts are always on the way to change and specifically constituted to perish. Did nature deliberately undertake to harm the parts of herself, to render them both exposed to harm and necessarily condemned to fall into harm, or did she not notice these consequences? Hard to believe either.

2   But if someone abandons the concept of nature and explains these things as 'just the way they are', how absurd it is to combine the assertion that the parts of the Whole are naturally subject to change with surprise or resentment as if this change was something contrary to nature – especially as the dissolution of each thing is into the elements of which it is composed. Dissolution is either a scattering of the component elements or the change of solid to earth and spirit to air, so that these too are subsumed into the Reason of the Whole, whether the Whole is periodically turned to fire or renews itself through eternal mutations.

3   And do not imagine that this solid and this spirit are the same as at original birth. All this was gathered only yesterday or the day before from the influx of food consumed and air breathed in. So what changes is the gathered influx, and not what your mother bore. Suppose now that this influx has close implication in your individual self: that, I think, has no bearing on the present argument.

8   Claim your entitlement to these epithets – good, decent, truthful; in mind clear, cooperative, and independent – and take care then not to swap them for other names: and if you do forfeit these titles, return to them quickly. Remember, too, that 'clarity of mind' was meant to signify for you discriminating attention to detail and vigorous thought; 'a cooperative mind' the willing acceptance of the dispensation of universal nature; 'independence of mind' the elevation of your thinking faculty above the calm or troubled affections of the flesh, above paltry fame or death or any other indifferent thing. So if you keep yourself

true to these titles, not just grubbing for this acclamation from others, you will be a new man and enter a new life.

To continue the same man as you have been up to now, to   2
be torn apart and defiled in this life you live, is just senseless self-preservation like that of half-eaten gladiators who, mauled all over and covered in blood by the wild beasts, still plead to be kept alive for the next day, when in their same state they will meet again those same claws and teeth.

Launch yourself, then, on these few claims. If you can stay   3
within them, stay there like a man translated to some paradise, the Islands of the Blest. But if you feel yourself falling away and losing control, retire in good heart to some corner where you will regain control – or else make a complete exit from life, not in anger, but simply, freely, with integrity, making this leaving of it at least one achievement in your life.

A great help to keeping these claims to virtue fresh in your   4
mind will be to keep your mind on the gods, remembering that what they want is not servile flattery but the development of all rational beings into their own image: they want the fig-tree to do the proper work of a fig-tree, the dog of a dog, the bee of a bee – and man the proper work of man.

Farce, war, frenzy, torpor, slavery! Day by day those sacred   9
doctrines of yours will be wiped out, whenever you conceive and admit them untested by natural philosophy. Every perception, every action must both satisfy the circumstantial and exercise the theoretical, so that you preserve the confidence of precise knowledge in every particular – this confidence unobtrusive, but not concealed.

Because when will you take your pleasure in simplicity? When in dignity? When in the knowledge of each individual thing – what is its essential nature, its place in the world, its natural span of existence, what are its components, to whom can it belong, who can give it and take it away?

A spider is proud to trap a fly. Men are proud of their own   10
hunting – a hare, a sprat in the net, boars, bears, Sarmatian prisoners. If you examine their motives, are they not all bandits?

11   Adopt a systematic study of the way all things change into one another: pay constant attention to this aspect of nature and train yourself in it. Nothing is so conducive to greatness of mind. One so trained has divested himself of his body: recognizing that in almost no time he will have to leave all this behind and depart from the world of men, he has devoted his entire self to justice in his own actions and to the nature of the Whole in all things external. He does not even give a thought to what others will say or suppose about him, or do against him, but is content to meet these two conditions – his own integrity in each present action, and glad acceptance of his present lot. He has abandoned all other preoccupations and ambitions, and his only desire is to walk the straight path according to law and, in so doing, to follow in the path of god.

12   What need of prompt or hint when it is open to yourself to discern what needs to be done – and, if you can see your way, to follow it with kind but undeviating intent. If you cannot see the way, hold back and consult your best advisers. If some other factors obstruct this advice, proceed on your present resources, but with cautious deliberation, keeping always to what seems just. Justice is the best aim, as any failure is in fact a failure of justice.

     A man following reason in all things combines relaxation with initiative, spark with composure.

13   As soon as you wake from sleep ask yourself: 'Will it make any difference to you if others criticize what is in fact just and true?' No, it will not. You have surely not forgotten what these people who whinny in praise or blame of others are like in their bed and at their board, the sort of things they do and avoid or pursue, their cheating and stealing, not with hands and feet, but with the most precious part of themselves, the part where – if allowed – there grows trust, decency, truth, law, the spirit of goodness.

14   Nature gives all and takes all back. To her the man educated into humility says: 'Give what you will; take back what you

will.' And he says this in no spirit of defiance, but simply as her loyal subject.

The time you have left is short. Live it as if you were on a mountain. Here or there makes no difference, if wherever you live you take the world as your city. Let men see, let them observe a true man living in accordance with nature. If they cannot bear him, let them kill him – a better fate than a life like theirs.   15

No more roundabout discussion of what makes a good man. 16 Be one!

Keep constantly in your mind an impression of the whole of 17 time and the whole of existence – and the thought that each individual thing is, on the scale of existence, a mere fig-seed; on the scale of time, one turn of a drill.

Consider any existing object and reflect that it is even now in 18 the process of dissolution and change, in a sense regenerating through decay or dispersal: in other words, to what sort of 'death' each thing is born.

What sort of people are they when eating, sleeping, coupling, 19 shitting, etc.? Then what are they like when given power over men? Haughty, quick to anger, punishing to excess. And yet just now they were slaves to all those needs for all those reasons: and shortly they will be slaves again.

What universal nature brings to each is brought to his benefit. 20 The benefit stands at the time of its bringing.

'Earth loves the rain, the proud sky loves to give it.' The whole 21 world loves to create futurity. I say then to the world, 'I share your love.' Is this not the source of the phrase, 'This loves to happen'?

Either you live on here, used to it now; or you retire, your own 22

decision to leave; or you die, your service done. No other choice.
Be cheerful, then.

23   Always have clear in your mind that 'the grass is not greener'
elsewhere, and how everything is the same here as on the top
of a mountain, or on the sea-shore, or wherever you will. Plato's
words you will find directly apposite: 'walling himself a fold on
a mountain, and milking his flock when they bleat'.

24   What is my directing mind to me? What am I turning it into
now, what use am I making of it? Is it drained of intelligence?
Is it divorced and broken off from society? Is it so interfused
and welded to the flesh that it sways with its tides?

25   A slave running from his master is a fugitive. Law is our master:
the law-breaker is therefore a fugitive. But also in the same way
pain, anger, or fear denote refusal of some past, present, or
future order from the governor of all things – and this is law,
which legislates his lot for each of us. To feel fear, then, pain
or anger is to be a fugitive.

26   A man deposits his sperm in a womb and goes away. Thereafter
another cause takes over, does its work, and produces a baby.
What a result from what a beginning! Then again. The child
takes food down its throat, and now another causal sequence
takes over, creating sensation and impulse, the whole of life
and strength, and all manner of other wonderful things.
        Look, then, at what happens in such mystery, and see the
power at work, just as we see the force which weighs things
down or carries them up – not with our eyes, but no less clearly.

27   Constantly reflect that all the things which happen now have
happened before: reflect too that they will happen again in the
future. Have in your mind's eye whole dramas with similar
settings, all that you know of from your own experience or
earlier history – for example, the whole court of Hadrian, the
whole court of Antoninus, the whole court of Philip, Alexander,
Croesus. All the same as now: just a different cast.

Picture everyone voicing pain or discontent at anything, as like   28
a pig at a sacrifice, kicking and squealing. Just the same is the
man who keeps it to himself, silently resentful on his bed. Think
of all the threads that bind us, and how only rational creatures
are given the choice of submitting willingly to events: pure
submission is forced on all.

Consider each individual thing you do and ask yourself whether   29
to lose it through death makes death itself any cause for fear.

Whenever you take offence at the wrong done by another, move   30
on at once to consider what similar wrong *you* are committing
– it could be setting value on money, or pleasure, or reputation,
and so on through the categories. This reflection will quickly
damp your anger, aided by the further thought that the man is
acting under compulsion – what else can he do? Or, if you can,
remove the cause of his compulsion.

When you see Satyrion or Eutyches or Hymen, picture them in   31
Socrates' circle; when you see Eutychion or Silvanus, picture
Euphrates; when you see Tropaeophorus, picture Alciphron;
when you see Severus, picture Crito or Xenophon; and when
you look at yourself, picture one of the Caesars – for each,
then, a parallel in the past. Then let this further thought strike
you: Where are those men now? Nowhere, or wherever. In this
way you will always look on human life as mere smoke and
nothing, especially if you remind yourself also that what has
once changed will be no more for the infinity of time. Why then
this stress? Why not be content with an orderly passage through
the brief span you have?

   And what material situation, what role are you seeking to
escape? What is all this other than an exercise for that reason
which has looked at all of life with close and scientific inquiry?
Stay on, then, until you have assimilated all this too, just as a
strong stomach assimilates all food, or a bright fire turns all
that you throw on it into flame and light.

Let no one have the chance to accuse you, with any truth, of   32 not being sincere or a good man: make sure that anyone taking this view of you is a liar. This is wholly up to you – who is there to prevent you being good and sincere? You must just decide to live no longer if you won't have these qualities. And reason too abandons the man who won't.

33   In any given material circumstance what can be done or said to soundest effect? Whatever that is, it is in your power to do it or say it – and make no pretence of 'obstacles in the way'. You will never cease moaning until you experience the same pleasure in making an appropriately human response to any circumstance you meet or face as the hedonist does in his indulgence – a response, that is, in keeping with man's constitution. Because you should regard as enjoyment any action you can take in accord with your own nature; and you can do that anywhere.

2   Now the roller does not have the gift of following its own movement wherever it will, nor does water or fire, or anything else subject to a nature or life without reason: there are many barriers or impediments in their way. But mind and reason have the power, by their nature and at their will, to move through every obstacle.

3   Keeping clear in your view this easy facility of reason to carry through all things – like fire rising, a stone falling, a roller on a slope – stop looking for anything more. Any remaining hindrances either come from the corpse which is our body, or – without the judgement and consent of our own reason itself – have no power at all to break or harm.

4   Otherwise, anyone meeting such hindrance would immediately become bad himself. With all other organisms any harm occurring to any of them makes them worse in themselves. But in our case, to put it so, a person actually becomes better and more praiseworthy for the right use of the circumstances he meets. Generally, remember that nothing harms the citizen of nature other than what harms the city: and nothing harms the city other than what harms the law. None of our so-called misfortunes harms the law. So what is not harmful to the law does not harm either city or citizen.

One bitten by the true doctrines needs only a very short and   34
commonplace reminder to lose all pain and fear – for instance:

> The wind scatters one year's leaves on the ground . . . so it is with
> the generations of men.

Your children are no more than 'leaves'. 'Leaves' too these loud
voices of loyal praise, these curses from your opponents, this
silent blame or mockery: mere 'leaves' likewise those with cus-
tody of your future fame. All these 'come round in the season
of spring': but then the wind blows them down, and the forest
'puts out others' in their stead. All things are short-lived – this
is their common lot – but you pursue likes and dislikes as if all
was fixed for eternity. In a little while you too will close your
eyes, and soon there will be others mourning the man who
buries you.

The healthy eye must look at all there is to be seen, and not say   35
'I only want pale colours' – this is a symptom of disease. The
healthy ear and nose must be ready for all sounds or smells,
and the healthy stomach must accept all food in the same way
that a mill accepts all it was made to grind. And so the healthy
mind too must be ready for all eventualities. The mind which
says 'my children must live', or 'there must be popular acclaim
for all I do', is the eye demanding pale or the teeth demanding
pap.

No one is so fortunate as not to have standing round his death-   36
bed some people who welcome the fate coming on him. Was
he the earnest sage? Then maybe there will be someone at his
final moment saying to himself: 'We can breathe again now, rid
of this schoolmaster. He was not hard on any one of us, but I
could feel his silent criticism of us all.' So much for the earnest
sage: but in our own case how many other reasons are there
for a general wish to be rid of us? You will think of this when
you are dying, and your departure will be the easier if you
reason to yourself: 'I am leaving the sort of life in which even
my colleagues – on whose behalf I have expended so much

effort, prayer, and thought – even they want me out of the way, doubtless hoping for some relief from my death.' So why should anyone cling to a longer stay here on earth?

Do not, though, for that reason feel any less warmth for them as you depart this life, but keep true to your own character – friendly, kind, generous. Again, your leaving of them should not be any wrench from life, but rather that easy slipping of the soul from the body's carapace experienced by those dying at peace. Nature bound you to them and made them your colleagues, but is now releasing you. My release is like parting from kinsmen, but I do not resist or need to be forced. This too is one of the ways to follow nature.

37 As far as you can, get into the habit of asking yourself in relation to any action taken by another: 'What is his point of reference here?' But begin with yourself: examine yourself first.

38 Remember that what pulls the strings is that part of us hidden inside: that is the power to act, that is the principle of life, that, one could say, is the man himself. So never give any equal thought to the vessel which contains it or the organs built round it. These are an instrument like an axe, differing only in their attachment to the body. There is no more use in these parts without the agency which starts or stops them than in the shuttle without the weaver, the pen without the writer, the whip without the driver.

BOOK 11

The properties of the rational soul. It looks on itself, it shapes 1
itself, it makes itself however it wishes to be, it gathers for
itself the fruit it bears – whereas the fruit of plants and the
corresponding produce of animals is gathered by others. It
achieves its own end wherever the limit of life is set. Unlike a
ballet or a play or suchlike, where any interruption aborts the
whole performance, in every scene and whenever it is cut off
the rational soul has its own programme complete and entirely
fulfilled, so it can say: 'I am in possession of my own.'

Further, the rational soul traverses the whole universe and 2
its surrounding void, explores the shape of it, stretches into the
infinity of time, encompasses and comprehends the periodic
regeneration of the Whole. It reflects that our successors will
see nothing new, just as our predecessors saw nothing more
than we do: such is the sameness of things, a man of forty with
any understanding whatsoever has in a sense seen all the past
and all the future.

Particular qualities too of the rational soul are love of neigh- 3
bour, truthfulness, integrity, no higher value than itself. This
last is a defining quality of law also. There is thus no difference
between the true principle of philosophy and the principle of
justice.

You will think little of the entertainment of song or dance or 2
all-in wrestling if you deconstruct the melodic line of a song
into its individual notes and ask yourself of each of them: 'Is
this something that overpowers me?' You will recoil from that
admission. So too with a comparable analysis of dance by each

movement and each pose, and the same again with wrestling. Generally, then, with the exception of virtue and its workings, remember to go straight to the component parts of anything, and through that analysis come to despise the thing itself. And the same method should be applied to the whole of life.

3   What a noble thing is the soul ready for its release from the body, if now must be the time, and prepared for whatever follows – extinction, dispersal, or survival! But this readiness must come from a specific decision: not in mere revolt, like the Christians, but thoughtful, dignified, and – if others are to believe it – undramatic.

4   Have I done something for the common good? Then I too have benefited. Have this thought always ready to hand: and no stopping.

5   What is your profession? Being a good man. But this can only come about through philosophic concepts – concepts of the nature of the Whole, and concepts of the specific constitution of man.

6   First, tragedies were brought on stage to remind you of what can happen, that these happenings are determined by nature, and that what moves you in the theatre should not burden you on the larger stage of life. You can see the way things must turn out and that even those who cry 'Oh Cithaeron!' must bear them.

    There are some useful sayings too in the tragedians. A prime example is:

> 'If I and my two sons are now no more
> The gods' concern, this too will have its cause.'

Again: 'Mere things, brute facts, should not provoke your rage.'
And: 'Ripe ears of corn are reaped, and so are lives.'
    And many others like that.

After tragedy the Old Comedy was introduced. There was 2
educational value in its unbridled frankness, and this plain
speaking was of itself a useful warning against pomposity –
Diogenes too adopted this trait to a similar end. After this,
examine the nature of Middle Comedy and the purpose of the
subsequent adoption of New Comedy, which gradually slipped
into the mere artistry of imitation. True, it is recognized that
these writers too said some useful things – but what was the
whole thrust and aim of this sort of poetry and drama?

How clearly it strikes you that there is no other walk of life so 7
conducive to the exercise of philosophy as this in which you
now find yourself!

A branch cut from its neighbouring branch is necessarily cut 8
away from the whole tree. In the same way a human being
severed from just one other human has dropped from the whole
community. Now the branch is cut off by someone else, but a
man separates himself from his neighbour by his own hatred
or rejection, not realizing that he has thereby severed himself
from the wider society of fellow citizens. Only there is this gift
we have from Zeus who brought together the human community: we can grow back again to our neighbour and resume
our place in the complement of the whole. Too often repeated,
though, such separation makes it harder to unite and restore
the divided part. In sum, the branch which stays with the tree
from the beginning of its growth and shares its transpiration is
not the same as the branch which is cut off and then regrafted,
whatever the gardeners say.
     Share their stock, but not their doctrines.

Just as those who try to block your progress along the straight 9
path of reason will not be able to divert you from principled
action, so you must not let them knock you out of your good
will towards them. Rather you should watch yourself equally
on both fronts, keeping not only a stability of judgement and
action but also a mild response to those who try to stop you or
are otherwise disaffected. To be angry with them is no less a

weakness than to abandon your course of action and capitulate in panic. Both amount equally to desertion of duty – either being frightened into retreat, or setting yourself at odds with your natural kinsmen and friends.

10 'No nature is inferior to art': in fact the arts imitate the variety of natures. If that is so, then the most perfect and comprehensive of all natures could not be surpassed by any artistic invention. Now all arts create the lower in the interests of the higher: so this is the way of universal nature too. And indeed here is the origin of justice, from which all other virtues take their being, since there will be no preservation of justice if we are concerned with indifferent things, or gullible and quick to chop and change.

11 The external things whose pursuit or avoidance troubles you do not force themselves on you, but in a way you yourself go out to them. However that may be, keep your judgement of them calm and they too will stay still – then you will not be seen either to pursue or to avoid.

12 The soul is a sphere which retains the integrity of its own form if it does not bulge or contract for anything, does not flare or subside, but keeps the constant light by which it sees the truth of all things and the truth in itself.

13 Someone despises me? That is his concern. But I will see to it that I am not found guilty of any word or action deserving contempt. Will he hate me? That is his concern. But I will be kind and well-intentioned to all, and ready to show this very person what he is failing to see – not in any criticism or display of tolerance, but with genuine good will, like the famous Phocion (if, that is, he was not speaking ironically). This should be the quality of our inner thoughts, which are open to the gods' eyes: they should see a man not disposed to any complaint and free of self-pity. And what harm can you suffer, if you yourself at this present moment are acting in kind with your own nature and accepting what suits the present purpose of

universal nature – a man at full stretch for the achievement, this way or that, of the common good?

They despise each other, but still toady to each other: they want   14
to win, but still grovel.

The rotten pretence of the man who says, 'I prefer to be honest   15
with you'! What are you on about, man? No need for this preface – the reality will show. It should be written on your forehead, immediately clear in the tone of your voice and the light of your eyes, just as the loved one can immediately read all in the glance of his lovers. In short, the good and honest man should have the same effect as the unwashed – anyone close by as he passes detects the aura, willy-nilly, at once. Calculated honesty is a stiletto. There is nothing more degrading than the friendship of wolves: avoid that above all. The good, honest, kindly man has it in his eyes, and you cannot mistake him.

Live through life in the best way you can. The power to do so   16
is in a man's own soul, if he is indifferent to things indifferent. And he will be indifferent if he looks at these things both as a whole and analysed into their parts, and remembers that none of them imposes a judgement of itself or forces itself on us. The things themselves are inert: it is we who procreate judgements about them and, as it were, imprint them on our minds – but there is no need for imprinting at all, and any accidental print can immediately be erased. Remember too that our attention to these things can only last a little while, and then life will be at an end. And what, anyway, is the difficulty in them? If they are in accord with nature, welcome them and you will find them easy. If they are contrary to nature, look for what accords with your own nature and go straight for that, even if it brings you no glory. Anyone can be forgiven for seeking his own proper good.

With each object of experience consider its origin, its constitu-   17
ents, what it is changing into, what it will be when changed – and that no harm will come to it.

18   *First.* How do I regard my relation to them, and the fact that we were all born for each other: and, turning the argument, that I was born to be their leader, as the ram leads his flock and the bull his herd? But start from first principles. If not atoms, then nature governing all: if so, then the lower in the interests of the higher, and the higher for each other.

2   *Second.* What sort of people they are at table, in bed, and so on. Most of all, what sort of behaviour their opinions impose on them, and their complacent pride in acting as they do.

3   *Third.* If what they do is right, no cause for complaint. If wrong, this is clearly out of ignorance and not their wish. Just as no soul likes to be robbed of truth, so no soul wants to abandon the proper treatment of each individual as his worth deserves. At any rate these people resent the imputation of injustice, cruelty, selfishness – in a word, crimes against their neighbours.

4   *Fourth.* You yourself have many faults and are no different from them. If you do refrain from some wrongs you still have the proclivity to them, even if your restraint from wrongs like theirs is due to the fear or pursuit of public opinion, or some other such poor motive.

5   *Fifth.* You are not even sure that they are doing wrong. Many things are done as part of a larger plan, and generally one needs to know a great deal before one can pronounce with certainty on another's actions.

6   *Sixth.* When you are high in indignation and perhaps losing patience, remember that human life is a mere fragment of time and shortly we are all in our graves.

7   *Seventh.* It is not their actions which trouble us – because these lie in their own directing minds – but our judgements of them. Well, remove these judgements, make up your mind to dismiss your assessment of some supposed outrage, and your anger is gone. And how to remove them? By reflecting that no moral harm is caused you. If moral harm were not the only true harm, it would necessarily follow that you your-self are guilty of causing much harm, and become a robber, a rogue!

8   *Eighth.* The greater grief comes from the consequent anger

and pain, rather than the original causes of our anger and pain.

Ninth. Kindness is invincible – if it is sincere, not fawning or   9
pretence. What can the most aggressive man do to you if you
continue to be kind to him? If, as opportunity arises, you gently
admonish him and take your time to re-educate him at the very
moment when he is trying to do you harm? 'No, son, we were
born for other purposes than this. There is no way that I can
be harmed, but you are harming yourself, son.' And show him
delicately how things are, making the general point that bees
do not act like this, or any other creatures of gregarious nature.
But your advice must not be ironic or critical. It should be
affectionate, with no hurt feelings, not a lecture or a demon-
stration to impress others, but the way you would talk to
someone by himself irrespective of company.

Keep these nine points in your mind – take them as gifts from   10
the Muses! – and begin at long last to be a human being, while
life remains. You should avoid flattery as much as anger in your
dealings with them: both are against the common good and
lead to harm. In your fits of anger have this thought ready to
mind, that there is nothing manly in being angry, but a gentle
calm is both more human and therefore more virile. It is the
gentle who have strength, sinew, and courage – not the indignant and complaining. The closer to control of emotion, the
closer to power. Anger is as much a sign of weakness as is pain.
Both have been wounded, and have surrendered.

Now, if you will, take a *tenth* gift from the Leader of the   11
Muses – the thought that it is madness to expect bad men to
do no wrong: that is asking for the impossible. But it is cruel
tyranny to allow them such behaviour to others while
demanding that they do no wrong to you.

There are four particular corruptions of the directing mind   19
for which you must keep constant watch, and eliminate them
whenever you detect them, in each case applying one of these
formulas: 'This mental image is superfluous'; 'This could
weaken the bond of community'; 'This would not be yourself
speaking' (to say what you do not feel should be regarded as the
height of contradiction). And the fourth case for self-reproach is

that in which the more divine part of you loses the contest and
bows to the lower, mortal part, the body and its gross pleasures.

20 All the elements of air and fire that are mingled in you have a
natural tendency to rise, but nevertheless obey the dispensation
of the Whole and are kept waiting here in the compound of the
body. And all the elements of earth and water in you, whose
tendency is to sink down, are nevertheless raised up and stay
in a position unnatural to them. So even the elements are obedient to the Whole: assigned their place, they are forced to stay
there, until the signal authorizing their dissolution once more
is given from that same source.

2   So is it not strange that it is only your intelligent part which
rebels and complains of the place given it? And yet there is
nothing forced on it, only what accords with its own nature.
But still it refuses to comply, and sets off in the opposite direction. Any movement towards acts of injustice or self-indulgence,
to anger, pain, or fear is nothing less than apostasy from nature.
Further, whenever the directing mind feels resentment at any
happening, that too is desertion of its proper post. It was constituted not only for justice to men but no less for the reverence
and service of god – this also a form of fellowship, perhaps yet
more important than the operation of justice.

21 'The man without one and the same aim in life cannot himself
stay one and the same throughout his life.' The maxim is incom-
plete unless you add what sort of aim that should be. Judgements vary of the whole range of various things taken by the
majority to be goods in one way or another, but only one
category commands a universal judgement, and that is the
good of the community. It follows that the aim we should set
ourselves is a social aim, the benefit of our fellow citizens. A
man directing all his own impulses to this end will be consistent
in all his actions, and therefore the same man throughout.

22 The hill mouse and the house mouse – and the frightened
scurrying of the house mouse.

Socrates used to call the popular beliefs 'bogies', things to 23
frighten children with.

At their festivals the Spartans would put seats for visitors in the 24
shade, and sit themselves wherever they could.

Socrates to Perdiccas of Macedon, declining the invitation to 25
visit him: 'to avoid dying the worst of deaths' – that is, the
inability to return in kind benefits received.

In Epicurean writings there is laid down the precept that one 26
should continually keep in mind one of those who followed the
path of virtue in earlier times.

The Pythagoreans say, 'Look at the sky at dawn' – to remind 27
ourselves of the constancy of those heavenly bodies, their perpetual round of their own duty, their order, their purity, and
their nakedness. No star wears a veil.

Think of Socrates in his underclothes when Xanthippe had 28
gone out with his coat: and what he said to his friends retiring
in embarrassment when they saw the state of his dress.

In writing and reading you must learn before you can teach. 29
Yet more so in life.

'You were born a slave: you have no voice.' 30

'And the heart within me laughed.' 31

'They will pour scorn on virtue and sting with their abuse.' 32

Only a madman looks for figs in winter: just as mad to hope 33
for a child when the time of this gift is past.

Epictetus used to say that when you kiss your child you should 34
say to yourself: 'Tomorrow you may be dead.' But these are
ominous words! 'No,' he replies, 'nothing is ominous which

points to a natural process. Otherwise it would be ominous to speak of the corn being reaped.'

35 Grapes unripe, ripened, raisined: all changes, not into non-existence, but into not-yet existence.

36 'No thief can steal your will' – so Epictetus.

37 Another saying of his. 'We must discover an art of assent, and in the whole field of our impulses take care to ensure that each impulse is conditional, has a social purpose, and is proportionate to the value of its goal. We must keep absolutely clear of personal motivation, and at the same time show no disinclination to anything outside our immediate control.'

38 Again. 'So this is not a contest for a trivial prize: at issue is madness or sanity.'

39 Socrates used to question thus. 'What do you want to have? The souls of rational or irrational beings?' 'Rational.' 'What sort of rational beings? The pure or the lower?' 'The pure.' 'Why then don't you aim for that?' 'Because we have it.' 'Why then your fighting and disagreements?'

BOOK 12

All that you pray to reach at some point in the circuit of your 1
life can be yours now – if you are generous to yourself. That is,
if you leave all the past behind, entrust the future to Providence,
and direct the present solely to reverence and justice. To reverence, so that you come to love your given lot: it was Nature
that brought it to you and you to it. To justice, so that you are
open and direct in word and action, speaking the truth, observing law and proportion in all you do. You should let nothing
stand in your way – not the iniquity of others, not what anyone
else thinks or says, still less any sensation of this poor flesh that
has accreted round you: the afflicted part must see to its own
concern.

   If, then, when you finally come close to your exit, you have 2
left all else behind and value only your directing mind and the
divinity within you, if your fear is not that you will cease to
live, but that you never started a life in accordance with nature,
then you will be a man worthy of the universe that gave you
birth. You will no longer be a stranger in your own country,
no longer meet the day's events as if bemused by the unexpected,
no longer hang on this or that.

God sees all our directing minds stripped of their material 2
vessels, their husks and their dross. His contact is only between
his own intelligence and what has flowed from him into these
channels of ours. If you train yourself to do the same, you will
be rid of what so much distracts you. Hardly likely, is it, that
one blind to the enveloping flesh will spend his time eyeing

clothes, houses, reputation, or any other such trappings and
stage scenery?

3 There are three things in your composition: body, breath, and
mind. The first two are yours to the extent that you must take
care for them, but only the third is in the full sense your own.
So, if you separate from yourself – that is, from your mind – all
that others say or do, all that you yourself have said or done,
all that troubles you for the future, all that your encasing body
and associate breath bring on you without your choice, all that
is whirled round in the external vortex encircling us, so that
your power of mind, transcending now all contingent ties, can
exist on its own, pure and liberated, doing what is just, willing
2 what happens to it, and saying what is true; if, as I say, you
separate from this directing mind of yours the baggage of passion, time future and time past, and make yourself like Empedocles' 'perfect round rejoicing in the solitude it enjoys', and
seek only to perfect this life you are living in the present, you
will be able at least to live out the time remaining before your
death calmly, kindly, and at peace with the god inside you.

4 I have often wondered how it is that everyone loves himself
more than anyone else, but rates his own judgement of himself
below that of others. Anyway, if a god or some wise tutor
appeared at his side and told him to entertain no internal
thought or intention which he won't immediately broadcast
outside, he would not tolerate this regime for a single day. So
it is that we have more respect for what our neighbours will
think of us than we have for ourselves.

5 However was it that the gods, who have ordered all else so well
and with such love for men, overlooked this one thing, that
some men, the very best of them, those who had conducted, as
it were, the most commerce with the divine and reached the
closest relation to it through their acts of devotion and their
observances – that these men, once dead, should meet perpetual
extinction rather than some return to existence?
     Now if this is indeed the case, you can be sure that if it should

have been otherwise the gods would have made it otherwise: because if that were right, it would also have been possible, and if in accordance with nature, nature would have brought it about. Therefore the fact that it is not otherwise (if indeed that is a fact) should assure you that it ought not to be otherwise. You can see for yourself that in raising this presumptuous question you are pleading a case with god. But we would not enter such debate with the gods if they were not supremely good and supremely just: and if that is so, they would not have let any part of their ordered arrangement of the world escape them through neglect of justice or reason.

Practise even what you have despaired of mastering. For lack   6
of practice the left hand is awkward for most tasks, but has a stronger grip on the bridle than the right – it is practised in this.

How one should be in both body and soul when overtaken by   7
death; the shortness of life; the immensity of time future and past; the feebleness of all things material.

Look at causation stripped bare of its covers; look at the ulterior   8
reference of any action. Consider, what is pain? What is plea-sure? What is death? What is fame? Who is not himself the cause of his own unrest? Reflect how no one is hampered by any other; and that all is as thinking makes it so.

The model for the application of your principles is the boxer   9
rather than the gladiator. The gladiator puts down or takes up the sword he uses, but the boxer always has his hands and needs only to clench them into fists.

See things for what they are, analysing into material, cause, and   10
reference.

What liberty man has to do only what god will approve, and   11
to welcome all that god assigns him in the course of nature!

Do not blame the gods: they do no wrong, willed or unwilled.   12

Do not blame men either: all their wrongs are unwilled. No one, then, should be blamed.

13 How absurd – and a complete stranger to the world – is the man surprised at any aspect of his experience in life!

14 Either the compulsion of destiny and an order allowing no deviation, or a providence open to prayer, or a random welter without direction. Now if undeviating compulsion, why resist it? If a providence admitting the placation of prayer, make yourself worthy of divine assistance. If an ungoverned welter, be glad that in such a maelstrom you have within yourself a directing mind of your own: if the flood carries you away, let it take your flesh, your breath, all else – but it will not carry away your mind.

15 The light of a lamp shines on and does not lose its radiance until it is extinguished. Will then the truth, justice, and self-control which fuel you fail before your own end?

16 Presented with the impression that someone has done wrong, how do I know that this was a wrong? And if it was indeed a wrong, how do I know that he was not already condemning himself, which is the equivalent of tearing his own face?

Wanting the bad man not to do wrong is like wanting the fig-tree not to produce rennet in its figs, babies not to cry, horses not to neigh, or any other inevitable fact of nature. What else can he do with a state of mind like his? So if you are really keen, cure his state.

17 If it is not right, don't do it: if it is not true, don't say it.

18 Your impulse on every occasion should be to a complete survey of what exactly this thing is which is making an impression on your mind – to open it out by analysis into cause, material, reference, and the time-span within which it must cease to be.

19 Realize at long last that you have within you something stronger

and more numinous than those agents of emotion which make you a mere puppet on their strings. What is in my mind at this very moment? Fear, is it? Suspicion? Desire? Something else of that sort?

First, nothing aimless or without ulterior reference. Second, no 20 reference to any end other than the common good.

That in a short while you will be nobody and nowhere; and the 21 same of all that you now see and all who are now alive. It is the nature of all things to change, to perish and be transformed, so that in succession different things can come to be.

That all is as thinking makes it so – and you control your 22 thinking. So remove your judgements whenever you wish and then there is calm – as the sailor rounding the cape finds smooth water and the welcome of a waveless bay.

Any one individual activity which comes to an end at the appro- 23 priate time suffers no harm from its cessation: nor has the agent suffered any harm simply because this particular action has ceased. In the same way, then, if the total of all his actions which constitutes a man's life comes to an end at the appropriate time, it suffers no harm from the mere fact of cessation: nor is the agent who brings this series of actions to a timely end exposed to any harm. The time and the term are assigned by nature – sometimes man's own nature, as in old age, but in any case by the nature of the Whole, which through the constant changing of its constituent parts keeps the whole world ever young and fresh.

Now anything which benefits the Whole is always fine and ripe. It follows that for each of us there is certainly no harm in the cessation of life, as there is no shame either – not self-chosen, not damaging to the common interest. Rather there is good, in that it falls in due season for the Whole, thereby both giving and receiving benefit. Thus too a man walks with god's support when his choice and his direction carry him along god's own path.

24 Three thoughts to keep at hand. *First*: in your own actions, nothing aimless or other than Justice herself would have done; in external happenings either chance or providence is at work, and one should not blame chance or indict providence. *Second*: the nature of each of us from conception to the first breath of soul, and from that first breath to the surrender of our soul; what elements form our constitution and will be the result of our dissolution. *Third*: that if you were suddenly lifted up to a great height and could look down on human activity and see all its variety, you would despise it, because your view would take in also the great surrounding host of spirits who populate the air and the sky; and that, however many times you were lifted up, you would see the same things – monotony and transience. Such are the objects of our conceit.

25 Jettison the judgement, and you are saved. And who is there to prevent this jettison?

26 When you fret at any circumstance, you have forgotten a number of things. You have forgotten that all comes about in accordance with the nature of the Whole; that any wrong done lies with the other; further, that everything which happens was always so in the past, will be the same again in the future, and is happening now across the world; that a human being has close kinship with the whole human race – not a bond of blood or seed, but a community of mind. And you have forgotten this too, that every man's mind is god and has flowed from that source; that nothing is our own property, but even our child, our body, our very soul have come from that source; that all is as thinking makes it so; that each of us lives only the present moment, and the present moment is all we lose.

27 Continually review in your mind those whom a particular anger took to extremes, those who reached the greatest heights of glory or disaster or enmity or any other sort of fortune. Then stop and think: where is it all now? Smoke and ashes, a story told or even a story forgotten. At the same time this whole class of examples should occur to you: Fabius Catullinus in his

country house, Lusius Lupus in his town gardens, Stertinius at Baiae, Tiberius in Capri, Velius Rufus – and generally any obsession combined with self-conceit. Think how worthless all this striving is: how much wiser to use the material given you to make yourself in all simplicity just, self-controlled, obedient to the gods. The pride that prides itself on freedom from pride is the hardest of all to bear.

To those who ask, 'Where then have you seen the gods? What   28
conviction of their existence leads you to this worship of them?', I reply first that they are in fact visible to our eyes. Secondly, and notwithstanding, that I have not seen my own soul either, and yet I honour it. So it is with the gods too: from my every experience of their power time after time I am certain that they exist, and I revere them.

The salvation of life lies in seeing each object in its essence and   29
its entirety, discerning both the material and the causal: in applying one's whole soul to doing right and speaking the truth. There remains only the enjoyment of living a linked succession of good deeds, with not the slightest gap between them.

One light of the sun, even though its path is broken by walls,   30
mountains, innumerable other obstacles. One common sub-stance, even though it is broken up into innumerable forms of individual bodies. One animate soul, even though it is broken up into innumerable species with specific individualities. One intelligent soul, even though it appears divided.

Now in all the above the other parts – such as mere breath, or that material which is insensate – have no direct affinity to each other: yet even here a link is formed by a sort of unity and the gravitation of like to like. But the mind has this unique property: it reaches out to others of its own kind and joins with them, so the feeling of fellowship is not broken.

What more do you want? To live on? Or is it to continue   31
sensation and impulse? To wax and then to wane? To make use of your voice, your mind? What in all this strikes you as

good cause for regret? But if every one of these objects is contemptible, go on then to the final aim, which is to follow reason and to follow god. To value these other things, to fret at their loss which death will bring, militates against this aim.

32   What a tiny part of the boundless abyss of time has been allotted to each of us – and this is soon vanished in eternity; what a tiny part of the universal substance and the universal soul; how tiny in the whole earth the mere clod on which you creep. Reflecting on all this, think nothing important other than active pursuit where your own nature leads and passive acceptance of what universal nature brings.

33   How does your directing mind employ itself? This is the whole issue. All else, of your own choice or not, is just corpse and smoke.

34   The clearest call to think nothing of death is the fact that even those who regard pleasure as a good and pain as an evil have nevertheless thought nothing of death.

35   For one whose only good is what comes in its own proper season, who is equally content with a greater or lesser opportunity to express true reason in his actions, to whom it makes no difference whether he looks on this world for a longer or a shorter time – for him even death has no terrors.

36   Mortal man, you have lived as a citizen in this great city. What matter if that life is five or fifty years? The laws of the city apply equally to all. So what is there to fear in your dismissal from the city? This is no tyrant or corrupt judge who dismisses you, but the very same nature that brought you in. It is like the officer who engaged a comic actor dismissing him from the stage. 'But I have not played my five acts, only three.' 'True, but in life three acts can be the whole play.' Completion is determined by that being who caused first your composition and now your dissolution. You have no part in either causation. Go then in peace: the god who lets you go is at peace with you.

Notes

The twelve Books of the *Meditations* contain between them 488 'chapters' – the conventional term for the discrete sections, which vary in length from three words (in the Greek text) to two or three pages. Some of the longer chapters are divided into sub-sections, marked in the text of the translation by marginal numbers in italics.

In these notes all initial references and cross-references are by Book and chapter (e.g. 1.3) or Book, chapter, and sub-section (e.g. 1.17.3).

All dates are AD unless otherwise indicated.

The notes do not pretend to offer a full commentary. Their purpose is rather to aid the general reader's understanding of Marcus and the *Meditations* by explaining the various historical, literary, and philosophical references, and by giving the reader the means of tracking Marcus' thought through what is inevitably a 'bitty' work, neither written in deliberate sequence nor requiring a consecutive reading. Many topics or themes recur several times throughout the *Meditations*, and the frequency of occurrence may well reflect the importance which Marcus attributed to them. There is therefore much internal cross-referencing in the notes, which I hope, together with the Indices, will enable the reader to place individual chapters or sections in a wider context, as relevant.

I have been relatively sparing in the provision of references to other ancient authors, which only the superhuman look up. Much of Marcus' philosophical thought has direct parallels in other writers on or within the Stoic tradition, especially **Cicero** (in particular his *Academica, On Duties, On Ends, On the Nature of the Gods, Tusculan Disputations*), **Seneca** (in particular his *Moral Epistles* and *On Anger*), and **Epictetus** (*Discourses* and *Handbook* [*Encheiridion*]). Readers wishing to explore Roman Stoicism further in primary sources are recommended to read these authors and cited works: translations of all are available in volumes of the Loeb Classical Library, and a

selection of Seneca's *Epistles* is published in the Penguin Classics series
(*Seneca: Letters from a Stoic*).

Several modern works of scholarship are referred to in the notes by
author's name (or joint initials) only. These are:

Birley: A. R. Birley, *Marcus Aurelius: A Biography*, revised
              edition (London, 1987).
Brunt: P. A. Brunt, 'Marcus Aurelius in his *Meditations*', *Jour-
              nal of Roman Studies* 64 (1974), 1–20.
Farquharson: A. S. L. Farquharson, *The Meditations of the Emperor
              Marcus Antoninus*, edited with a translation and com-
              mentary, 2 vols (Oxford, 1944). The only full-scale
              edition and commentary since Thomas Gataker's, pub-
              lished in 1652.
Long: A. A. Long, *Hellenistic Philosophy*, second edition
              (Berkeley and Los Angeles, 1986).
LS: A. A. Long and D. N. Sedley, *The Hellenistic Philo-
              sophers*, 2 vols (Cambridge, 1987). References are
              mostly to sections (e.g. LS, 47) but sometimes to vol-
              ume and page.
Rutherford: R. B. Rutherford, *The* Meditations *of Marcus Aurelius,
              a Study* (Oxford, 1989).
Sandbach: F. H. Sandbach, *The Stoics*, second edition (London
              and Indianapolis/Cambridge, 1989).

BOOK 1

Book 1 has a special character, a unity of theme and composition,
which distinguishes it from the other eleven Books of the *Meditations*,
where the sequence and treatment of material, and the varying degrees
of elaboration, suggest the random jottings of a busy and preoccupied
man, sometimes tired, sometimes at leisure to write more expansively.
(For the relative unity of Book 2 and Book 3, and the valedictory
nature of Book 12, see the introductory notes to those Books.) Book
1 was clearly conceived as a whole, perhaps as a later summation,
composed at a time of relative leisure, to consolidate and console.
Despite the structure, giving culminating emphasis to Marcus' debt to
Antoninus Pius (ch. 16) and to the gods (ch. 17), the haphazard
arrangement of material and the impenetrably personal nature of some
references confirm that Marcus was writing for himself, without any
thought of publication.

Something of the purpose of the list of obligations and gratitude in this Book can be gathered from 6.48: 'Whenever you want to cheer yourself, think of the qualities of your fellows – the energy of one, for example, the decency of another, the generosity of a third, some other merit in a fourth. There is nothing so cheering as the stamp of virtues manifest in the character of colleagues – and the greater the collective incidence, the better. So keep them ready to hand.' Here Marcus is in unusually tolerant form. His regular manner is to denigrate his contemporaries and associates and to praise (with reservations) those of an earlier generation (see notes on 3.4.4, 4.6, 5.10.1). This Book records his genuine gratitude.

The format 'From X . . .:', followed verblessly by a list of qualities or virtues, does not imply that Marcus thought that he himself had acquired those qualities or exemplified those virtues (far from it: his usual mode is self-castigation, not self-congratulation). Rather the sense is 'From X I learned the value of this quality or that virtue': though the construction increasingly varies, and later chapters often mix elements of character sketch with a statement of moral or practical lessons learnt.

There is much illuminating discussion of Book 1 in Rutherford, chapters 2 and 3. Rutherford observes (p. 48) that 'There is quite simply nothing else like Book 1 of the *Meditations* in the whole of classical literature.'

For Marcus' family and forebears see in general the standard biography by Birley.

1.1 *my grandfather*: Marcus Annius Verus, three times consul, who adopted Marcus as a very young boy on the premature death of Marcus' father. For Marcus' view of the mistress taken by his grandfather after the death of his wife, see 1.17.2. His grandfather died in 138, at nearly ninety years of age.
     a mild temper: Marcus was in fact very conscious of his irascibility. See notes on 1.17.1 and 11.18.

1.2 *my natural father*: Also named Marcus Annius Verus. He died young, probably in 124, when Marcus was three years old.

1.3 *my mother*: Domitia Lucilla, a lady of considerable inherited wealth. Marcus' affection for her is expressed in 1.17.7. See also note on that section.

1.4 *my great-grandfather*: On his mother's side, Lucius Catilius Severus.

1.5 *my tutor*: Unnamed. Probably an educated slave, in charge of Marcus' general development as a young boy.

Green or Blue . . . Lights or Heavies: The Greens and Blues were rival chariot-racing teams: such teams, denoted by their colours, attracted a passionate following comparable to that of modern football or baseball teams. The Lights and Heavies were two types of gladiators, distinguished by their weapons and the weight of their armour. The entertainments in the amphitheatre bored Marcus: see note on 6.46.

1.6 *Diognetus*: Marcus' instructor in painting (he also had an instructor in music). It is clear that Diognetus' influence extended far beyond the art class.

Baccheius . . . Marcianus: Nothing is known of these three philosophers.

1.7 *Rusticus*: Quintus Junius Rusticus, a Stoic politician, descendant (son or grandson) of Q. Arulenus Junius Rusticus, a 'Stoic martyr' executed by Domitian in 93. Rusticus was one of the most important intellectual influences on Marcus from his mid-twenties on, instrumental in turning him from rhetoric to philosophy and fostering his interest in Stoicism. Marcus made Rusticus consul (for the second time) in 162, and prefect of the city in 163, in which role Rusticus condemned Justin Martyr to death in 165.

Marcus' debt to Rusticus is expressed again in 1.17.5. For a different side of the relationship see 1.17.7.

On this chapter and Marcus' 'conversion' see Rutherford, pp. 103–7.

1.7.2 *Sinuessa:* A coastal town (modern Torre S. Limato) on the Via Appia, close to the Latium/Campania border.

1.7.3 *Epictetus*: The philosopher most influential on Marcus' thought, who is often quoted or paraphrased in the *Meditations* (see Index of Quotations). He lived in the second half of the first century AD and the first third of the second century: exact dates are not known.

Originally from Hierapolis in Phrygia, Epictetus was a slave in Rome until freed by his master, Epaphroditus. Banished, with other philosophers, by Domitian in 89, he established a school at Nicopolis in Epirus. Epictetus left no writings of his own, but the content of his teaching was compiled and published by his pupil Arrian (*c.*86–160) in eight volumes of *Discourses*: four of these survive. This is the work to which Marcus refers.

1.8 *Apollonius*: A Stoic philosopher and professional lecturer from Chalcedon on the Bosporus, whom Antoninus Pius invited back to Rome to instruct Marcus. Marcus' evident high regard for

Apollonius (see also 1.17.5) is at odds with the criticisms (largely of arrogance) laid against him in some other writers.

1.9 *Sextus*: A professional philosopher from Chaeronea in Boeotia, central Greece: the nephew of Plutarch, the renowned and prolific biographer and essayist. Marcus continued to attend Sextus' lectures even after he became emperor.

life lived according to nature: See note on 1.17.6 for this Stoic ideal.

1.10 *Alexander the grammarian*: From Cotiaeum in Phrygia, Asia Minor. One of Marcus' tutors, eminent in his day, particularly for his Homeric scholarship. Alexander also taught the great sophist and man of letters Aelius Aristides, whose obituary eulogy of his teacher is still extant.

1.11 *Fronto*: Marcus Cornelius Fronto (*c.*95–166/7), from Cirta in Numidia, North Africa, leading lawyer and orator in Rome, and consul in 143, was appointed by Antoninus Pius in 138/9 as Marcus' tutor in rhetoric. The two men remained close and affectionate friends (despite Marcus' secession from rhetoric to philosophy) for the rest of Fronto's life. The warmth of this mutual affection glows in the extensive correspondence they exchanged throughout the years of their friendship: a large number of these letters, hitherto unknown, was discovered in 1815. The complaint that Romans lack human affection – and even lack a native Latin word for it – is made twice by Fronto in the extant correspondence.

The discovery of these letters has brought Fronto alive, some warts and all, and has also shed largely attractive light on Marcus' own character and generosity of feeling. Fronto was clearly pained by Marcus' abandonment of rhetoric and embrace of Stoic philosophy, but their friendship happily survived this 'agreement to differ'. Nevertheless, it is indicative of Fronto's relative influence on Marcus' thought and development that in this Book's retrospective record of debts owed and lessons learnt Marcus makes no mention of Fronto's formal instruction, and that the positioning, length, and content of this tenuous tribute to Fronto contrasts strongly with that to Rusticus (1.7 and 1.17.5).

'Patricians': the privileged classes, aristocrats of birth or imperial favour.

1.12 *Alexander the Platonist*: A philosopher/rhetorician from Seleucia in Cilicia, Asia Minor, whom Marcus appointed as his Greek secretary when he was based in Pannonia: he could well have been still in that post when Marcus wrote this of him. Alexander was nicknamed 'Peloplaton' – 'the Plato of clay'.

1.13 *Catulus*: Cinna Catulus, mentioned once elsewhere as a Stoic whose lectures were attended by Marcus, but otherwise unknown.

Domitius and Athenodotus: The references and the relation are obscure. Athenodotus was one of Fronto's teachers. This Domitius *may* be Gnaeus Domitius Afer, who taught Quintilian and *may* have taught Athenodotus. A story here escapes us.

1.14 *Severus*: Probably Gnaeus Claudius Severus Arabianus, consul 146, whose son married one of Marcus' daughters. Evidently a politician with a deep interest in political philosophy.

1.14.1 *Thrasea, Helvidius, Cato, Dio, Brutus*: Heroes and martyrs, in unchronological order, of the Stoic and/or republican opposition to the tyrannical abuse of power. Publius Clodius *Thrasea* Paetus was forced to kill himself in 66 for his attempts to preserve senatorial freedom under Nero. His son-in-law *Helvidius* Priscus, who witnessed Thrasea's suicide, was himself executed in 75, under Vespasian, for a similar assertion of independence: Helvidius' son of the same name was executed by Domitian in 93. Marcus Porcius *Cato*, a staunch republican and after his death revered as a martyr to the cause, killed himself after the battle of Thapsus in 46 BC rather than surrender to Julius Caesar. Marcus Junius *Brutus*, Cato's son-in-law, was one of the assassins of Julius Caesar on the Ides of March 44 BC, and committed suicide after the defeat of his forces by Antony and Octavian at the battle of Philippi in 42 BC: he too was subsequently revered as a champion of Roman freedom against despotism.

The identity of the *Dio* included in this list by Marcus is less certain. Either Dio of Syracuse, a pupil and disciple of Plato in the fourth century BC, who made an ultimately catastrophic attempt to reform or replace tyranny in Syracuse with some sort of Platonic philosopher-kingship, and was assassinated in 353 BC (in Plutarch's *Parallel Lives* this Dio is linked with Brutus): or else Dio Cocceianus of Prusa in Bithynia, later called Chrysostomos ('the golden-mouthed'), an orator and Stoic philosopher who was banished by Domitian; a substantial quantity of his writings survives.

A balanced constitution . . . the liberty of the subject: The summation of Severus' instruction in the history of the opposition to despotism, and a clear template for Marcus' own rule.

1.15 *Maximus*: Claudius Maximus, Stoic senator, who was consul in
c.142, governor of Upper Pannonia 150–54, and proconsul of
Africa in the late 150s. In this last capacity he presided over the
trial, on the charge of practising magic, of the philosopher, orator, and writer Apuleius, best known now for his remarkable
picaresque novel *The Golden Ass*. Extant also is Apuleius' published speech in his defence, the *Apology*: he was presumably
acquitted. In this speech Apuleius addresses and refers to
Maximus in the most flattering terms, which accord, doubtless
from rather different motives, with the picture here painted by
Marcus, which is that of a Stoic ideal.

Further mention of Maximus is made in 1.16.10 (as here, his
resolution in illness), 1.17.5 (one of the three men Marcus is
most grateful to have known), 8.25 (buried by his wife Secunda
– the year of his death is not known).

1.16 *my [adoptive] father*: Antoninus Pius, emperor from 10 July 138
(in succession to Hadrian) to his death on 7 March 161, when
Marcus succeeded as emperor.

Antoninus was in fact Marcus' uncle, having married the
daughter of Marcus' grandfather, Marcus Annius Verus. A condition of Antoninus' adoption by the ailing Hadrian in early 138
was that Antoninus should himself adopt both Marcus (then
aged sixteen) and Lucius Ceionius Commodus (then aged seven),
the son of Hadrian's originally intended successor, Lucius Aelius
Caesar, who had died on 1 January 138. Later that year Marcus
was betrothed to Antoninus' daughter Faustina: they were married in 145.

This chapter, by far the longest tribute in this Book of tributes,
breathes genuine affection and admiration. It should be read
in conjunction with the shorter, but equally warm, tribute to
Antoninus in 6.30.2. See also 1.17.3.

1.16.8 *Lorium ... Lanuvium*: Antoninus was born in Lanuvium
(modern Lanuvio) in Latium, about 18 miles south-east of Rome
along the Via Appia: and was brought up, and died, on his family
estate at Lorium (modern Castel di Guido) in Etruria, about 12
miles west of Rome along the Via Aurelia. The detail of these
references, and of that to Antoninus' treatment of *the apologetic
customs officer*, are obscure to us, though obviously clear in
Marcus' own recollection (he was writing for himself). Presumably they are adduced as evidence of Antoninus' frugality, down-
to-earthness, and 'common touch'.

Tusculum: A hill-town (modern Tuscolo) in Latium, about 10 miles south-east of Rome along the Via Latina, a favourite summer resort of wealthy Romans.

1.16.9 *Socrates*: The famous Athenian philosopher, executed in 399 BC at the age of seventy, was renowned both for his remarkable physical endurance and for his ability to drink any man under the table (Plato, *Symposium*, 176c, 220a). On Socrates, a paramount influence on Stoic philosophy, see note on 7.66.

1.16.10 *Maximus*: See 1.15 and note.

1.17 *From the gods*: See note on 6.44 for Marcus on the gods.

1.17.1 *a good sister*: Annia Cornificia Faustina, Marcus' only sibling, born perhaps two years after him. On her marriage Marcus settled the whole of his paternal inheritance on her. She died young, at no more than thirty, in 152, leaving two children.
that I did not blunder into offending any of them: Marcus was acutely aware of, and bothered by, his irascible tendency. See especially 11.18 and note.

1.17.2 *my grandfather's mistress*: See 1.1 note. We can only guess at Marcus' objection to this period of his upbringing, perhaps linked to his gratitude for the retention of sexual innocence. See also 1.17.7.

1.17.3 *a ruler and a father*: Antoninus Pius, emperor 138–161, and Marcus' adoptive father. See 1.16 and note. For the realization that 'a good life can be lived in a palace' see 5.16 and note.

1.17.4 *a brother*: His adoptive brother Lucius Ceionius Commodus (see note on 1.16). On his accession in 161 Marcus made Lucius joint emperor, naming him Lucius Aurelius Verus. Lucius married Marcus' eldest surviving daughter, Lucilla, in 164 (when she was aged fourteen). Lucius died suddenly of a stroke in 169, aged thirty-nine. The ancient historical and biographical tradition was not kind to Lucius, presenting him – probably in exaggerated contrast to Marcus – as something of a ne'er-do-well. Marcus' own picture is pleasantly generous.
my children: Marcus and Faustina, married in 145, had fourteen children (including two sets of boy twins), of whom seven (six boys and one girl) died in infancy or early childhood: see Birley, pp. 247–8, and note on 9.3.1. When Marcus died in 180, his only surviving son Commodus, then aged eighteen, succeeded him as emperor. His was an increasingly disastrous reign, cut short by assassination at the end of 192. Ausonius, writing in the fourth century AD, gives the terse verdict: 'The only harm Marcus

did to his country was to have a son.' For Marcus on children and the loss of a child see note on 11.34.

That I did not make further progress in rhetoric . . . my right path: For Marcus' decisive shift in study and interest from rhetoric to philosophy, see 1.7 (Rusticus) and note, and note on 1.11.

1.17.5 *quick to raise my tutors to . . . public office*: We do not have much detail. Marcus made Rusticus consul in 162, and prefect of the city in the following year (see 1.7 and note), but Rusticus then was hardly in his youth.

Apollonius, Rusticus, Maximus: See 1.8, 1.7, 1.15 and notes.

1.17.6 *life according to nature*: The Stoic ideal, and a constant underlying theme in the *Meditations*. This ideal is of a life lived in conformity with *reason*, the rationality inherent both in human nature and in the nature of the universe (the Whole), of which human nature is a part. See in particular 1.9.1 (the influence of Sextus), 2.9, 3.2.3 ('one who has developed a genuine affinity for Nature and her works'): cf. 4.48.2 ('in tune with nature'), 3.4.4, 6.58, 9.1.4, 10.15, 12.1.2. Marcus rises to an almost devotional exaltation in 4.23: 'Nature, all that your seasons bring is fruit to me: all comes from you, exists in you, returns to you.' See also note on 6.33. See further Sandbach, pp. 52–9; Long, pp. 179–84; LS, 63 B–C.

The reference in this section to *communications* and *promptings/instructions* from the gods, together with the mention of *help through dreams* in 1.17.9, suggests strongly that Marcus' religious experience and belief went beyond conventional piety. See Rutherford, pp. 192–5. For his metaphysical devotion see 4.23 and note.

1.17.7 *Benedicta or Theodotus*: Unknown, but presumably slaves in Antoninus' household, with whom sexual relations, whether heterosexual or homosexual, would have been no disgrace, and even expected. For Marcus' sexual constraint see also 1.17.2, 3.2.3: he commends similar restraint in Antoninus in 1.16.8. His reductive analysis of the mechanics of sexual intercourse in 6.13 suggests a fastidious distaste. See also note on 5.10.1.

my mother: See 1.3 and note. Domitia Lucilla was still alive in 155, and dead by 161. *Fated to die young* is a relative judgement. Marcus' mother was at least fifty when she died.

1.17.8 *my wife*: Annia Galeria Faustina, daughter of Antoninus Pius, who was married to Marcus in 145, and bore him fourteen children (see note on 1.17.4 above). She accompanied Marcus to

the front on some of his campaigns, earning thereby the title
Mater Castrorum, 'Mother of the camp'. She was with Marcus in
the eastern provinces when she suddenly died in 175 at Halala in
Cappadocia, aged about forty-five. She was deified by the senate,
and Marcus renamed Halala Faustinopolis in her memory.

The rumour-mill, grinding matter readily accepted and passed
on by the subsequent historical tradition, accused Faustina of
infidelity and sedition – the two combined in the allegation of an
affair with Avidius Cassius, the governor of Syria, who instituted
a serious but short-lived rebellion in spring 175. There is no
substantiating evidence, and Marcus' words here (the present
tense implies that Faustina was still alive when these words were
written) speak only of affection and trust.

1.17.9 *the oracle at Caieta*: The oracle of Apollo at Caieta (modern
Gaeta), situated on a promontory about seventy-five miles south-
east of Rome. Neither the nature nor the occasion of the inquiry
is known. That Marcus relates here the response of Apollo's
priest (or at least part of it) confirms his belief in the validity of
divine communication. See further Rutherford, pp. 195–200.

for all my love of philosophy: For Marcus as philosopher *manqué*
see note on 8.1.

'*the help of gods and Fortune's favour*': The rhythm of the Greek
suggests a verse quotation, but the origin is unknown.

BOOK 2

The second book of the *Meditations* also has a distinct character, with
an overall unity suggesting linked composition in a single frame of
mind. In the seventeen chapters of this Book Marcus sets out much of
the philosophy and most of the principles or thoughts which are
recurrent themes in the remainder of the *Meditations*. They can be
tracked through the General Index. Many of these themes are summarized, as a sort of aide-memoire or check-list, in 12.26.

The main themes, listed in the order of their presentation, are:

· The true nature of good and evil (2.1, 2.6, 2.11, 2.13, 2.17.2).
· The kinship of all men (2.1, 2.13).
· The divinity within us (2.1, 2.4, 2.12, 2.13, 2.17.2).
· The case against anger (2.1, 2.10, 2.16).
· The subordination of body to mind, passion to reason (2.2, 2.5, 2.10,
  2.12, 2.13, 2.16).

- The need to accept one's lot (2.2, 2.5, 2.13, 2.16, 2.17.2).
- The interrelation of all parts of nature, under necessity/providence, to the benefit of the Whole (2.3, 2.4, 2.9, 2.12, 2.16, 2.17.2).
- The shortness of life, and of opportunity (2.4, 2.6, 2.11.1, 2.12, 2.14, 2.17.1).
- The principles of purposeful action and thought (2.5, 2.7, 2.11.1, 2.16).
- No cause for fear of death (2.11, 2.12, 2.14, 2.17.2).
- The beneficence of god/the gods/nature (2.11, 2.13, 2.17.2).
- The 'indifferent' nature of externals (2.11.4, cf. 2.7).
- The futility and tawdriness of things temporal (2.12).
- The nature and evanescence of fame (2.12, 2.17.1, cf. 2.6).
- The eternal sameness of things (2.14).
- 'All is as thinking makes it so' (2.15).
- The duty of truthfulness (2.16, 2.17.2).

It is characteristic of the *Meditations*, and hardly surprising, given their wholly personal nature and intent, that a good number of themes or thoughts – philosophical, moral, or practical – recur frequently throughout the Books (indeed within this one Book) in either near-identical or varied terms. It is fair to assume that the relative frequency reflects Marcus' own preoccupations, and that the variety of expression, and weighting, reflects the emotional or psychological need at the moment of writing (it could be vexation, self-exhortation, self-consolation, or more serene reflection). Even in this second Book, Marcus does not preach, unless it is preaching to himself: 'You' in the *Meditations* is always self-referential, and the frequent imperative 'Always remember this . . .', or the like, is an exhortation to himself.

One aspect of variety of expression needs particular note. Marcus makes frequent and devout reference to a universal world-order, governed beneficently in the interest of all its parts and the inclusive whole, whence comes the dispensation of his lot to each individual. The governing principle of this world-order is variously referred to as God, the gods, Zeus (three times), Nature, universal Nature, the Whole, the nature of the Whole, the Universe, 'the governor of all things' (or similar formulations), Law, Providence, Fate. These are equations, essentially interchangeable, differing only perhaps in the emotional response, at various times and in various contexts, to the same principle. Marcus gives a clear statement of unitary Stoic doctrine in 7.9: 'There is one universe out of all things, one god pervading all things, one substance, one law, one common reason in all intelligent beings, and one truth.' See further note on 6.44. The final chapter of the

Meditations (12.36) movingly equates law, nature, and god as the benign agents of dismissal from life's stage.

Written among the Quadi on the River Gran: Only Books 2 and 3 (*'Written in Carnuntum'*) have prescripts indicating the place and occasion of their composition.

The Gran (Hron) is a northern tributary of the Danube, joining at modern Esztergom in Hungary. The Quadi, against whom Marcus was campaigning in the early 170s, were a Germanic tribe north of the Danube, in modern Slovakia. For these northern campaigns see Birley, ch. 8.

2.1   *first thing in the morning*: Several times Marcus exhorts himself to early morning meditation, or, it may be, fortification for the coming day (this chapter, 5.1, 10.13: cf. 6.2, 8.12). He also urges himself to get up (5.1, 8.12)! In his later years he suffered badly from insomnia.

true good and evil: Stoic ethics adopted from Socrates an intellectual concept of virtue and vice. Virtue is knowledge (of what is truly good): to know good is inevitably to do it. Vice is the result of ignorance: hence Socrates' famous paradox that 'no one willingly (i.e. knowingly) does wrong'. The only true harm which can befall a human being is that which he does to himself – i.e. making himself morally worse. Therefore no external agent, circumstance, or event has the ability to do him true harm. Compare 8.55 ('. . . wickedness does no harm to the recipient: it is only harmful to the perpetrator') and 9.4 ('The sinner sins against himself: the wrongdoer wrongs himself, by making himself morally bad').

If fully believed, this virtually watertight ethical system has clear power to fortify and console. Elements of it recur frequently in the *Meditations*, sometimes taken to what we would consider implausible excess (e.g. 4.39, 7.68, 8.41).

For sin/error as ignorance, therefore unwitting, therefore pardonable or at least intelligible, see also 4.3.2, 7.22 ('they go wrong through ignorance, not intent'), 7.62, 8.14, 9.42.2 ('gone astray'), 10.30, 11.18.3, 12.12. For the consequent obligation to teach the ignorant see 2.13 note.

For the inability of any external to do one true harm see also 2.11.2, 4.8, 4.39, 5.19, 6.41, 7.14, 7.16, 7.22, 7.64, 8.1, 8.28, 8.41, 8.55, 8.56, 9.42.2, 11.18.7.

For self-harm as the only true harm see 2.6 and note.

On Stoic ethics see Sandbach, ch. 3; Long, pp. 179–209; LS, 56–67.

kinship . . . fragment of divinity: Interfused with the ethical philosophy in this carefully composed chapter are two other linked axioms of central importance to Marcus' thinking: the essential kinship and community of all men (presented in the *Meditations* both as a theological or metaphysical argument and as a moral imperative to social action); and 'the divinity within us'. The ruling principle of the Universe is (divine) reason. The ruling principle in a human being, his 'directing mind', which he shares with his kin, is the analogue within him (or the 'emanation', 2.4) of that universal reason. God and Nature are differently nuanced but ultimately equivalent expressions for the ruling principle of the universe. Marcus generally prefers the latter. See further note on 6.44.

For the *kinship* of men, see also 2.13, 3.4.4, 3.11.3, 4.29, 7.13, 7.22 ('all men are brothers'), 9.22, 10.6.2, 10.36, 11.9, 12.26, 12.30. The moral imperatives Marcus derives from this axiom of kinship vary in warmth: sometimes a duty of care and kindness (see note on 9.11), sometimes a more resigned duty of tolerance ('bear and forbear' – see note on 5.33).

Marcus speaks of 'the divinity within us' with particular frequency in Book 3 (see introductory note to that Book) and Book 12 (12.1.2, 12.2, 12.3.2, 12.26). See also 2.13, 2.17.2, 5.10.2, 5.27, 6.35, 8.45. The final formulation in the *Meditations* (12.26) rings with profound conviction: 'every man's mind is god.'

We were born for cooperation: See note on 7.13.

2.2   *flesh, breath, and directing mind*: For this tripartite division, and associated conclusions, see also 12.3: similar in 3.16. For disdain of the flesh/body (*'blood, bones . . .'*) see 3.3 and note. On the mind/body dualism see note on 6.32. For the 'directing mind' see notes on 2.1 and 5.21.

Quit your books: This terse instruction to himself is repeated in 2.3 ('give up your thirst for books'): cf. 3.14, 7.67, 8.8. Clearly a personal struggle of inclination, and a lingering regret.

'you are old': The *Meditations* were probably written in Marcus' last decade, in his fifties. When he died in March 180, he was one month short of fifty-nine. Marcus' references to old age and the proximity of death (this chapter, 2.6, 4.17, 4.37, 5.31, 7.70, 8.2, 8.5, 10.15, 10.34, 12.1.2) may reflect the exhaustion of the moment and/or his more general view, often expressed, of the insignificant brevity of human life *sub specie aeternitatis* (see note on 3.10).

jerking to the strings of selfish impulse: The striking and eloquent image of the marionette is a favourite of Marcus: see also 3.16, 6.16.1, 6.28, 7.3, 7.29, 10.38, 12.19.

2.3   Another carefully composed chapter, of which Farquharson (p. 285) observes:

> The chapter is an example of the simplicity and yet extreme difficulty of the writer. He is simple because he states with conviction a conclusion which has sunk into the common consciousness of religious men and women; difficult because of his deep knowledge of a system every tenet of which had been discussed and criticized, and because of his parsimony of words, his reference to suppressed arguments.

But Marcus, writing for himself, can say, 'Let this be enough for you': his own need is for a compressed reminder, not a treatise.

the changes in the elements: A central doctrine of Stoic physics is that the elements whose combination forms the physical universe and every object in it are constantly interchanging and recombining, giving constant renewal and regeneration ('so that the world is always young', 7.25: cf. 6.15, 12.23). See especially 2.17.2, 4.46 (Heraclitus), 5.13, 6.15, 7.47, 10.7.

For the general doctrine – 'the universe is change' (4.3.4), change expressed in creation, transformation, and regeneration (9.1.5, 10.1, 10.18, 12.21) – see also 4.36, 6.17, 7.25, 8.6, 9.19, 10.11, 12.23. The universe/nature of the Whole 'loves' or 'delights in' change: 4.36, 7.18, 9.35. Its operation can be compared to that of a master-craftsman: 7.23, 8.50.

For the rapidity of change see 4.3.4, 7.10, 7.23, 7.25, 9.28, 9.32. For the dissolution of constituent elements at death see 2.17.2 and note.

Marcus puts this doctrine to various uses in the *Meditations*: for consolation against fear of death or any other harm (2.17, 8.6, 9.35, 10.7, 10.18, 11.17, 12.23); to underline the transience of life and the futility of any temporal values (6.15, 9.32); to 'wash away the filth of life on the ground' (7.47); as an aid to 'divesting of the body' (10.11).

2.5   *as if it were the last of your life*: This powerful prescription for focus, perhaps linked to Marcus' brooding sense of mortality, is used again in 2.11.1, 3.12, 7.69. Compare also 7.56.

lack of aim: For Marcus' insistence on the importance of a clear aim or purpose in every action, impulse, or thought see 2.7, 2.16

(a failure in this respect is one of the ways in which a soul 'harms itself'), 2.17.2, 3.4.2, 4.2, 8.17, 9.28 (even if the universe is purposeless, 'you should not be without purpose yourself'), 11.21, 12.20, 12.24.

2.6 *Self-harm, my soul*: The only true harm done to a human being (or his soul) is that done by himself (or itself): see note on 2.1, *'true good and evil'*. 2.16 explores the ways in which a soul can harm itself. See also 4.26 ('Someone does wrong? He does wrong to himself'), 6.21, 8.55, 9.4, 9.38, 12.26.

but let your own welfare depend on other people's souls: That is, by paying attention, or too much attention, to what others think, believe, or value. This chapter should be read in conjunction with 2.8 (and compare 8.56), and there is a clear link with the more positive (or defiant) thought, 'there is no one who can prevent you . . .', in 2.9 (see below). The need for independence of others and their opinions is a recurrent theme, especially in Book 3 (see introductory note to Book 3). See further notes on 4.12 and 5.3.

2.9 *there is no one who can prevent you*: Marcus often feels the need to bolster his resolve with such a reminder of the independence of his own moral will. See also 3.12 ('and nobody is able to stop you'), 4.49, 5.10.2, 5.29, 6.58, 8.32, 8.47, 9.11, 10.32, 12.25; and cf. 9.29.

2.10 *the common man's distinctions*: Strict Stoic ethics regarded all sins as equal. See LS, 61; Sandbach, pp. 41–8: Long (p. 204) observes that 'in Stoic ethics a miss is as bad as a mile'.

Theophrastus: Greek philosopher, scientist, and polymath, c.371–287 BC, pupil of Aristotle and his successor, from 322 BC, as head of his school, the Lyceum: an exceptionally able man, of wide-ranging intellect, who almost single-handedly established the science of botany. A good number of his writings survive, but not the work to which Marcus here refers.

lust . . . anger: Is there a personal agenda in this otherwise out-of-context discussion of the relative gravity of offences of lust and anger? In the *Meditations* Marcus makes little mention of the distractions of lust, but is almost obsessed with the analysis and control of anger: see note on 11.18. Marcus knew his own faults.

2.11 A chapter weaving together arguments against fear of death, the conviction of divine/natural providence and beneficence, and the crucial distinction between true harm (which can only be self-inflicted, and so *'absolutely in man's power to avoid'*: see notes on 2.1 and 2.6) and popularly supposed (good and) harm, which falls indiscriminately (see also 9.1.3). For Marcus on the gods see note on 6.44. Compare the arguments in 10.7 and 12.5.

2.11.2 *cannot make a human being worse*: The same thought and conclusion in 4.8.

2.11.4 *death and life, fame and ignominy ... poverty*: The major polarities of those externals, commonly regarded as goods or evils, which to the Stoic are 'indifferent' – i.e. with no ability of themselves (other than through his own judgement of them) to affect a person's 'directing mind' or inner state: not therefore *'inherent good or evil'*. For the 'indifferents' see in particular 9.1.4–5: and notes on 5.12 and 5.20. See further Sandbach, pp. 28–31; LS, 58.

2.12 The argument of the previous chapter is couched in calm, measured, and almost formal terms. This chapter rehearses much of the same argument in a more earthy and expostulatory manner, equally characteristic of Marcus. Two different days?
how cheap they are, how contemptible, shoddy, perishable, and dead: See note on 5.10.1 for Marcus' constant reminders of the shoddiness of things temporal.
What is death: See note on 2.14 below. For death as *'a function of nature'* compare 4.5, 6.2 (death 'is one of the acts of life'), 9.3.1.

2.13 *in Pindar's words*: The Greek text does not actually name the author of this quotation, a fragment of Pindar (fr. 292 Snell), which is also used by Plato (*Theaetetus*, 173e). Pindar was the leading Greek lyric poet in the first half of the fifth century BC.
the divinity within himself: See note on 2.1 (*'fragment of divinity'*).
their ignorance of good and evil: See note on 2.1, *'true good and evil'*, for the Socratic/Stoic view that virtue is knowledge and vice ignorance. Moral blindness, then, is an involuntary state, properly exciting pity rather than anger: and it is incumbent on the morally sighted to do what they can to educate their less fortunate fellows into a clearer vision (see 5.22, 5.28, 6.27, 7.26, 8.17, 8.59, 9.11, 9.42.2, 10.4, 10.30, 11.13, 11.18.9, 12.16). A charming practical example in 11.18.9.

2.14 Two arguments of 'consolation' against fear of death. The argument that death is only the loss of the present moment recurs in 3.10 and 12.26. It is fair to conclude from the *Meditations* that Marcus, at least in his later years, was preoccupied with death (and with the associated themes of the trivial shortness of life

and our *post mortem* destination, if any). Marcus touches on or
discusses these themes with great frequency: his treatment varies,
doubtless according to mood and circumstance, from austere and
high-minded philosophy to world-weariness and almost brutal
realism.

Many of Marcus' considerations of death fall into one or more
of these four categories:

- Arguments of consolation and/or reasons not to fear death:
  2.11.1, 2.14 (similar in 3.10, 12.26), 3.3, 4.50, 8.58, 9.3, 9.21,
  10.7, 10.29, 12.23, 12.35.
- Death as a function of a beneficent universal nature, so no harm
  in it or cause for fear: 2.12, 2.17.2, 4.5, 5.4, 5.10, 6.2, 8.20,
  9.3.1, 12.23.
- Reflections, with varying degrees of focus, on the inevitability of
  death ('where are they now?') for the greatest of men, the wisest
  of men, ordinary men, those who buried others: 3.3, 4.32, 4.33,
  4.48, 4.50, 6.24, 6.47, 7.19, 8.25, 8.31 (the whole court of
  Augustus), 8.37 ('all stench and corruption in a bag of bones'),
  10.31, 12.27.
- A more cynical consolation – death as the relief from life: 5.10,
  6.28, 9.3.2, 10.36, 12.31.

See also notes on 3.1 (suicide) and 3.5 ('ready to depart').

For the trivial shortness of life see notes on 3.10, 4.48.2, and
5.10.1. On the 'present moment' see note on 4.26.

For the *post mortem* possibilities see note on 3.3.

For Marcus on death and dissolution see also Rutherford,
pp. 244–50.

2.14.2 *see the same things*: The eternal sameness of things is another
frequent theme in the *Meditations*, taking two widely disparate
forms. One (as here) derives from the belief of orthodox Stoicism,
evidently accepted by Marcus, that from eternity to eternity the
world goes through an endless succession of identical cycles (so
that all that happens has happened before, and will happen
again): see especially 9.28, and also 5.13 (and note), 5.32, 6.37,
8.6, 9.35, 10.7.2, 11.1.2, 12.26. For the doctrine of everlasting
recurrence see LS, 52; Sandbach, pp. 78–9.

The other is the expression of a world-weary and often dismissive view that 'there is no new thing under the sun' (Ecclesiastes
1:9) in human life, behaviour, and depravity: with a few years'
experience (in 7.49 and 11.1.2 Marcus puts it at forty) you have

'seen it all'. See also 4.32, 4.44, 6.46, 7.1, 8.25, 9.14, 9.33, 10.27, 12.24 ('monotony and transience').

2.15 *'All is as thinking makes it so'*: By this anticipation of Hamlet Marcus means that the nature and impact (for good or ill) of any external event or circumstance – all 'indifferent' things – is determined solely by the rational judgement of it formed by the directing mind, not by the event itself. See in particular 4.7: 'Remove the judgement, and you have removed the thought "I am hurt": remove the thought "I am hurt", and the hurt itself is removed'; 4.39: 'So no such judgement, and all is well . . . [the directing mind] should assess nothing either bad or good which can happen equally to the bad man or the good: because what can happen to a man irrespective of his life's conformity to nature is not of itself either in accordance with nature or contrary to it'; and 8.40: 'If you remove your judgement of anything that seems painful, you yourself stand quite immune to pain.'

The theme recurs, in the same phrasing, in 12.8, 12.22, 12.26. Compare also 3.9, 4.3.4, 5.26, 8.47, 9.13, 9.32, 9.42.2, 11.16, 11.18.7, 12.25: and notes on 4.7 and 5.19.

Monimus: A Cynic philosopher of the fourth century BC. The 'clear retort' to Monimus is that his saying refutes its own truth, being only what he thinks.

2.16 The last two chapters of Book 2, each building up to a weighty and resonant final sentence, form an eloquent summary, in contrasting styles, of many of the themes of the preceding chapters.

For the conception of a soul's self-harm see notes on 2.1 and 2.6. A similar list, in the context of offences/sins against nature/god, in 9.1.

For the noble idea, central to Stoicism, of the universe as the 'great city', see in particular 4.4: also 3.11.2, 4.3.2, 4.23, 12.36, and compare 4.40, 6.44, 10.15. See LS, 67.

2.17.1 *his existence a flux*: See note on 4.48.2 for Marcus on human life as short and cheap.

a visit in a strange land: Contrast 12.1.2 ('You will no longer be a stranger in your own country') and note.

the only lasting fame is oblivion: See notes on 3.10 and 7.34 for Marcus' view of fame.

2.17.2 *What then can escort us on our way*: For Marcus' view of philosophy and its function in human life see note on 8.1.

the dissolution of the elements: For the Stoic doctrine of the constant change, dissolution, and recombination of the elements which constitute all matter – a doctrine here used as another argument to assuage fear of death – see note on 2.3, *'the changes in the elements'*. For the dissolution of the constituent elements at death (and recombination thereafter) see also 4.5, 4.14, 4.32.2, 5.13, 8.18, 10.7.2, 11.20.1, 12.24. For *'accordance with nature'* see note on 6.33.

BOOK 3

Like Book 2, also written on campaign, Book 3 suggests a relative unity of composition (considered paragraphs, constant themes, few random jottings) reflecting place, opportunity, and mood. 'This Book has a happier tone than the second, and the language is less abstract and impersonal; the writer seems to be in a clearer atmosphere, above the mists of difficulty and doubt, the melancholy sense of transience and human futility which lies at least on the surface of Book 2. The sentences convey an impression of personal devotion to a religious ideal, an evident warmth of feeling, a sentiment which rarely occurs in the *Meditations* until we reach the closing Book' (Farquharson, p. 297).

The core of the Book is a detailed exploration of what it means to be a good man, taking the form of a set of precepts, abstract or practical, for living a good life, and set in the context of duty both to men and to god – the god within and the god without (the good man 'is in some way a priest and minister of the gods', 3.4.3).

As in Book 2, Marcus brings this section of his *Meditations* to an eloquent and sonorous conclusion ('. . . pure, at peace, ready to depart, in unforced harmony with his fate', 3.16.2).

The themes given particular emphasis in Book 3 are:

- The divinity within us (3.3, 3.4.3, 3.5, 3.6.2, 3.7, 3.12): see note on 2.1.
- Preparation/readiness for death (3.1, 3.3, 3.5, 3.7, 3.14, 3.16.2: cf. 3.10).
- Precepts for the good life (3.4–9, 3.11, 3.12, 3.16.2).
- Glad acceptance of one's lot (3.4.3, 3.6.1, 3.16.2).
- Independence of others and their opinions (3.4.1, 3.4.3, 3.4.4, 3.5, 3.8).
- Duty of care for one's fellow men (3.4.4, 3.6.2, 3.9, 3.11.3).
- The interfusion of the human and the divine (3.1, 3.4.3, 3.9, 3.13).

Written in Carnuntum: See note on the prescript to Book 2.

Carnuntum (modern Hainburg in Austria), just south of the border between the Roman province of Upper Pannonia and the hostile tribes of free Germany, was Marcus' headquarters for the northern campaigns of the early 170s.

3.1 *whether the time has come to leave this life*: i.e. by suicide, allowed by Stoic ethics under certain circumstances (both the founding father of Stoicism, Zeno of Citium, and his pupil and successor Cleanthes are said to have committed suicide, in 263 BC and 232 BC respectively). Further references to suicide in 3.7 (?), 5.29, 8.47, 9.2, 9.3.2 (?), 10.8.3, 10.22, 10.32, 11.3. See also note on 10.8.3.

3.2 *even the incidental effects*: See 6.36 for a similar thought, and compare 8.50.

3.2.3 *seductive charm*: See note on 1.17.7.

3.3 Two more arguments of 'consolation' (see 2.14 and note). The first, from the inevitability of death for even the cleverest and the most powerful, recurs in more cynical form in 4.48 (cf. also 6.47). The tone here is rather one of irony – the physician could not heal himself, the philosopher who speculated about universal fire was destroyed by internal water.

Hippocrates of Cos lived in the fifth century BC, a contemporary of Socrates. Surprisingly little is known of the physician revered since antiquity as 'the father of medicine'.

Chaldean: i.e. Babylonian.

Alexander the Great (356–323 BC), *Pompey* (106–48 BC), *Julius Caesar* (100–44 BC): archetypes of the outstanding military leader. See also 8.3 and note.

Heraclitus of Ephesus: a pre-Socratic philosopher who flourished at the turn of the sixth and fifth centuries BC.

the conflagration of the universe: Heraclitus' cosmology seems to have included the prediction that the entire universe would turn to fire (fr. B66 Diels-Kranz). This was taken as authority for the Stoic doctrine of the periodic conflagration and regeneration of the universe (see notes on 2.14.2 and 5.13): see LS, 46; Sandbach, pp. 78–9.

Vermin were the death of Democritus, and vermin of another sort killed Socrates: Democritus of Abdera in Thrace was a fifth-century BC philosopher (born *c.*460 BC). The reference to Democritus seems to be a lapse of memory (another such in 11.25): it was another philosopher, Pherecydes of Syros (mid-sixth century BC), who was said to have died of an infestation of lice. '*Vermin of another sort*' refers to the Athenian jury which condemned Socrates to death in 399 BC.

If it is to another life: There are nearly twenty passages in the *Meditations* where Marcus speculates on, or argues from, the various *post mortem* possibilities, without committing himself to any one view. The three possibilities 'for whatever follows' are listed succinctly in 11.3: 'extinction, dispersal, or survival'. All three together also in 7.32 ('Either dispersal if we are atoms: or, if we are a unity, extinction or a change of home'), and 8.25. Elsewhere Marcus speaks of extinction (insensibility, unconsciousness) or some form of survival (3.3, 5.33, 8.58); of dispersal or survival (6.24, 7.50); of dispersal/dissolution only (4.5, 4.32.2, 6.10, 8.18, 12.24); or of survival (in some form) only (4.14, 4.21.1, 5.13, 6.47). See also 9.21, 12.5, 12.21.

From this welter it is clear both that Marcus was bothered by *post mortem* considerations and that he had no constant view, vacillating between austere physical theory (dispersal of the atoms, or dissolution of the elements, of which we are composed) and the more emotional hope of some form of personal survival: 'another life' (3.3); 'translation' (5.33); change of abode to 'that other world' (6.47); 'change of home' (7.32); 'migration' (8.25); 'a different consciousness' (8.58). Dissolution shades into survival in the notion that after death our constituent elements are 'taken up into the generative principle of the universe' (4.14, 4.21.1, 6.24, 9.1.5).

no longer in thrall to a bodily vessel: The mind/body dualism is a frequent theme in the *Meditations*: see note on 6.32. For the mind as '*divinity*' see note on 2.1. For the disdainful reference to the material composition of the body ('*a clay of dust and blood*') compare 2.2, 2.17.1, 7.68, 8.37, 10.33.3 ('the corpse which is our body'), 12.1.1.

3.4   This chapter begins an extensive exploration of the nature of the good life and the characteristics of the good man (3.4–9, 3.11, 3.12, 3.16.2). In more brusque and impatient mood Marcus can tell himself, 'No more roundabout discussion of what makes a good man. Be one!' (10.16). Compare 4.17: 'While you live, while you can, become good'; and 8.22: 'You would rather become good tomorrow than be good today.' See Rutherford, pp. 169–72 for a discussion of this chapter.

3.4.3 For the ideal man here described compare the questions asked of Socrates' soul in 7.66. The acceptance of one's lot is an insistent theme in the *Meditations*, and a cardinal tenet of Marcus' philosophy. See note on 5.8.

3.4.4 *what sort of people they are*: Despite Marcus' insistence on the kinship of mankind and the duty of care to our fellow men, another voice often breaks through in the *Meditations*, with which Marcus refers to an unspecified 'they' in contempt, indignation, or irritation. He was not impressed by his associates, let alone by the ignorant masses (cf. 9.41: 'the ignorant chatter of the uneducated layman'). For the contemptuous use of 'they' see, for example, 3.15, 6.18, 6.59, 7.62, 8.4, 9.18, 9.34, 10.13, 10.19, 11.14, 11.18.2. See also notes on 4.6 and 5.10.1.

3.5 *like a soldier waiting for the Retreat from life to sound*: For the metaphor of life as a form of military service see note on 7.7.
     ready to depart: The thought recurs in 3.7, 3.16.2, 4.48.2 (the ripe olive ready to fall), 11.3. A rather different tone in 5.10, 5.33, and 9.3.2.
     Your duty is to stand straight – not held straight: Repeated, in even terser form, but interestingly varied in 7.12 (see note). Compare 1.15.3.

3.6.2 *as Socrates used to say:* Not exactly matched in the extant sources, but close is Plato, *Phaedo*, 83 a–b.

3.6.3 *the praise of the many . . . the enjoyment of pleasure*: For Marcus on praise see note on 4.20, and note on 8.10 for Marcus on pleasure.
     '*But better is what benefits*': For sharper effect Marcus often casts his arguments in dialogue form. The supposed interlocutor is sometimes an imagined objector, sometimes Marcus himself.
     Only make sure that your scrutiny is sound: For the methods of analysis Marcus recommends to himself see notes on 3.11 (reductive analysis – 'stripping bare') and 4.21.2 (analysis into material, cause, and reference). See also 4.3 and note (retreat into oneself); 8.13, 8.22, 10.11, 11.19. Compare 'Ask yourself this question . . .', or the like, in e.g. 5.11, 8.2, 8.14, 10.37.

3.7 *the bodily envelope of his soul*: See 3.3 and note. Indifference to the length of life is a constant theme: see 2.14.2, 4.15, 4.47, 4.50, 6.23, 6.49, 7.46, 9.33, 12.35, 12.36. The starkest formulation is in 4.50: in the perspective of eternity 'what is the difference between an infant of three days and a Nestor of three generations?'

3.8 A combination of favoured medical (see note on 3.13) and dramatic (see note on 10.27) analogies or metaphors. Compare in particular 11.1.1.

3.10 *each of us lives only in the present moment*: For this thought, both consolation and spur, see also 2.14, 8.36, 12.26, and note on 4.26.

life is a small thing: The insignificance, in the wider scheme of things and *sub specie aeternitatis*, of human life, habitation, and fame is a melancholy note struck often in the *Meditations*.

For human life as an infinitesimal part of eternal time see also 4.48, 4.50, 5.23, 5.24, 6.15, 6.36, 9.32, 10.17, 12.32.

For geographical insignificance see also 3.11.2, 4.3.3, 6.36, 8.21, 12.32.

For the uncertainty and evanescence of fame see also 2.17.1, 4.3.3, 4.19, 4.33, 7.6, 7.21, 9.30, and note on 7.34.

3.11 *stripped bare to its essential nature*: For this reductive mode of analysis, applicable in both moral and material contexts, see further 6.13, 8.36, 9.34, 9.36, 10.9, 11.2 ('go straight to the component parts of anything'), 11.17, 12.2, 12.8. See also notes on 4.21.2 and 9.34.

3.11.2 *Nothing is so conducive to greatness of mind*: Identical language in 10.11.

this highest City: See 2.16 and note.

3.13 A medical analogy (in itself traditional) which suggests that at least one of Marcus' purposes in writing the *Meditations* was self-therapy (see Rutherford, pp. 15–21). Compare 5.9: 'Do not come back to philosophy as schoolboy to tutor, but rather as a man with ophthalmia returns to his sponge and salve, or another to his poultice or lotion.' Further medical analogies in 3.8, 5.8, and 10.35.

have your doctrines ready: A constant exhortation, taking various forms. To Marcus his doctrines or principles are comfort (4.3.1, 4.16, 6.12, 10.34), guides (8.1) and armoury (12.9), 'living things' (7.2) which can 'bite' a man (10.34) and can be carelessly 'wiped out' (10.9). For 'readiness' compare 4.12.

3.14 *No more wandering*: See 2.2 and note. Similar exhortations not to 'wander' in 2.7, 4.22: cf. 8.1.

jottings ... histories ... extracts: The 'jottings' could well be some early part of these *Meditations*; it is not known what is meant by the 'histories' (perhaps a compilation, conceivably by Marcus himself, of the deeds of great men of the past); 'extracts' suggest a personal anthology or commonplace book, some evidence of which is seen in Marcus' use of quotations (a particular concentration in 7.35ff. : cf. 11.6 and 11.22–39) – see Index of Quotations.

3.15 *They*: See note on 3.4.4.

a different sort of vision: See 2.13 and note.

3.16 Starting from a tripartite division similar to that in 2.2, this final chapter provides an effective summary and amalgamation of most of the main themes of Book 3.

3.16.1 *catamites*: See note on 5.10.1.

a Phalaris or a Nero: Types of depraved tyranny. Phalaris, tyrant of Acragas in Sicily in the first half of the sixth century BC, was notorious for his sadistic cruelty. Nero, Roman emperor from 54 to his suicide in 68, quickly became a by-word for paranoid excesses of cruelty and vice (including matricide).

Compare 6.34: 'As for pleasure, pirates, catamites, parricides, and tyrants have enjoyed it to the full.'

BOOK 4

4.1 *sets out on its objects in a conditional way*: This idea, that the rational man sets out on any object or course of action 'conditionally' (or 'with reservation'), i.e. ready to adapt to circumstances, absorb or circumvent obstacles, and turn the revised situation to a new exercise of virtue, is explored further in 5.20 ('The mind adapts and turns round any obstacle to action to serve its objective: a hindrance to a given work is turned to its furtherance, an obstacle in a given path becomes an advance'), 6.50 ('. . . so using the obstacle to bring forth a different virtue'), 7.58, 8.32, 8.35, 8.41, 10.33 (and note), 11.37. An 'unconditional aim', ignoring the limits of the possible (6.50), is an offence against reason (8.41). Marcus is here, as often, using a technical term of Stoicism. A similar, simpler, thought in 8.50 ('Brambles in the path? Go round them').

4.2 *No action . . . without aim*: For this insistent theme in the *Meditations* see note on 2.5.

4.3 Framed in the context of 'retreat into yourself', this chapter gathers and recapitulates many of the themes which are central to Marcus' theoretical, moral, and practical philosophy: the backbone of doctrines (3.13 note), the kinship of men (2.1 note), wrongdoing not deliberate (2.1 note), glad acceptance of one's lot (5.8 note), the universe as community (2.16 note: fully articulated in the following chapter, 4.4), the mind/body dualism (6.32 note), the evanescence of fame (3.10 note), the tininess of man's time and place (3.10 note), the immunity of the mind to externals ('all is as thinking makes it so': 2.15 note and 5.19 note), the constancy and rapidity of change (2.3 note). The terse and eloquent summary, 'The universe is change: life is judgement', may be a quotation, of uncertain source.

A comparable vade mecum recapitulation in 12.26.

4.3.1 *retreat into yourself*: Marcus here gives a personal and persuasive endorsement of what was a commonplace philosophical argument, that a change of place is not a change of mind. Similar in 10.23. The notion of retreat or withdrawal into one's own mind recurs in stronger form and military analogy in 8.48 (the mind free from passions is an impregnable fortress). See also 7.28 ('Withdraw into yourself...'), and 7.59 ('Dig inside yourself...'), and compare 5.2, 6.11 ('...quickly return to yourself'), 7.67 ('drawing a boundary around yourself'), and 10.8.3. For the means of inducing calm see also 5.2, 7.28, 12.22.

4.3.2 *providence or atoms*: These alternative models of the universe are frequently presented and contrasted in the *Meditations*. 'Providence' is shorthand for the Stoic view of the universe as a coherent, ordered, and purposeful whole, created, preserved, and governed by a beneficent rational principle variously termed Providence, God, or Nature (for these equations see introductory note to Book 2). 'Atoms' is shorthand for the Epicurean doctrine that all matter is the result of a random combination of atoms. Not surprisingly, Marcus largely adheres to the Stoic view, though in 9.28 he protects his position by asserting the validity of human purpose even if the atomist theory is true: 'The Whole is either a god – then all is well: or if purposeless – some sort of random arrangement of atoms or molecules – you should not be without purpose yourself.'

The alternatives, variously formulated and in various contexts of argument, are set out further in 4.27, 6.4, 6.10, 6.24, 9.28, 9.39, 10.6.1, 11.18.1. Compare also 7.32, 8.17, 12.14.

4.4   For the universe as the 'great city' see 2.16 note.

4.5   For this consolatory view of death see notes on 2.3, 2.14, 2.17.2.

4.6   *With such people*: For Marcus' largely cynical and sometimes despairing view of at least some of his associates and contemporaries see notes on 3.4.4 and 5.10.1. In this context Marcus speaks with two voices. He is conscious of the moral obligation, based on the kinship of men and the doctrine that wrongdoing is involuntary (2.1 note), to understand, tolerate, forgive, and educate (see notes on 2.13, 5.33, and 9.11). The harsher, more worldly view of an inevitable link between character and action (a combination of 'By their fruits ye shall know them' and 'Do men gather grapes of thorns, or figs of thistles?') is nevertheless prominent in the *Meditations*: see in particular 5.17, 5.28, 7.71, 8.14–15, 9.42.3–4, 10.30, 11.18.2, 11.18.11, 12.16.

The same fig-tree analogy is used again in 12.16 (and similar in 8.15): see also 10.8.4, 11.33. Fig-juice was used as rennet, to curdle milk.

4.7 *Remove the judgement*: For this doctrine, frequently rehearsed in the *Meditations*, that hurt or harm (including physical hurt) is only a matter of perception (i.e. rational judgement), see notes on 2.15 and 5.19. Closest to this passage is 12.25 : 'Jettison the judgement, and you are saved.' An ingredient is the Socratic belief, adopted by Stoic ethics, that the only true harm is (moral) harm done to oneself: on this see notes on 2.1 and 2.6. The next chapter, 4.8, is a firm statement of this belief (similar in 2.11.2). For Marcus on pain see note on 7.33.

4.10 *'All's right that happens in the world'*: This appears to be a quotation, or at least a popular saying, but the source is unknown. For the 'justice' of men's allotted experience, and the obligation to accept it gladly – a very frequent theme in the *Meditations* – see note on 5.8.

4.12 *to change your ground*: Despite Marcus' almost obsessive insistence (to himself) on the retention of his independence of others' opinions and values (see notes on 2.6 and 5.3), he also recognizes the need to accept advice, correction, and help. For advice/correction see 1.16.1 and 6.30.2 (the example of Antoninus), 6.21, 8.16. For the acceptance of help see 7.5, 7.7 ('Do not be ashamed of help'), 7.12, 10.12.

4.14 See note on 2.17.2.

4.15 For indifference to the length of life (this is the point of the image of the grains of incense) see 3.7 note.

4.17 For the exhortation to 'become good' compare 4.10, 4.25, 7.15, 10.16, and see introductory note to Book 3 and note on 3.4.

4.18 *the black characters either side*: The reference is obscure (yet more so that to the 'black character' in 4.28), but presumably this striking expression is a fusion of two of Marcus' favourite themes – the unworthiness of his associates and contemporaries (see notes on 3.4.4, 4.6, and 5.10.1), and the need to remain independent of the influence of others (see notes on 2.6 and 5.3). For the right path, along which one should 'run the straight race' ('the line' is death), see note on 5.4.

4.19 Fame and its shorter-term analogue, praise, both fascinate and sicken Marcus. For the evanescence of fame see notes on 3.10 and 7.34. For Marcus' views on praise and its worth, see note on the next chapter, 4.20.

Something is missing from the text at the end of this chapter.

4.20 Marcus on praise ('what is the point of praise?', 4.19). Marcus rejects the seduction of mere popularity: in 3.6.3 he groups 'the praise of the many' with power, wealth, and pleasure as the great seducers, and see also 6.16.1 ('the praise of the masses is the mere rattle of tongues') and 10.35 (unhealthy to demand that 'there must be popular acclaim for all I do'). His professed fastidious distaste for and suspicion of praise is based on its irrelevance to the inherent quality of any thing or action (this chapter) – a position which is philosophically tendentious and politically dangerous; on the poor quality of most of those who give or withhold praise (so they can be ignored: 3.4.4, 8.52–3, 9.34); and on their fickleness (4.3.3, 9.30, 10.34). Doubtless personal experience, vexation, and disappointment contributed to this defensively austere view.

4.21 For Marcus' consideration of the various *post mortem* possibilities see note on 3.3. He himself expresses no certain view. This chapter, while retaining an agnostic position, seems an over-earnest counter to an over-literal objector (possibly Marcus himself).

4.21.2 *By distinguishing the material and the causal*: A mode of analysis (see notes on 3.6.3 and 3.11) which Marcus frequently recommends to himself. To each thing, event, or action there is both inert content (substance, material) and an activating causal principle with a discernible reference. A simple, practical example is given in 10.38 ('the shuttle without the weaver, the pen without the writer, the whip without the driver'). See LS, 44.

For analysis into cause and material see also 5.13 ('I am made up of the causal and the material'), 7.29, 8.3, 8.11, 9.25, 9.37, 12.29 ('The salvation of one's life lies in seeing each object in its entirety, discerning both the material and the causal aspects of it'). For analysis into cause, material, and reference see 12.8, 12.10, 12.18.

4.22 *No wandering*: See notes on 2.2 and 3.14.

4.23 This remarkable chapter, eloquent of a state of spiritual exaltation, comes close to a devotional hymn. A similar exaltation breathes in 7.9 and 10.21. For the proper season of all things see also 9.10, 12.23, and 12.35.

'*Dear city of Cecrops*': The quotation is from the comic poet

Aristophanes (c.450–386 BC), fr. 112 Kassel-Austin. Cecrops was a mythical king of Athens, regarded by Athenians as the ancestral hero-founder of their city. By 'Dear city of Zeus' Marcus means the universe, the 'great city' (see 2.16 note).

4.24 For Democritus see 3.3 note. This quotation is fr. B3 Diels-Kranz.

4.26 *He does wrong to himself*: See notes on 2.1, 2.6, and 2.13.
make your gain from the present moment: The insistence in the *Meditations* on the importance of the present moment is the corollary of the equal insistence on the shortness and futility of human life (see notes on 3.10, 4.48.2, and 5.10.1). See 2.14, 3.10 and note, 6.32, 7.29, 7.68, 8.36, 8.44, 9.29, 9.41, 11.13, 12.3.2 ('seek only to perfect this life you are living in the present'), 12.26.

4.27 *Either an ordered universe, or a stew*: For these alternatives see note on 4.3.2, and for 'stew' see note on 6.10.

4.28 The reference, specific or general, of this vitriolic chapter is obscure (for 'black characters' see also 4.18). This very obscurity confirms that Marcus was writing for and to himself.

4.29 *a stranger in it*: Compare 12.1.2 and note.
For the notion of severance from the community (human society or universal nature), see also 5.8.5, 8.34, 11.8: and compare 8.52 and 9.9.3. Regrafting is allowed in 8.34 and 11.8.

4.30 Marcus probably has in mind here philosophers of the Cynic persuasion, who practised extreme simplicity of living.

4.32–33 In these clearly linked chapters Marcus combines two familiar themes – the eternal sameness of things (see note on 2.14.2) and the fleeting transitoriness of human life and memory/fame (see note on 3.10) – and from this combination draws conclusions about the proper objects of esteem and endeavour in human life, always in glad acceptance of god's will. Compare 7.3: 'But bear in mind that a person's worth is measured by the worth of what he values.' The next four chapters (4.34–37) more briefly reinforce these thoughts.
For similar 'Where are they now?' reflections on the annihilation of death see note on 2.14 and the passages there cited, and notes on 3.3 and 6.24.

4.32 *Vespasian* was emperor from 69 to 79, *Trajan* from 98 to 117.

4.32.1 *People marrying, having children ... kingships*: Similar lists expressing the miscellany of human life in 7.48 and (more cynical) 7.3. Compare also 9.30.

4.33 *Camillus, Caeso, Volesus, Dentatus*: Great men of the early

Roman republic. Marcus Furius *Camillus* was credited with the recovery of Rome after the Gallic sack in 390 BC; no detail is known of this *Caeso*, though a Quinctius Caeso is linked with M. Furius Camillus in Cicero, *Pro Domo*, 86; nor is it known to which *Volesus* (the family name of the Valerii) Marcus here refers; Manius Curius *Dentatus* (died 270 BC), Roman statesman and general, defeated Pyrrhus in 275 BC.

Scipio: Of the many famous Scipios Marcus probably means Publius Cornelius Scipio Africanus (236–183 BC), the conqueror of Hannibal.

Cato: Probably Marcus Porcius Cato 'the Censor' (234–149 BC), a contemporary of Scipio Africanus, rather than his great-grandson of the same name (for whom see note on 1.14.1).

Augustus: (63 BC–AD 14) The first Roman emperor.

Hadrian: Emperor from 117 to 138.

Antoninus: Marcus' adoptive father (see 1.16 and note, and 6.30.2–4), emperor from 138 to 161.

'*beyond sight, beyond knowledge*': A quotation from Homer's *Odyssey* (1.242) – Telemachus' despairing words to Athene about his missing father, Odysseus.

speech incapable of lies: See note on 9.1.2 for Marcus on truth and truthfulness.

4.34 *Clotho*: 'The Spinner', one of the three Fates (the other Fates are Lachesis and Atropos). For the equation of Fate, Providence, God, Nature etc. as the source of man's allocation in life see introductory note to Book 2.

4.36 For constant change as a principle of the universe see note on 2.3.

4.39 *So no such judgement, and all is well*: For this constantly repeated doctrine, that any apparent external harm or hurt is only a matter of judgement (and therefore removing the judgement removes the harm), see notes on 2.1, 2.6, 2.15, 4.7, 5.19.

subjected to knife or cautery ... mortify: A similarly extreme formulation in 8.41 ('The mind cannot be touched by fire, steel, tyranny, slander, or anything whatever . . .'), and compare 7.68.

4.40 For the conception of a unitary and unified universe compare in particular 4.45 and 7.9: and see note on 6.38.

4.41 This trenchant quotation (fr. 26 Schenkl: not from the extant volumes of the *Discourses* of Epictetus) is repeated in 9.24. On *Epictetus* see note on 1.7.3.

4.43 For the image of the rapid river of time/existence see also 2.17.1, 5.23, 6.15, 7.19, 9.29. The image is perhaps derived from two sayings of Heraclitus: 'All is in a state of flow' and 'We do not step into the same river twice' (frs A1.8, A6, B12, B49a, B91 Diels-Kranz).

4.46 On *Heraclitus*, 'who was a kind of prophet to the Stoics' (Farquharson, p. 323), see note on 3.3. For the changes of the elements into each other see note on 2.3. Some of these fragments of Heraclitus (frs B76, B71–4 Diels-Kranz) are recollected or reflected elsewhere in the *Meditations*, especially in 4.29 and 12.13.

their everyday experience takes them by surprise: Compare 12.1.2 ('you will . . . no longer meet the day's events as if bemused by the unexpected') and 12.13 ('How absurd . . . is the man surprised at any aspect of his experience in life!').

4.48 One of Marcus' most eloquent discourses on the triviality of both life and death. See in general the note on 2.14. For the serene image of the ripe olive ready to fall, see note on 3.5.

4.48.1 *Helice*: a Greek city in Achaea which suddenly sank into the sea in 373 BC. *Pompeii* and *Herculaneum*: Roman cities in Campania famously destroyed by the eruption of Vesuvius on 24 August AD 79.

4.48.2 *You should always look on human life as short and cheap*: A constant theme in the *Meditations*, treated starkly in vigorous language. See 2.17.1, 5.10 ('all this murk and dirt'), 5.33, 7.47 ('the filth of life on the ground'), 8.24 (the image of bath-water), 8.37 ('It is all stench and corruption in a bag of bones'), 9.28, 10.31 ('In this way you will always look on human life as mere smoke and nothing'), 12.27 ('smoke and ashes'), 12.33 ('corpse and smoke').

4.49 *Be like the rocky headland*: Marcus has in mind a passage in Homer's *Iliad* (15.618ff.), describing the initial Achaean resistance to Hector's attack on their ships: 'They closed wall-like against him and stood their ground, like a huge sheer cliff at the edge of the grey sea, which stands against the shrill winds on their rapid pathways and the waves that swell large and burst on it.' The image was imitated by Vergil (*Aeneid*, 7.586ff.).

4.50 For arguments to 'put death in its place' see note on 2.14.

Caedicianus . . . Lepidus: These presumably long-lived people cannot be identified with any certainty. A nice illustration of Marcus' point.

in such poor company: For Marcus' largely unfavourable view of his associates and contemporaries see notes on 3.4.4, 4.6, and 5.10.1.

a Nestor of three generations: Nestor, king of Pylos, 'ruled over three generations of men' (*Odyssey*, 3.245). For indifference to the length of life see note on 3.7.

4.51 For '*nature's road*' see 4.18 and note on 5.4. The meaning of the final sentence of this chapter is obscure. Probably Marcus means that 'the short road', implying a consciousness of the brevity of life and the consequent focus of values and endeavour as argued in 4.32–33, relieves one of the burden of wider, and by implication futile, ambition.

BOOK 5

5.1 *when you are reluctant to get up*: See note on 2.1.

what I was born for: Marcus often speaks of 'man's proper nature' or 'constitution' – 'the nature of a rational and social being' (5.29: cf. 6.44.2) – linking it to the principle of universal nature (2.9, 5.3, 6.58, 7.55, 11.5). He offers at least partial definitions in 4.49 (a list of virtues 'whose combination is the fulfilment of man's proper nature': cf. 8.1), 7.55 (a set of principles), 8.26 ('man's proper work'): the simplest statement is in 9.42.4 ('man was made to do good'). See also 5.15, 5.25, 6.16.1 (analogy with crafts), 7.20, 7.53, 8.5, 9.31, 10.8.4, 10.33.

There may be in Marcus' mind also the consciousness of his specific duties as one 'born into the purple'. The *Meditations* are surprisingly reticent on the vocation or the responsibilities of an emperor. The strongest statements are in 1.17.3, 9.29 (see note), and 11.18.1 ('. . . I was born to be their leader, as the ram leads his flock and the bull his herd'): passing references in 1.11, 1.14.1, 3.5, 4.12, 6.39, 7.36, 8.1, 11.7. See notes on 5.16 and 6.2.

Can you not see plants, birds, ants, spiders, bees: 'Go to the ant, thou sluggard: consider her ways, and be wise' (Proverbs 6:6). Marcus is fond of drawing comparisons with, or lessons from, the ordered and instinctive world of insects and animals: see 5.6 (horse, dog, bee), 6.54 (bee), 9.9.2 (hives, flocks, birds), 10.10 (spider), 11.18.9 (bees).

5.2 This thought is elaborated in 4.3: similar in 7.28 and 12.2.2. For the immunizing effect of the erasure of impressions or removal of judgements see 2.15 note.

5.3 *subsequent criticism or persuasion from anyone*: See notes on 2.6 and 4.12. Compare in particular 10.13: 'As soon as you wake from sleep ask yourself: "Will it make any difference to you if

others criticize what is in fact just and true?" No, it will not.'
Marcus' insistent assertion throughout the *Meditations* of the
independence of his own moral and practical will, the irrelevance
of public or Court opinion, and his indifference to posthumous
repute suggests the constant need to bolster his resolve against
insecurity, frustration, and, it may be, temptation. In 2.6 he
castigates himself for letting his 'own welfare depend on other
people's souls'. His more positive approach is expressed with
direct simplicity in 7.15: 'Whatever anyone does or says, I must
be a good man.'

See also 2.17.2, 3.4, 3.5, 4.18, 4.29, 7.55, 8.56, 10.11, 12.1,
12.3.1, 12.4 (*contra* 6.53). Compare 9.39: 'Say to your directing
mind . . . "are you herding with the rest and sharing their feed?"'

5.4   *I travel on by nature's path*: The lyricism of this chapter is the
more touching for its rarity.

The straight/true/right/proper path or road is a frequent image
in the *Meditations*, expressive of a clear conviction. As in 5.3
above, Marcus sees the path prescribed by man's proper nature
as coterminous with the path of universal nature (cf. also 4.51);
with the path of reason (5.14, 5.34, 8.7, 11.9); and with the path
of god (10.11, 12.23). The fullest definition of 'the right path'
for a rational nature is given in 8.7; 6.17 speaks of 'a path hard
to understand'.

See also 3.16.2, 6.22, 7.53, 7.55; and notes on 4.18 and 4.51.

5.5   The commonplace disjunction of intellect and virtue is here given
sharp and personal application, with a characteristic element of
impatient disgust. For practice in the face of apparent inadequacy
see 5.9 ('Do not give up in disgust or impatience . . .') and 12.6
('Practise even what you have despaired of mastering').

Marcus often lists virtues which he does, or could, or should
display: see 3.4.3, 3.6.1, 3.11.2, 4.49.2, 5.9, 5.31, 6.30.1, 7.52,
7.63, 7.67, 8.1, 8.8, 10.8.

5.6   For kindness as an end in itself, and a kind action its own reward,
see also 7.73, 9.42.4.

5.7   Marcus discusses the nature of prayer more fully in 9.40. See
also 6.44, 12.14.

5.8   The Stoic doctrine (see Sandbach, pp. 35–7) that it is not only
the duty but also the delight of a good man to accept and welcome
all that is allotted to him (even if his lot is apparent ill) is an
insistent theme in the *Meditations*, occurring in various formulations and contexts over thirty times, and may be taken as a
cardinal tenet of Marcus' own philosophy, theology, and cos-

mology. This chapter is his fullest and most carefully argued treatment: see also, in particular, 4.33, 6.44, 10.1, 10.6.

The determining agent of a man's lot is variously given as Fate, Clotho (one of the Fates: 4.34), the gods, God, Zeus (5.8.4), Nature, universal Nature, the Whole, Law (10.25), 'that other source' (2.17.2), 'the universal source' (8.23), 'god ... in the course of nature' (12.11). For the essential equation of these terms see introductory note to Book 2.

Doubtless according to mood and circumstance, the mode of acceptance urged varies from 'passive' (3.6.1, 12.32), through 'glad welcome' (e.g. 4.33, 4.34, 6.44, 8.7, 12.11), to the exaltation of love (e.g. 3.4.3, 3.16.2, 12.1.1). The level of argument likewise varies from a simple fatalism to a profound conviction of divine benevolence and cosmic order. Whatever happens to an individual was 'prepared' for him 'from everlasting' (10.5), may be a 'prescription' for his own good, and, such is the interrelation of all things, must be a contributory part of the universal good (e.g. 6.44). One's own lot should therefore be accepted without question or complaint, and positively welcomed, inasmuch as the interest of the individual is subordinate to that of the whole. 'I am part of the Whole ... Nothing which benefits the Whole can be harmful to the part, and the Whole contains nothing which is not to its benefit' (10.6.1: cf. 5.22, 6.54). See also notes on 6.38 and 6.54.

5.8.1 *Asclepius*: The Greek god of healing, whose sanctuary and cult centre at Epidaurus in the Peloponnese was famous in antiquity from the fifth century BC. The Latin form of the name is Aesculapius.

5.8.2 *as masons speak of the 'fit' of squared stones*: Marcus is fond of illustrating his point by analogy or contrast with trades and crafts. See, for example, 5.1.3 (smith, etc.), 5.8.1 (medicine), 6.16.1 (crafts in general), 6.35 (architect, doctor), 6.55 and 8.15 (ship's captain, doctor), 8.50 (carpenter/cobbler).

5.8.5 *And you do sever something*: On severance, and the possibility of regrafting, see note on 4.29.

5.9 'Medical treatment reminds the writer that philosophy is the medicine of the soul: that he is himself an invalid, at best a convalescent' (Farquharson, p. 330).

For the comfort and guidance of philosophy see also 2.17.2 and 6.12. In 8.1 Marcus despairs that he is 'far from philosophy', ruefully observing that his 'station in life is a contrary pull': a different view in 11.7 ('How clearly it strikes you that there is no other walk of life so conducive to the exercise of philosophy as this in which you now find yourself!').

For medical analogies see note on 3.13.

5.10 One of the most despairing chapters in the *Meditations*. Marcus passes quickly from philosophical bafflement to real-life disgust at the 'murk and dirt' in which he must live, taking comfort only in a sort of solipsism and the hope of early release. The next chapter extends this disgust to himself. A similar despondency in 5.33.

5.10.1 *several philosophers of distinction*: Marcus is thinking of the Sceptics, who denied the possibility of knowledge, and therefore of informed judgement. See Long, ch. 3, and for the Stoic theory of knowledge LS, 41.

how short-lived they are, how shoddy: Marcus frequently, and vigorously, reminds himself of the shoddiness and futility of things temporal, and the contempt they deserve. See 2.12 ('how cheap they are, how contemptible, shoddy, perishable, and dead'), 3.6.2 ('small and paltry'), 5.33 ('empty, rotten, puny'), 6.13 ('. . . see their shoddiness'), 8.24 (as disgusting as bathwater), 9.14 ('transient in time, sordid in substance'), 9.36 ('water, dust, bones, stench'), 12.7 ('the feebleness of all things material').

For Marcus' wider view of all human life as short and cheap see note on 4.48.2.

a catamite, a whore, a thief could own them: For the thought, and the language, compare 3.16.1 and 6.34. Marcus seems to reserve a particular abhorrence for catamites: cf. also 1.16.2, his specific approval of Antoninus' 'putting a stop to homosexual love of young men'.

it is hard to tolerate even the best of them: Despite his evidently genuine conviction of the kinship of all men and the consequent duties of care and tolerance (see notes on 2.1, 2.13, 3.4.4, 5.33, 9.11), Marcus had clear difficulty in persuading himself into any respect, let alone admiration, for his fellow men, whether ordinary citizens or close associates. The *Meditations* are peppered with expressions of indifference, suspicion, fastidious distaste, or overt contempt, even hatred. His approval is limited to those (evidently few) 'who live their lives in agreement with nature' (3.4.4) – i.e. those who share and evince in their lives Marcus' own philosophy.

The relation 'to your fellows and contemporaries' is one of the three relations Marcus sets himself in 8.27, but he also observes

'how wearisome it is to live out of tune with your fellows' (9.3.2).
This dissonance echoes throughout the *Meditations*: 'they and
the polluting company they keep' (3.4.4), 'black characters'
(4.18, 4.28), 'in such poor company' (4.50), death brings relief
from 'the sort of characters which will no longer contaminate
your soul' (9.3.2), 'how worthless are these little men in the
public eye . . .' (9.29). Characteristic is the frequent dismissive
reference to an unspecified 'they', on which see 3.4.4 note:
Marcus shows at times an almost prurient distaste for 'their'
presumed habits, especially in bed (3.4.4, 10.13, 10.19, 11.18.2).
See also 2.1, 3.11.3, 5.28, 8.4, 8.44, 9.2, 9.27, 9.42, 10.15 (to
be killed by 'them' is 'a better fate than a life like theirs'), 10.36.
Marcus' most devastating conclusion is that in 9.24: 'Children's
tantrums and toys, "tiny spirits carrying corpses" – the Underworld in the *Odyssey* strikes more real!'

   And yet Marcus, conscious of his misanthropic tendency (cf.
7.65), tried hard to argue himself into love for his fellow men.
'Love these people among whom destiny has cast you – but your
love must be genuine' (6.39): see also 7.13, 7.63, 10.36. His best
effort is in 6.48: 'Whenever you want to cheer yourself, think of
the qualities of your fellows . . .'

5.10.2 *In all this murk and dirt*: Similarly graphic language in 7.47:
'. . . such imaginings wash away the filth of life on the ground.'
       the divinity within me: See note on 2.1.
       no one can force me: See note on 2.9.

5.12 *'too many goods to make room'*: The *comic poet* is Menander
(344/3–292/1 BC), the leading writer of New Comedy, whose
play *The Ghost*, extant only in papyrus fragments, makes use of
this 'popular saying' with its coarse conclusion. The quotation is
fr. 42 Sandbach.

   The radical difference between the common man's and the
philosopher's concept of 'goods' is a frequent topic, explicit or
implicit, in the *Meditations*. What the common man takes to be
'goods' – wealth and health, 'clothes, houses, reputation, or any
other such trappings and stage scenery' (12.2) – Marcus and the
Stoics class as 'indifferents' (see notes on 2.11.4 and 5.20), disdain of which is an index of virtue (5.15). See further 5.36, 6.14,
6.16, 6.45, 7.26, 8.10, 8.14, 11.21.

5.13 For *the causal and the material* see note on 4.21.2.
       For the *sequence of change* see note on 2.3.
       even if the universe is subject to the completion of cycles: Stoic
doctrine held that the universe is periodically consumed by

conflagration and regenerated. See notes on 2.14.2 and 3.3, and also 5.32, 6.4, 9.28, 10.7.2, 11.1.2. See LS, 46, 52.

5.15 For Marcus' conception of *man's nature* see note on 5.1.

5.16 *souls are dyed by thoughts*: The same striking image, with a play on the literal meaning, is used as a warning in 6.30.1: 'Take care not to be Caesarified, or dyed in purple.' A similar thought in 7.3: 'bear in mind that a person's worth is measured by the worth of what he values.'

a good life can be lived in a palace: Marcus was acutely aware of the possible or perceived incompatibility between the life of palace and Court and the 'good life' as he defined it. See 1.17.3, 6.12, 6.30, 8.9. In 11.7, in different mood, he recognizes the unique opportunity which his position affords for the exercise of philosophy.

each creature is made in the interest of another: Marcus uses the *scala naturae* to argue that (rational) men are born for each other ('*we are born for community*'): see also 5.30, 7.55, 9.9, 11.18.1, and note on 7.13.

The inanimate/animate/rational sequence and distinctions are pressed into frequent service in the *Meditations*, for various purposes in a variety of contexts. See, for example, 3.6.3, 3.16.1, 6.14, 6.16, 6.22, 6.23, 8.7, 8.41, 8.46, 9.2, 9.8–9, 10.2, 11.10, 12.30. See in general LS, 53 and 57A.

5.17 For the inevitable link of character (or opinion) and action, a favourite topic, see note on 4.6.

5.18 *beyond its own natural endurance*: Similar in 8.46 and 10.3 ('All that happens is an event either within your natural ability to bear it, or not').

5.19 *Things of themselves cannot touch the soul at all*: The immunity of the soul/mind to all external events or circumstances, subject only to the judgements the soul/mind chooses to make of them, is a cardinal tenet of Marcus' and Stoic philosophy. See notes on 2.1, 2.6, 2.15, and 4.7. Compare in particular 4.3.4 ('*things* cannot touch the mind: they are external and inert; anxieties can only come from your internal judgement'), 5.34, 6.8, 6.52, 7.14, 7.16, 11.11, 11.16.

5.20 *the category of things indifferent to me*: For the Stoic doctrine of 'indifferents' see also notes on 2.11.4 and 5.12: other chapters of particular relevance are 5.36, 6.32, 8.14, 9.1.4–5, 11.16.

Marcus takes this doctrine for granted (indeed it is essential to his moral and practical philosophy), but nevertheless offers several implied definitions of 'indifferents' in the course of his

Meditations: 'matters which are morally neutral' (3.11.3); 'assess nothing either bad or good which can happen equally to the bad man or the good' (4.39); 'things which do not belong to man's portion incumbent on him as a human being' (5.15); 'to the mind all that is not its own activity is indifferent' (6.32); 'things which universal Nature treats indifferently ... I mean that they happen impartially by cause and effect to all that comes into being' (9.1.4–5).

As examples of 'indifferents' Marcus gives death and life, fame and ignominy (2.11.4, 9.1.4, 10.8.1), pain and pleasure (2.11.4, 3.6.3, 9.1.4, 10.30), wealth and poverty (2.11.4, 3.6.3, 10.30), praise (3.6.3, 6.16), power (3.6.3). The Stoics recognized some 'indifferents' as 'preferable' (i.e. worth having rather than not, but still not inherent goods with any bearing on virtue): these 'preferable indifferents' are what the majority regard, mistakenly, as true 'goods' (see 5.12 note). Marcus takes the severe view that 'anyone who feels the need of any of these things is necessarily sullied' (6.16.2).

There is a clear link with the doctrine that material things or circumstances are inert and cannot touch the soul (5.19 note).
there is conditional commitment: See note on 4.1 for the sense of 'conditional'.

5.21 *the ultimate power in yourself*: So 4.1, 'the power within us', 6.40 ('immanent' power), 10.38 ('that is the power to act, that is the principle of life, that, one could say, is the man himself'). This power is our 'directing mind', which is derived from, and virtually identical with, the 'divinity within us', 'that fragment of himself which Zeus has given each person to guard and guide him' (5.27: see note on 2.1). This chapter should be read in conjunction with 5.26 and 5.27.

On the 'directing mind' (man's 'own guiding principle, which he has in common with the gods': 6.35), its nature, purpose, importance, and fragility, see also 2.2, 3.9, 4.3.2, 5.32, 6.8, 7.16, 7.28, 9.7 ('keep your directing mind its own master'), 9.15, 9.26, 11.19 (the 'four particular corruptions of the directing mind'), 11.20.2, 12.14. For the ideal state of the directing mind ('pure and liberated') see 12.3. See also Long, pp. 171–2; Sandbach, pp. 83–4.

An overlapping concept is that of the 'rational soul', for which see particularly 11.1 ('The properties of the rational soul').

5.22 For the main thought compare 5.35, 6.54, and 10.6.1, and see note on 5.8.

For the obligation to educate the wrongdoer see note on 2.13.

5.23–4 Familiar themes. See notes on 3.10 and 4.43.

5.25 *Another does wrong*: For the 'let him see to it' response compare 7.16 ('let him do so') and 11.13 ('that is his concern'): and see note on 7.29.

5.26–7 See notes on 2.1, 2.15, 5.21.

5.26 *immune to any current in the flesh*: Compare 9.41 (Epicurus), 'how the mind shares in such disturbances of the flesh while still preserving its calm and pursuing its own good': and 10.8.1, 'the elevation of your thinking faculty above the calm or troubled affections of the flesh'. In general, see note on 6.32 for the mind/body dualism. For the chapter as a whole compare in particular 7.16.

5.27 *'Live with the gods'*: For Marcus' view of the relation between man and god, of which this is the most intimate expression, see note on 6.44.

5.28 This pungent chapter combines Marcus' concern with anger (11.18 note), the link of character/circumstance to action (4.6 note), and the obligation to educate (2.13 note).
Neither hypocrite nor whore: A puzzle. Marcus may mean that he must neither shirk the issue nor tolerate the effects.

5.29 *'The fire smokes and I leave the house'*: A quotation from Epictetus (1.25.18: cf. 4.10.27). For comparable passages on suicide see note on 3.1.
the nature of a rational and social being: See 6.44.2 ('my nature is both rational and social'), and notes on 5.1 and 6.7.

5.30 See 5.16 and note, and compare 7.55, 11.10, and 11.18.1.

5.31 *'say no evil, do no evil'*: A loose quotation from Homer, *Odyssey*, 4.690.
your service completed: Compare 10.22 ('. . . or you die, your service done') and see note on 7.7 for the metaphor of life as a form of military service.

5.32 For *appointed cycles* see note on 5.13.

5.33 See 5.10 and note for comparison with the despondency of this chapter.
puppies snapping at each other: A similar image, in similar context, in 7.3 ('a bone thrown to puppies').
children squabbling: cf. 9.24: 'Children's tantrums and toys'.
'fled up to Olympus': The quotation is from Hesiod, *Works and Days*, 197 (in the context of a degenerate age of men left to their own misery).
whatever it is, either extinction or translation: See note on 3.3.

Only to worship and praise the gods, and to do good to men: Marcus frequently sums up the 'good life' in these two commandments of duty to god and duty to men: see 3.6.2, 3.9, 6.7, 6.16.2, 6.23, 6.30.1 ('Revere the gods, look after men'), 7.31 ('Love mankind. Follow god'), 7.54, 7.66 ('a life of justice shown to men and piety to the gods'), 11.20.2. See in general note on 6.44 for Marcus' religious convictions.

to bear and forbear: A maxim of Epictetus (fr. 10 Schenkl). Marcus often feels the need to remind himself of the duty of tolerance, not an easy virtue for one whose general view of his fellow men was so poor (5.10.1 note): see 4.3.2 ('Tolerance is a part of justice'), 5.20, 6.47, 7.3 ('amid all this you must keep yourself tolerant'), 7.26, 7.52, 7.63, 8.8, 8.59 ('either teach or tolerate'), 9.3.2. Brunt observes (p. 10) that Marcus 'insists most in the *Meditations* on duties he found hardest'.

5.34 *the right path*: See note on 5.4.

immune to any external impediment: See note on 5.19.

5.36 *the loss of something indifferent*: For 'indifferents' see note on 5.20.

the old man in the play: The reference here is obscure: neither the play nor the story is known.

For the sense of this chapter compare 7.43: '"Don't join in mourning, or in ecstasy."'

5.37 Marcus may have in mind the saying of Heraclitus (fr. B119 Diels-Kranz) that 'character is destiny'.

BOOK 6

6.2 *If you are doing your proper duty*: The concept of duty, broadly interpreted, underlies Marcus' whole philosophy of human behaviour *sub specie aeternitatis*: the duty is both to man and to god (on these 'two commandments' see note on 5.33). It is interesting, and indicative of the purely personal nature of the *Meditations*, that an emperor who spent many of his years on campaign should set little of his reflection on duty in a specifically imperial or military context: see note on 5.1, and for military analogy or metaphor 3.5, 5.31, 7.7 (note), 7.45, 10.22.

Marcus sees his duty primarily as that incumbent on 'a rational and social being' (5.29), generalized into the 'duty to be a good man' (8.5: cf. 7.15, 'I must be a good man'), 'one's proper use of oneself, one's accurate assessment of the gradations of duty'

(3.1). Marcus gives various formulations of the virtues and actions thereby required in 2.5, 3.4.3, 3.12, 4.33, 7.5, 8.1, 8.26 ('Man's joy is to do man's proper work'). His consciousness of particular demands is eloquent in 5.5 ('display those virtues which are wholly in your own power') and 6.39 ('Fit yourself for the matters which have fallen to your lot').

See also 1.12, 6.22 ('I do my own duty: the other things do not distract me'), 6.26 ('remember that every duty is the completed sum of certain actions'), and 11.9 (anger or capitulation in the face of opposition 'both amount equally to desertion of duty').

whether you are sleepy or well-slept: Marcus was very conscious of his need for, and lack of, sleep. See note on 2.1, and 7.64 (drowsiness as one of 'the unrecognized analogues of pain').

even this, the act in which we die, is one of the acts of life: For this paradox, part of Marcus' panoply of consolation against fear of death (see note on 2.14), compare 2.12 (death is 'nothing more than a function of nature'), 4.5 ('Death, just like birth, is a mystery of nature'), 9.3.1 ('one further part of nature's will . . . one of the functions of nature').

6.4 Alternative eschatological views, as often presented in the *Meditations* (see 4.3.2 note). 'Turned into vapour' reflects the Stoic doctrine of periodic conflagration of the universe (see notes on 2.14.2 and 5.13). 'Scattered in atoms' is the Epicurean view (see LS, 13). For the general doctrine that 'all that exists will soon change' see note on 2.3.

6.7 *to move on from social act to social act*: An essential element in Marcus' concept of duty and 'man's proper work' (see notes on 6.2 and 5.1). The social imperative springs from the conviction of the kinship of mankind (see note on 2.1) and the consequent duty of care and kindness (see note on 9.11).

For Marcus, social responsibility is a direct consequence of man's rational nature (10.2: 'rational directly implies social'): 'For a rational nature the right path is . . . to direct its impulses solely to social action' (8.7). And social action (i.e. action 'for the common good': 7.5, 11.4, 11.13, 11.21, 12.20) is a necessary function of man's specific constitution and nature: 'the main principle in man's constitution is the social' (7.55); 'it is your constitution and man's nature to perform social acts' (8.12); '. . . impulse and action fulfilled in that social conduct which is an expression of your own nature' (9.31).

Despite Marcus' often acerbic view of his fellow men (see note on 5.10.1), there is no doubting the sincerity and centrality of his social principles. 'The one harvest of existence on earth is a godly habit of mind and social action' (6.30). His final words on this subject are also his warmest: 'There remains only the enjoyment of living a linked succession of good deeds' (12.29).

See also 3.4.2, 3.6.3, 3.7, 4.24, 5.29, 6.14, 6.44, 7.68, 9.23, 10.6.2.

6.8   For 'the directing mind' see note on 5.21.

6.10 *Either a stew ... or ... providence*: For these alternatives see notes on 3.3 and 4.3.2. The Greek word (*kukeon*) rendered as 'stew' here and in 4.27 and 9.39 signifies any concoction of mixed ingredients: this venerable word occurs in Homer (*Odyssey*, 10. 290 and 316) and also (which might have suggested its use to Marcus) in Heraclitus, fr. B125 Diels-Kranz.

to become 'earth unto earth': This may be a reminiscence of Homer, *Iliad*, 7.99 (Menelaus to the Achaeans: 'may you all rot into water and earth').

6.11 *quickly return to yourself*: For the notion of return/retreat/ withdrawal to oneself, and the consequent calm, see note on 4.3.1.

6.12 See notes on 3.13 and 5.9 for the 'comfort' of philosophy: and note on 5.16 for Marcus' uneasiness with Court life. Step-mothers in the Greek and Latin literary tradition were notorious for cruelty.

6.13 It may be that the contrast of Court and philosophy in the previous chapter prompted these extreme examples of the reductive analysis ('stripping bare') which Marcus elsewhere recommends: see note on 3.11, and Rutherford, pp. 143–7. Similar ('your clothing is animal hair, your purple is fish blood'), but much more bitter, in 9.36.

Falernian wine: a prized wine produced in north Campania.

soaked in shell-fish blood: Purple dye was produced from the secretions of the mollusc *murex* – a complicated and costly process which gave purple its cachet as a badge of wealth and status.

sexual intercourse: Marcus is rather prim on sexual matters: see notes on 1.17.7 and 5.10.1.

show them naked, see their shoddiness: For this frequent theme see note on 5.10.1.

what Crates says even about Xenocrates: Crates was a Cynic philosopher and poet of the second half of the fourth and the beginning of the third century BC: Xenocrates was a disciple of Plato, and head of the Academy from 339 to 314 BC. The point of Marcus' reference is lost, but it is probably relevant that Xenocrates is elsewhere (Diogenes Laertius, 4.11) described as 'the least pretentious of men'.

6.14 *Most of the things valued by the masses*: For Marcus' view of the common man's values see note on 5.12. For the inanimate/animate/rational sequence see note on 5.16. For 'rational and social activity' see note on 6.7.

cohesion: The Greek word (*hexis*) is a technical term of Stoic physics. See LS, 47.

6.15 *Flows and changes ... eternity ever young*: For the doctrine of constant change (creation, transformation, regeneration) see note on 2.3: cf. in particular 7.25 ('... so that the world is always young') and 12.23 ('the nature of the Whole ... through the constant changing of its constituent parts keeps the whole world ever young and fresh').

For the river image see note on 4.43.

For Marcus on the transience of human life see note on 3.10.

6.16 This careful chapter gives an extended answer to the question posed in the previous chapter, 'what should anyone prize of all that races past him?' In this discussion of values, false and true, Marcus deploys and draws together many of his constant themes and images: the *scala naturae* (5.16n.), the 'puppet-strings of impulse' (2.2n.), the vacuity of praise (4.20n.), man's 'proper constitution' (5.1n.), the analogy of skills and crafts (5.8.2n.), the common man's mistaken concept of 'goods' (5.12n.) which sets value on 'indifferents' (5.20n.), the 'two commandments' of obligation to god and man (5.33n.), the glad acceptance of one's lot (5.8n.). See also 6.41.

6.17 *the motions of the elements*: See note on 2.3.

6.18 See note on 3.4.4 for Marcus' contemptuous use of 'they'.

6.21 For Marcus' recognition of the potential value of advice and correction see note on 4.12. For his insistence on the truth and truthfulness, see note on 9.1.2.

6.22 See note on 6.2 for Marcus' concept of duty, and note on 5.4 for 'the true way'.

6.23 *in all things call on the gods*: For Marcus' evidently profound religious conviction see note on 6.44.

6.24 Famous men dead and gone, 'levelled in death', provide Marcus with a ready set of themes: see notes on 2.14, 3.3, 3.10, and 7.34. See 3.3 (Alexander, Pompey, Julius Caesar and others), 4.33, 6.47, 7.6, 7.19, 8.5 (Hadrian and Augustus), 8.37, 10.31, 12.27.

For the *post mortem* alternatives see note on 3.3. 'Taken up into the . . . generative principles of the universe' (also in 4.14, 4.21.1) reflects the Stoic view, 'dispersed into atoms' the Epicurean: see note on 4.3.2.

6.26 A puzzling chapter, curiously expressed. There seems a fusion of several ideas: the importance of method and planned sequence in the completion of any proposed act of duty (cf. the reference to an 'accurate assessment of the gradations of duty' in 3.1), the need for patience and tolerance in the persuasion of others (see notes on 2.13 and 5.33), the avoidance of anger (see note on 11.18). The next chapter continues some of these lines of thought. For the name Antoninus see note on 6.44.

6.27 A similar quasi-sympathetic condescension in 11.18.11. For the duty to teach the ignorant see note on 2.13 (compare especially 8.59: 'either teach or tolerate').

6.28 For the 'consolation' of death as the relief from life see note on 2.14.

6.30.1 A fine passage in assertion of human and divine obligation against the potential corruption of absolute power.
dyed in purple: For the metaphorical sense compare 5.16, 'souls are dyed by thoughts': for the literal see note on 6.13.

6.30.2 *Always as a pupil of Antoninus*: See the more extensive tribute in 1.16 to the emperor Antoninus Pius, Marcus' uncle and adoptive father. This passage may be a preliminary draft for that larger treatment.
How he was content with little: Simplicity of living (a lesson from his mother: 1.3) is a virtue which Marcus admired in others and tried to practise himself: see also 1.5, 1.6, 1.16.8, 1.17.3, 7.67 ('the happy life depends on very little'), 10.1.

6.32 *I am made of body and soul*: Other formulations are: 'flesh, breath, and directing mind' (2.2), 'body, soul, mind' (3.16), directing mind, 'sensual soul', body (7.16), 'body, breath, and mind' (12.3).

The mind/body dualism is a frequent theme in the *Meditations* (in this context 'mind' and 'soul', and 'body' and 'flesh', are synonyms), expressed in contempt of 'the poor passions of the flesh' (7.66: compare 'the body and its gross pleasures' in 11.19) and in an austere asceticism inherently capable of extremes – 'You are a soul carrying a corpse' (4.41, quoted, evidently with approval, from Epictetus: also in 9.24, 'tiny spirits carrying corpses', and compare 'the corpse which is our body' in 10.33.3).

The mind/soul is the divine part ('the divinity within us': see

note on 2.1), the 'poor body' the corrupting and corruptible. See
in particular 3.3 ('. . . no longer in thrall to a bodily vessel which
is a master as far inferior as its servant is superior. One is mind
and divinity: the other a clay of dust and blood'), and 11.19
('. . . the fourth case for self-reproach is that in which the more
divine part of you loses the contest and bows to the lower, mortal
part, the body and its gross pleasures'). Death is the release of
the soul from bondage, 'when your soul will slip this bodily
sheath' (9.3.1: cf. 10.36, 'that easy slipping of the soul from the
body's carapace').

The dualism is most in evidence when Marcus is insisting on
the mind's independence from and immunity to 'any current in
the flesh, smooth or troubled' (5.26, and note). The main 'cur-
rents', 'disturbances' (8.29, 9.41), or 'affections' (10.8.1) of the
flesh are pain and pleasure/passion, through and above which
the mind should keep 'inviolate and free from harm' (2.17.2),
'preserving its calm and pursuing its own good' (9.41). 'It is the
specific property of rational and intelligent activity to isolate
itself and never be influenced by the activity of the senses or
desires' (7.55). On pleasure/passion see note on 8.10. On pain
see notes on 7.14 and 7.33.

See also 4.3.2, 5.26, 6.29, 7.16, 8.28, 10.24, 10.38, 12.1, 12.2,
12.14: and note on 3.3 for disdain of the material composition
of the body.

For the meaning of 'indifferent' see notes on 5.12 and 5.20.

6.33 *there is nothing contrary to nature in pain . . . not an evil either*:
Marcus sees 'accordance with nature' as a universal validating
principle, providing guidance, support, or consolation (which
only the superhuman or saintly would find effective). So 'nothing
harmful is in accordance with nature' (2.17.2), and 'nothing will
happen to me which is not in accordance with the nature of the
Whole' (5.10.2: similar in 6.58). See also 2.1, 4.39, 5.3, 7.11 ('to
act in accordance with nature is also to act in accordance with
reason'), 7.74, 11.16; and for 'life according to nature' note on
1.17.6.

For Marcus' philosophy in relation to pain see note on 7.33.

6.34 Similar in 3.16.1 (wild beasts, catamites, tyrants – including a
matricide). For Marcus' particular aversion to catamites see note
on 5.10.1.

Keeping us 'above pleasure and pain' is one of the functions
of philosophy as the 'escort' through life (2.17.2). Marcus is firm

in his austere view of pleasure and its heightened categorization as 'passion of the flesh': see further note on 8.10.

6.35 See note on 5.8.2 for Marcus' fondness for analogy or contrast with trades and crafts. It is clear that Marcus respected and admired the professionalism and dedication of the skilled craftsman.

6.36 Familiar themes of global insignificance and evanescence in the context of the infinite: compare especially 3.10 and note.

Mount Athos is the easternmost promontory of the triple-pronged peninsula of Chalcidice in northern Greece, rising to a peak of 1,935 metres.

So even the lion's gaping jaws . . . mischief: See 3.2 for similar thoughts and examples of the 'incidental effects of the processes of Nature', which 'have their own charm and attraction'. Compare 8.50.

6.37 For the eternal sameness of things (a frequent theme) see note on 2.14.2.

6.38 The conception of a unitary and unified universe is a central tenet of Marcus' philosophy and cosmology, presented both as abstract theory (sometimes tinged with an almost devotional wonder – e.g. 4.23) and as the source and argument for human imperatives – those flowing from the kinship of men (see note on 2.1), and the individual's obligation to accept his lot as part of and contributory to a universal scheme (see note on 5.8).

Marcus speaks of the interrelation of all things sometimes in objective terms ('the very web and mesh of it all', 4.40: cf. 7.9 and 10.5 for 'mesh'), but more often with an admiring warmth suggestive of a quasi-religious conviction: 'collective embrace' (2.16), 'the universe is a kind of community' (4.4), 'harmony' (4.23 and 5.8), 'all things are meshed together, and a sacred bond unites them' (7.9).

See in particular 4.40, 4.45, 5.8, 7.9: also 2.3, 2.16, 3.11.2, 4.4, 4.23, 4.27 ('all things, distinct as they are, nevertheless permeate and respond to each other'), 6.25, 6.37 ('all things are related and the same'), 7.19, 7.75, 8.23, 9.39, 10.6, 12.30.

6.39 *but your love must be genuine*: Marcus was intellectually convinced of the imperative to love his fellow men: but this caveat is perhaps his own recognition of the difficulty he had in giving practical expression to this conviction. See note on 5.10.1, and compare 7.13 ('. . . you do not yet love your fellow men from your heart: doing good does not yet delight you as an end in itself; you are still doing it as a mere duty, not yet as a kindness to yourself').

6.41 For the thought in this chapter see notes on 2.1 (*'true good and evil'*), 2.15, 5.12, 5.19, and 6.16. For blame of the gods and/or hostility to men as a consequence of attributing values to 'externals' as good or evil, see 6.16.2.

6.42 *Heraclitus* (see notes on 3.3 and 4.46): the quotation is fr. B75 Diels-Kranz.

Chrysippus: (*c*.280–207 BC), from Soli in Cilicia (southern Asia Minor), was the leading Stoic theorist in the third century BC, becoming head of the Stoa in 232: see also note on 10.33. The reference here is to a passage of Chrysippus' extensive writings which is preserved (for us) in Plutarch, *Moralia*, 1065D [Stoicorum Veterum Fragmenta, 2.1181].

Chrysippus' 'note' was that vice, reprehensible in itself, nevertheless has its contribution to the overall tapestry of the universe, just as cheap jokes contribute their charm in the context of a whole play. Marcus, not surprisingly, wishes his contribution to be in the higher category.

6.43 For *Asclepius* see note on 5.8.1.

the goddess of harvest is Ceres (in the Greek pantheon, Demeter).

6.44 Marcus on the gods (for Stoic theology in general see LS, 54, and for Marcus and the supernatural Rutherford, ch. 5). There is no doubt that Marcus had a profound religious conviction, which was both guide and sustenance to him. The focus of his devotion, and of his philosophical or human response to it, is sometimes fogged by an ambiguity of reference to the source of the beneficent governing world-order (see introductory note to Book 2, and note on 2.1): this varies in specificity from 'the nature of the Whole' through 'the gods' to Zeus (4.23, 5.8.4, 11.8) – but for the most part Marcus' discussion of the transcendent divine order is couched in overtly religious terms of a personal relation between man and god.

Other than this chapter, the passages most indicative of Marcus' view of the gods, and the relation of man to god, are 1.17 ('From the gods . . .'), 2.11, 2.12 ('How does man touch god . . . ?'), 3.3 ('nothing is empty of the gods'), 3.4.3 ('a priest and minister of the gods'), 3.13, 7.9 ('one god pervading all things'), 7.70, 9.40, 10.1, 12.5, 12.28.

See also note on 2.1 for 'the divinity within us', note on 5.7 on prayer, and note on 5.33 on the 'two commandments' of duty to god and duty to men.

Marcus was convinced:

- that gods exist (2.11, 12.28);
- that they are good (2.3, 2.13, 12.5) and do no wrong (12.12);
- that they care both for the common good (6.44, 10.1) and for men (2.11, 7.70, 8.34, 12.5);
- that they communicate with, help, and inspire men (1.17.6, 1.17.9, 9.11, 9.27);
- that they see our inner thoughts (11.13) and our minds 'stripped of . . . their husks' (12.2);
- that gods and men share both reason (7.53) and law (8.2), and that there is a fragment of god in each of us (2.1 note);
- that we owe them duty and service.

This duty and service – man's proper response to god – is to 'follow' god (7.31, 10.11, 12.23, 12.31) in piety (1.3, 7.66), obedience (3.9, 12.27), honour, reverence, worship, and praise (5.33, 6.30, 7.54, 11.20.2, 12.28), 'with your mind on god' (6.7, 10.8.4) and 'sincere commitment of all your being to the gods' (4.31); 'see to your relation to the gods' (9.37); 'in all things call on the gods' (6.23).

In sum, 'live with the gods' (5.27), for they 'are with us and share our lives' (6.44).

Philosophy and religion meet and meld in 'the final aim, which is to follow reason and follow god' (12.31), and the conviction that 'every man's mind is god' (12.26). There is a touching concentration of devotion and faith in the last Book of the *Meditations*, leading to the final *Nunc dimittis*: 'Go then in peace: the god who lets you go is at peace with you' (12.36).

As Antoninus: On his accession as emperor in March 161, Marcus took the surname Antoninus in tribute to his predecessor and adoptive father Antoninus Pius. Marcus' full imperial title was Imperator Caesar Marcus Aurelius Antoninus Augustus.

these two cities: For the world/the universe as the 'great city' see note on 2.16, and in particular 10.15 ('Here or there makes no difference, if wherever you live you take the world as your city').

6.45 An inversion, of uncertain application and dubious truth, of the general maxim expressed in the first sentence, on which see 6.54 note. For the 'popular application' of the concept of benefit see note on 5.12, and for the sense of 'indifferent' see note on 5.20.

6.46 *all the business of the amphitheatre*: Marcus did not enjoy the public entertainments (races, gladiatorial combats) he was duty-bound to attend in the amphitheatre (see 1.5). It is notable that the offence in his eyes was the monotony, not the morality, of the content: in 10.8.2 he speaks of 'half-eaten gladiators', but only as an example of 'senseless self-preservation'.

How much longer, then: For this world-weariness see note on 2.14.2.

6.47   For the theme of this chapter – the inevitability, and therefore the triviality, of death for people of every class, station, and persuasion – compare 3.3 and 4.48 (and notes), and see in general the note on 2.14. The theme is discussed in Rutherford, pp. 161–7.

Philistion, Phoebus, and Origanion: Three unknowns, by implication recently dead. The names suggest that they may have been slaves of the imperial household.

We too are bound to change our abode to that other world: For Marcus' speculations on the *post mortem* possibilities see note on 3.3.

Heraclitus, Pythagoras, Socrates: Three Greek philosophers of the greatest distinction. For Heraclitus (turn of the sixth and fifth centuries BC) see notes on 3.3 and 4.46: for Socrates (469– 399 BC) see notes on 1.16.9 and 7.66. Pythagoras of Samos (second half of the sixth century BC), a mysterious figure, had a huge influence in the fields of philosophy, religion, mathematics, and music.

Eudoxus, Hipparchus, Archimedes: Three Greek scientists. Eudoxus of Cnidus (first half of the fourth century BC) was an outstanding mathematician and astronomer. Hipparchus of Nicaea (second half of the second century BC) was an astronomer deeply versed in the observations and procedures of Babylonian astronomy. Archimedes of Syracuse (*c.*287–212/211 BC) was the greatest mathematician of the ancient world.

Menippus of Gadara in Syria (first half of the third century BC) was a Cynic writer who invented satire: his works are lost, but their influence is seen in Lucian and Varro. The inclusion of 'Menippus and his kind' in this list of the famous, the infamous, and the ordinary bears out the statement in 6.42 that in the world-order 'there is room even for the critic'.

tolerant of those who are neither true nor just: For the duty of tolerance, not always easy for Marcus, see notes on 5.10.1 and 5.33.

6.48   Here Marcus takes an unusually warm and generous view of his colleagues and contemporaries, comparable to that elaborated in some of the individual expressions of gratitude in Book 1: see introductory note to Book 1. For Marcus' more usual and critical view of his fellows see notes on 3.4.4, 4.6, and 5.10.1.

6.49 For indifference to the length of life see note on 3.7.

6.50 *you set out on a conditional course*: For the sense of 'conditional', and the turning of obstacles to constructive use, see note on 4.1.

6.52 *things of themselves . . . our judgements*: Compare 4.3.4 ('*things* cannot touch the mind . . .'), and see note on 5.19 ('Things of themselves cannot touch the soul at all') for this central tenet of Marcus' and Stoic philosophy.

6.53 *enter into the mind of the speaker*: Compare 7.30 ('Stretch your thought to parallel what is being said. Let your mind get inside what is happening and who is doing it') and 8.61 ('Enter into the directing mind of everyone, and let anyone else enter your own').

Admirable sentiments, but more often Marcus advocates the penetration of others' minds as a means of identifying their deficiencies (4.38, 9.18, 9.22, 9.27, 9.34), and equally often dismisses consideration of what others are thinking as a distractive waste of time (2.8, 2.13, 3.4, 4.18). For all his good intentions, Marcus did have great difficulty in reconciling himself to others.

6.54 A nice epigram, using Marcus' fondness for analogy with the world of insects and animals (see 5.1 note) to point an important truth about the interrelation of interest between individual and community, which Marcus applies at both the human and the cosmic level. See in particular 5.22 ('What is not harmful to the city does not harm the citizen either'), 6.45 ('All that happens to the individual is to the benefit of the Whole'), 10.6.1 ('Nothing which benefits the Whole can be harmful to the part'), 10.33.4 ('nothing harms the citizen of nature other than what harms the city'): and notes on 5.8 and 6.38.

6.55 See note on 5.8.2 for analogies with trades and crafts. Doubtless Marcus had in mind criticism of his own captaincy and political health-care.

6.58 *No one will prevent you*: See note on 2.9. For 'the principle of your own nature' see note on 5.1, and for the general thought compare 5.10.2, 'nothing will happen to me which is not in accordance with the nature of the Whole'.

6.59 For the contemptuous use of 'they' see note on 3.4.4.

BOOK 7

7.1   For the eternal sameness of things see note on 2.14.2.

7.2   *Your principles are living things*: Marcus' principles or doctrines
       were of constant importance to him, to be kept alive and ready
       at all times. See note on 3.13.

       You can live once more: Similar, and in similarly strong language,
       is the 'wake-up call' in 6.31. Marcus was given to moods of
       self-disgust, and did not spare himself.

7.3   Marcus was fond of colourful lists expressive of the miscellany
       of human life (see 4.32 and note, 7.48, 9.30): this is the liveliest
       and most cynical. For 'a bone thrown to puppies' compare 5.33,
       'puppies snapping at each other': for 'puppets dancing on their
       strings' (a favourite image) see note on 2.2.

       It is characteristic of Marcus' fastidious benevolence to com-
       bine recognition of the virtue and obligation of tolerance (see
       5.33 note) with an effective 'but only so far' caveat: for the
       thought of this final sentence see 5.16 note.

7.5   For Marcus' recognition of the need to accept advice, correction,
       or help see note on 4.12: a clear statement in 7.7, sharpened to
       epigram in 7.12.

       the common benefit and harmony: See note on 6.7 for the nature
       and basis of Marcus' strong sense of social responsibility.

7.6   A familiar theme. See notes on 3.10 and 7.34.

7.7   *Do not be ashamed of help*: See notes on 7.5 and 7.12.

       your assigned duty: See note on 6.2 for Marcus' concept of duty.
       The metaphor of life as a form of military service, *militia vitae*,
       recurs in 3.5 ('one who has taken his post like a soldier waiting
       for the Retreat from life to sound'), 5.31 ('your service com-
       pleted'), 7.45 (quotation from Socrates' *Apology*), 10.22,
       11.20.2. Starkest in 2.17.1: 'life is warfare'. The metaphor is
       Platonic (*Apology*, 28d; *Phaedo*, 61e).

7.9   For Marcus' conception of a unitary and unified universe see
       note on 6.38.

       ordered together . . . the one order of the universe: In the Greek
       here there is a sort of word-play: Marcus makes a serious point
       of the fact that the Greek word *kosmos* means both 'order' and
       'universe'.

       There is one universe . . . one truth: Marcus writes here with an
       almost religious exaltation: compare his tone in 4.23 and 10.21.

7.10   See note on 2.3 for the thought of this chapter.

7.11 For 'accordance with nature' see notes on 1.17.6 and 6.33. A similar identification of nature and reason in 7.24.

7.12 Compare 3.5, 'Your duty is to stand straight – not held straight.' The change from '*not* held straight' to '*or* held straight' suggests at least a different mood at a different time of composition (reflected also in 7.5 and 7.7), and possibly a development of thought from an austere self-reliance to a greater awareness of the value of others' help.

7.13 That 'rational creatures are born for each other's sake' (4.3.2) is a central tenet of Marcus' philosophy, presented variously as the conclusion of an argument from the *scala naturae* (see 5.16 and note), as part of the disposition of the nature of the Whole (5.30, 9.1.1), or as a simple fact (2.1, 4.3.2, 7.13, 7.55, 8.56, 8.59, 11.18.1). It is characteristic of Marcus to combine philosophical and intellectual conviction of this tenet with occasional recoil from the practical application (8.56, 9.9).

    Closest to the formulation in this chapter is that in 2.1, 'We were born for cooperation, like feet, like hands . . .': compare also 4.29 and 7.19. Tersest is that in 8.59: 'Men are born for the sake of each other. So either teach or tolerate.' See also note on 2.1 for the kinship of men, and note on 9.11 for the consequent duty of care and kindness.

the change of one letter: The point depends on the similarity of two Greek words: *melos* means 'limb', and *meros* means 'part'.

you do not yet love your fellow men from your heart: For Marcus' difficulty in persuading himself into true love of his fellows see notes on 5.10.1 and 6.39 ('but your love must be genuine').

7.14 For the philosophical basis of this view that no external can do true harm see notes on 2.1 and 2.6: and for harm/evil as a matter of judgement see notes on 2.15, 4.7, and 5.19.

they, if they wish, can complain: A striking expression of the dissociation of mind and body (see 6.32 note), and curiously favoured by Marcus: similar in 5.26, 7.16, 7.33, 8.28, 8.40, 12.1.1. See further note on 7.33 for Marcus on pain.

7.15 *I must be a good man*: See notes on 4.17 and 5.3.

7.16 Compare in particular 5.26, and see notes on 5.19, 5.21, and 7.14 above.

7.17 A chapter of impenetrable personal reference. Is this Marcus' equivalent of Churchill's 'black dog'?

7.18 For change as inherent in the nature of the Whole see note on 2.3.

7.19 For the image of the swirling stream see note on 4.43.

How many a Chrysippus, a Socrates, an Epictetus: For the general thought see notes on 2.14, 3.3, and 6.47. For Chrysippus see note on 6.42; for Socrates notes on 1.16.9 and 7.66; for Epictetus note on 1.7.3.

7.22 For the ideas underpinning the charitable and humane thought of this chapter (the brotherhood of man, wrongdoing as ignorance, the inability of anything external to harm the mind/soul) see notes on 2.1.

7.23, 7.25 For the doctrine of constant and rapid change in the substance of the universe, see note on 2.3. For the 'recycling' of finite material see in particular 8.50 ('The marvel of its craft' is that the nature of the Whole 'creates afresh from this same material').

7.24 A puzzling chapter, evidently making a connection or drawing an analogy between physiognomy and ethics (the pseudo-science of physiognomy was popular and oddly influential in the Greek and Roman worlds). The point seems to be that habitual abuse or non-use can cause the moral muscles to atrophy just like the facial: conscience can die like a smile. Similar use of a physiognomic analogy in 7.37, 7.60, 11.15.

7.25 *so that the world is always young*: A happy expression, of which Marcus was fond: see also 6.15 ('Flows and changes are constantly renewing the world, just as the ceaseless passage of time makes eternity ever young') and 12.23 ('the nature of the Whole . . . through the constant changing of its constituent parts keeps the whole world ever fresh and young').

7.26 *what judgement of good or evil led him to wrong you*: This chapter draws together, in the context of relations and responses to ordinary fallible people, several tenets of Marcus' philosophy: wrongdoing as ignorance (2.1n.), the contrast between the common man's and the philosopher's concept of 'goods' (5.12n.), the category of 'indifferents' (5.20n.), the obligation of tolerance (5.33n.), and the duty to educate the 'unsighted' (2.13n.).

7.27 Compare 1.16.4, in Marcus' tribute to his adoptive father Antoninus Pius: 'In those things which conduce to the comfort of life – and here fortune gave him plenty – to enjoy them without pride or apology either, so no routine acceptance of their presence or regret in their absence.'

7.28 For withdrawal/retreat into yourself, and the means of inducing calm, see note on 4.3.1. Similar in 9.41 (Epicurus).

7.29 A terse summary of imperatives. For 'the puppet-strings of

impulse' see note on 2.2. For analysis into causal and material
see note on 4.21.2.

Think of your final hour: Compare 6.30.2, further appreciation
of Antoninus Pius: 'So may your own last hour find you with a
conscience as clear as his.'

Leave the wrong done by another where it started: Similar in
9.20 ('You should leave another's wrong where it lies') and 12.26
('. . . any wrong done lies with the other'). Compare also 5.25
and note: 'Another does wrong? What is that to me? Let him see
to it . . .'

7.30 See note on 6.53.

7.31 *Love mankind. Follow god*: For these two commandments of
duty to god and duty to men, frequently rehearsed in the *Meditations*, see note on 5.33.

For Democritus see 3.3 note. The reference here is to fr. B9 (=
B125) Diels-Kranz. The text and interpretation of the final words
of this chapter are uncertain.

7.32 See notes on 3.3 and 4.3.2.

7.33 Marcus on pain. Marcus was interested in pain, both physical
and emotional, which presents a particular problem to the philosopher: and we should remember that both the incidence and the
tolerance of physical pain were much greater in Marcus' time
than they are in most (but not all) societies now.

Marcus was trained to tolerate pain (1.5), and admired those
'unchanged in sudden pain, in the loss of a child, in lingering
sickness' (1.8.1: cf. 1.16.10). His philosophical position ('all that
you have heard and agreed about pain and pleasure', 4.3.2) is
based on the mind/body dualism (6.32 note) and the ability or
obligation of the mind to dissociate itself from the body (7.14
note), leaving the body to its own devices ('The body should take
care, as far as it can, to avoid harm', 7.16: 'so let the body give
its evidence', 8.28). Pain is an 'indifferent' (4.39, 9.1.4–5: on
'indifferents' see notes on 5.12 and 5.20), and not therefore 'a
moral evil' (6.33, 7.64, 8.28). As an 'indifferent' pain only
acquires significance or even recognition according to the judgement made of it by the directing mind (7.16: and the mind both
can and should withhold its recognition. 'The mind preserves its
own serenity by withdrawal', 7.33; 'But the soul can preserve its
own clear sky and calm voyage by not accepting pain as an evil',
8.28; 'If you remove your judgement of anything that seems
painful, you yourself stand quite immune to pain', 8.40.

Few would find genuine comfort in this austere philosophy, still less when Marcus goes on to classify pain together with anger and fear, giving way to any of which is condemned as 'nothing less then apostasy from nature' (11.20.2) and incurs the stigma of being a 'fugitive' from the universal law (10.25). Worse, Marcus speaks of pain as 'a sign of weakness' (11.18.10), and of the failure to be indifferent to pain as a 'sin' (9.1.4). The most practical advice Marcus can offer is in fact derived from Epicurus (7.64), a quotation echoed at the beginning of this chapter.

For emotional pain, specifically the loss of a child, see note on 11.34.

7.34 Marcus on fame. Although Marcus was undoubtedly sensitive to criticism and to public opinion, and sometimes vexed with himself for being so (cf. 9.18, 11.18.4, 12.4), his regular mode is to insist on the uncertainty, the evanescence, and the futility of fame, both contemporary and posthumous. 'The only lasting fame is oblivion' (2.17.1); 'will a little fame distract you?' (4.3.3); 'In no time at all ashes or bare bones, a mere name or not even a name: and if a name, only sound and echo' (5.33: more moderate in 8.44, 'What, anyway, is it to you if this is the echo in future voices and this the judgement they make of you?'); 'But what in any case is everlasting memory? Utter emptiness' (4.33); 'Reflect that neither memory nor fame, nor anything else at all, has any importance worth thinking of' (9.30).

In the brief view of history, let alone the perspective of eternity, all are dead and forgotten (4.33, 7.6, 7.21, 8.25, 10.34). See note on 6.24 for famous men dead and gone.

See also 3.10 (and note), 4.6, 4.19, note on 4.20 (Marcus on praise), 4.35, 6.18, 10.8.1.

7.35–52 Most of these chapters are quotations, largely without comment, suggesting that Marcus kept a personal anthology or commonplace book: similar evidence in 11.6 and 11.22–39. See note on 3.14.

7.35 Plato, *Republic*, 486a.

7.36 Antisthenes (mid-fifth to mid-fourth centuries BC), fr. 20b Caizzi.

7.37 See note on 7.24 for the analogy between physiognomy and ethics.

7.38 Euripides, *Bellerophon*, fr. 287, 1f. Nauck², quoted also in 11.6.

7.39 Unknown. The Greek hexameter suggests an epic source.

7.40 Euripides, *Hypsipyle*, fr. 757, 6f., quoted also in 11.6.

7.41 Euripides, *Antiope*, fr. 208, 1f., again quoted in 11.6.

7.42 Euripides, fr. 918, 3.

7.43 Source unknown. For the thought compare 5.36.

7.44 Plato, *Apology*, 28b.

7.45 Plato, *Apology*, 28d. For the metaphor of life as a form of military service, see note on 7.7.

7.46 Plato, *Gorgias*, 512d–e. For indifference to the length of life see 3.7 note.

7.47 *the changes of the elements into each other*: See 2.3 note.
    For observation of the heavenly bodies as antidote to 'the filth of life on the ground' (cf. 5.10.2) see also 11.27.

7.48 *view earthly things ... from some point high above*: The same conceit in 9.30 ('Take a view from above . . .') and 12.24 ('. . . if you were suddenly lifted up to a great height . . .'). For the philosophical and literary history of this theme see Rutherford, pp. 155–61.
    all the medley of the world: For such lists see notes on 4.32 and 7.3.

7.49 See note on 2.14.2. Compare especially 11.1.2: 'such is the sameness of things, a man of forty with any understanding whatsoever has in a sense seen all the past and all the future.'

7.50 Euripides, *Chrysippus*, fr. 839, 9–11.
    Or else this: For the *post mortem* possibilities see notes on 2.17.2 and 3.3, and for 'providence or atoms' as alternative models of the universe see note on 4.3.2.

7.51 The first quotation is from Euripides, *Suppliants*, 1110–11. The second is a fragment of unknown source (Fr. Trag. Adesp. 303 Nauck[2]).

7.52 The reference is to a story about a Spartan wrestler beaten in a contest. When it was observed to him that his opponent had proved the better man, he replied, 'Not at all – just better at throwing his man.' Marcus reinterprets in the context of moral worth. For the duty and virtue of tolerance see 5.33 note.

7.53 *along the proper path, following our own human constitution*: For the 'proper path' see note on 5.4: for 'our own human constitution' see note on 5.1.

7.55 *Do not look around at the directing minds of other people*: See note on 5.3.
    the lower exists for the higher: For Marcus' use of the *scala naturae* see note on 5.16. Compare in particular 5.30, 11.10, and 11.18.1.
    rational beings are here to serve each other: See note on 7.13.

For the social principle see note on 6.7. For the sovereignty of mind over body (the senses and desires) see notes on 6.32 and 7.66.

7.58 *they will be raw material in your hands*: Compare 7.68 ('raw material for the exercise of rational and social virtue') and 8.35 ('the rational being can . . . convert every obstacle into material for his own use'): and see note on 4.1 for the concept of a 'conditional' course of action, making virtues of obstacles.

7.59 *Dig inside yourself*: For the reservoir of inner resources see note on 4.3.1, and compare the 'everlasting spring' in 8.51.

7.60 See note on 7.24 for physiognomic analogies.

7.61 For the analogy with wrestling, see 3.4.3: the ideal man is 'a wrestler for the greatest prize of all, to avoid being thrown by any passion'. In 12.9 the preferred image is that of the boxer.

7.62 For 'these people' see 3.4.4 note. For 'unwitting error' see note on 2.1.

7.63 Not a direct quotation from Plato, but as paraphrased by Epictetus (*Discourses*, 1.28.4). Very close in Plato's actual words are *Republic*, 412e–413a and *Sophist*, 228c. The same thought, in the same words, in 11.18.3.
this will make you more gentle to all: For the duty of care and kindness see note on 9.11.

7.64 For Marcus on pain see note on 7.33. The quotation from Epicurus is fr. 447 Usener. For Epicurus see note on 9.41.

7.66 *Telauges*: Largely obscure: he is the subject of one of the lost dialogues written by Aeschines 'Socraticus' (fourth century BC), a follower of Socrates who was present at the trial and death of his master. 'The passage illustrates Marcus' command of his literary sources and his use of some which are a little off the beaten track. If we had these sources we should be able to understand much in him that is now obscure to us' (Farquharson, p. 364). On this chapter see also Rutherford, pp. 216–17.
Socrates (469–399 BC) was the greatest Greek philosopher of the fifth century BC, and a major influence on the Stoics (see note on 2.1 for his intellectual concept of virtue and vice, adopted by Stoic ethics). He himself wrote nothing, but his philosophy was transmitted and elaborated by Plato (429–347 BC) in a magisterial set of dialogues of critical centrality to the western philosophical tradition. Socrates was executed by hemlock in an Athenian prison after trial and conviction by jury on the charges of atheism and 'corruption of the young': Plato's *Apology* (from which Marcus makes quotation in 7.44 and 7.45) is a moving and

convincing idealization of Socrates' speech in his own defence.

For 'a whole night out in the frost' see the stories told by Alcibiades in Plato, *Symposium*, 220a–d. Marcus is conflating two incidents there related: one of Socrates out lightly clothed and barefoot in a severe frost, and the other of him standing immobile in contemplation of a philosophical problem for a whole day and night.

For Leon of Salamis see Plato, *Apology*, 32c–d: in the reign of terror in Athens under the 'Thirty Tyrants' in 404/3 BC Socrates refused, or rather simply ignored, an order to join a posse for the arrest, leading to his execution, of the innocent Leon.

'Swaggered in the streets' refers to the description, with comic exaggeration, of Socrates' characteristic gait in Aristophanes, *Clouds*, 362 – quoted also in Plato, *Symposium*, 221b.

On Socrates see also 1.16.9 (and note), 3.3 ('vermin of another sort killed Socrates'), 3.6.2, 6.47, 7.19, 8.3, 11.23, 11.28, 11.39.

For the questions asked of Socrates' soul compare Marcus' description of the ideal man in 3.4.3.

the poor passions of the flesh: See note on 8.10 for Marcus on pleasure.

7.67 *drawing a boundary around yourself*: See note on 4.3.1.
      the happy life depends on very little: See note on 6.30.2.
      you have given up hope of becoming a philosopher or a scientist: See 2.2n., 5.5n., and 8.1n.

7.68 A combination of some of Marcus' more extreme views, put into curious dialogue form, which he may have borrowed from Cleanthes: Cleanthes, on whom see note on 9.9.3, has a verse dialogue between Reason and Passion (fr. 7 Powell: see LS, 65, I and Sandbach, p. 65). For the preservation of the mind in tranquillity, despite whatever afflictions of the flesh, see notes on 2.1, 6.32, and 7.33: and compare 4.39, 8.41, 8.51.

7.69 *to live each day as if it were your last*: Compare 2.5, and note.

7.70 For the gods' care for men see note on 6.44.

7.73 See 5.6, and note.

BOOK 8

8.1 A remarkable chapter of regret and resolve, drawing together several strands of 'true perception'.
     you are far from philosophy: With characteristic self-doubt, Marcus questions and rejects any claim he might have to be a

philosopher. Did he ever want to be? The *Meditations* suggest ambivalence, and a lingering tension between the academic urge and the practical life (in this chapter Marcus speaks of 'a contrary pull', and experience of his 'wanderings'). Full Stoic philosophy combined ethics, logic, and physics (i.e. natural science): though deeply interested in ethics (i.e. moral philosophy), Marcus was not much drawn to the other elements of the orthodox trivium. In 1.17.9 he thanks the gods 'That, for all my love of philosophy, I did not fall in with any sophist, or devote my time to the analysis of literature or logic, or busy myself with cosmic speculation.' For academic regret countered, as here, by resolute assertion of an alternative set of values for the good life, see 2.2 and note ('Quit your books'), 7.67 ('And do not think, just because you have given up hope of becoming a philosopher or a scientist, you should therefore despair of a free spirit, integrity, social conscience, obedience to god'), 8.8 ('Not possible to study. But possible to . . .').

Marcus saw philosophy, as he interpreted and practised it, as guide (2.17.2: 'What then can escort us on our way? One thing and one thing only: philosophy'), therapy (3.13, 5.9), comfort (6.12), and retreat (4.3.1 and note).

your station in life is a contrary pull: A different view in 11.7: 'How clearly it strikes you that there is no other walk of life so conducive to the exercise of philosophy as this in which you now find yourself!' Ambivalence again. See note on 5.1 for Marcus on his 'station in life'.

in all your wanderings: See 3.14 ('No more wandering') and note.

what man's nature requires: For Marcus' view of man's proper nature or constitution see note on 5.1.

What are these principles: For Marcus' principles or doctrines see note on 3.13. For good and evil defined solely in terms of moral effect see note on 2.1.

8.2 *Ask yourself this about each action*: Similar in 5.11, 10.37.

sharing one law with god: See note on 6.44 for Marcus' view of the relation between man and god.

8.3 A contrast between philosophers who explained the world and military commanders intent on imposing their will on the world. Similar distaste for conquerors and kings in 3.3 (this same trio: see note) and 9.29.

Diogenes of Sinope (south coast of the Black Sea) was a leading and notoriously ascetic Cynic philosopher of the fourth century BC. For *Heraclitus* see notes on 3.3 and 4.46, and for *Socrates* notes on 1.16.9 and 7.66.

its causes and its material: See 8.11 note.

8.4   For the contemptuous use of 'they' see notes on 3.4.4, 4.6, and 5.10.1.

8.5   *as is true now even of Hadrian and Augustus*: For similar 'Where are they now?' reflections see notes on 2.14, 3.3, and 6.24.

your duty to be a good man: For Marcus' concept of duty see note on 6.2.

what man's nature demands: See note on 5.1.

8.6   For the general doctrine that 'the universe is change' (4.3.4) see note on 2.3.

All is familiar: For the eternal sameness of things see note on 2.14.2.

8.7   Marcus uses the *scala naturae* (the inanimate/animate/rational sequence) frequently and for a variety of purposes. See note on 5.16.

the right path: See note on 5.4.

to direct its impulses solely to social action: See 8.12 and note on 6.7 for this social imperative.

to welcome all that is assigned to it by universal nature: For this constant theme see note on 5.8.

8.8   See notes on 8.1 and 5.5 for the disjunction of intellect/academic study and virtuous practice, which requires no specific intelligence (cf. 5.5) or investment of time.

8.9   For Marcus on palace life see 5.16 ('A good life can be lived in a palace') and note.

8.10 Marcus on pleasure. The tight argument in this chapter gives apparent logical validation to what may have been, at least partly, a matter of personal disdain, springing from an austerely fastidious temperament.

       Certainly, for Marcus and the Stoics pleasure, like pain, is an 'indifferent' (see notes on 5.12 and 5.20), so to attribute inherent value to pleasure is to make an error of judgement: indeed 'the pursuit of pleasure as a good' constitutes a 'sin' (9.1.3–4). But ordinary human experience (not always of the greatest interest to Marcus) revolts against the denial of any benefit in pleasure: Marcus deals with this objection in 3.6.3. Here, as elsewhere, Marcus' philosophical position stands counter to psychology, and it is hard to resist the conclusion that Marcus was emotionally, as well as philosophically, averse to pleasure, seeing it as something dangerous and almost improper. Even so, he recognizes an austere 'joy' in the performance of duty (6.7, 8.26, 8.43, 12.29).

Marcus' tone is set by his scything comment in 6.34: 'As for pleasure, pirates, catamites, parricides, and tyrants have enjoyed it to the full.' Philosophy 'consists in keeping the divinity within us inviolate and free from harm, master of pleasure and pain' (2.17.2). Various formulations of the implied ideal man include: 'a social being who has no regard for the fancies of pleasure or wider indulgence' (3.4.2); 'unsullied by pleasures . . . a wrestler for the greatest prize of all, to avoid being thrown by any passion' (3.4.3); withdrawal 'from all inducements of the senses' (3.6.2); 'devoid of passion' (6.16.2); 'resistance to the promptings of the flesh' (7.55); 'disdain for the stirrings of the senses' (8.26); 'a mind free from passions is a fortress' (8.48).

The mind/body dualism (see note on 6.32) lends force to the denigration of pleasure and its heightened categorization as 'passion of the flesh': so 'the body and its gross pleasures' (11.19); the commendation of Socrates for 'not lending his mind to share the poor passions of the flesh' (7.66); the need to 'separate from this directing mind of yours the baggage of passion' (12.3.2). A similar concept underlies Marcus' favoured image of the body as a marionette, 'jerking to the strings of selfish impulse' (2.2 and note).

In 3.6.3 Marcus groups 'the enjoyment of pleasure' with popularity, power, and wealth as potential seducers away from 'the rational and social good': 'All these things may seem to suit for a little while, but they can suddenly take control and carry you away.'

See also 1.9.3, 2.10 (Theophrastus on offences committed under the influence of pleasure), 3.16.1, 4.3.2, 5.1 ('Were you then born for pleasure?'), 8.19.

For the Stoic orthodoxy on pleasure/passion see Sandbach, pp. 59–67; Long, pp. 206–7; and LS, 65, where note in particular i. 421: 'Pleasure only becomes a passion when a person assents to false judgements concerning the desirability and goodness of pleasurable experiences.'

For Marcus on pain see note on 7.33.

8.11 For this frequently recommended analysis into causal and material elements see notes on 3.6.3 and 4.21.2. Similar in 8.13 and 10.9.

8.12 *When you are reluctant to get up from your sleep*: Compare 5.1, and see note on 2.1.

8.14 The link between (mistaken) value-judgements and moral habit of life, stressed again in 8.15, is created by the individual's response to the status of 'indifferents' such as those listed here (see notes on 5.12, 5.20, and 8.10). See more generally note on 4.6. Marcus also charitably recalls the Socratic view that sin/ error is ignorance, and that no one willingly does wrong (see 2.1 note). Compare 9.42.3: 'where is the harm or surprise in the ignorant behaving as the ignorant do?'

8.15 For the fig-tree analogy see 4.6 note. For the analogy with doctor and ship's captain see notes on 5.8.2 and 6.35.

8.16 See note on 4.12 for Marcus' recognition of the need to change course and accept correction.

8.17 *atoms or gods*: See note on 4.3.2 for these alternative models of the universe.
  There is no blame: Compare 12.12.
  If you can, put him right: For the obligation to teach the morally ignorant/unsighted see notes on 2.1 and 2.13.
  Nothing should be done without purpose: An insistent theme in the *Meditations*: see 2.5n.

8.18 For the changes in the elements of the universe, and the 'recycling' of all that dies, see notes on 2.3, 2.17.2, 3.3, and 8.50.

8.19 *For your pleasure*: See note on 8.10 for Marcus on pleasure. Marcus here rejects the Epicurean view (see LS, 21) of pleasure as the ultimate good.

8.20 *like someone throwing up a ball*: A similar image in 9.17.

8.21 See note on 3.10 for the constant theme of the insignificance of human life and habitation in 'a mere point in space'.

8.22 *You would rather become good tomorrow*: For Marcus' impatience with his own moral progress see note on 3.4, and note on 4.17 for the exhortation to 'become good'.

8.23 *I accept it*: See note on 5.8 for Marcus' insistence on the duty to accept and welcome one's lot.
  from which all things spring interrelated: For the interrelation of all things see note on 6.38.

8.24 One of Marcus' most vigorous expressions of contempt for the squalor of all things temporal. A frequent theme – see notes on 4.48.2 and 5.10.1.

8.25 One of a sequence of 'Where are they now?' reflections, linked to thoughts on the brevity of life and the evanescence of fame – evidently much in Marcus' mind at the time of this Book's composition (see 8.31 and 8.37). See notes on 2.14, 6.24, 7.34.
  Lucilla: Domitia Lucilla, Marcus' mother (see note on 1.3).

Verus: presumably Marcus Annius Verus, Lucilla's husband and
Marcus' natural father, who died young (see note on 1.2). For
Maximus see note on 1.15: *Secunda* was presumably his wife.
Nothing is known of *Epitynchanus* or *Diotimus* (mentioned as
mourning Hadrian in 8.37). *Faustina* was the wife of Marcus'
uncle and adoptive father *Antoninus* (see note on 1.16): she died
early in her husband's reign. *Celer* was Marcus' tutor in oratory.
Hadrian: either the emperor (died 138), or a sophist of that name.
Charax: unknown. *Demetrius:* probably the Cynic philosopher of
that name who was banished by Vespasian. *Eudaemon:* the name
of Hadrian's Greek secretary, who may be the referent here.
The same story always: See note on 2.14.2.
So remember this . . . elsewhere: Marcus frequently canvasses the
various *post mortem* possibilities: see note on 3.3.

8.26 *man's proper work:* See notes on 5.1 and 6.2.
disdain for the stirrings of the senses: For this aspect of 'proper
work' see note on 8.10.

8.27 Of these three relations, it was the third, 'to your fellows and
contemporaries', which Marcus found most difficult to maintain:
see note on 5.10.1.

8.28 For Marcus on pain, and on the capacity of the mind/soul to
dissociate itself and '*preserve its own clear sky*', see notes on
7.33, 6.32, and 7.14. For the inability of any external to harm
the soul see note on 2.1: the most striking formulations are in
4.39, 7.68, 8.41, and 8.51. The thought of this chapter is continued in the next.

8.30 For Marcus' insistence on sincerity and truthfulness see notes on
9.1.2 and 11.19.

8.31 Further meditation on the universal erasure of time and death:
see note on 8.25.
Augustus (63 BC–AD 14) was the first Roman emperor. *Areius*,
a Stoic philosopher born in Alexandria, was philosopher-in-
residence at Augustus' court, and highly regarded by Augustus.
Agrippa and *Maecenas* were the two closest and most important
associates and ministers of Augustus while they lived. Marcus
Vipsanius Agrippa (64/63–12 BC) was Augustus' principal general. Gaius Maecenas (died 8 BC) is best known for his extreme
wealth and his literary patronage – especially of Horace, Vergil,
and Propertius.
Pompeys: the immediate descendants of Gnaeus Pompeius
Magnus (106–48 BC) were, like him, killed in the civil wars.

8.32 The right approach to obstacles encountered in any proposed
course of action – to accept, absorb, circumvent, or turn them to
advantage – is a constant theme in the *Meditations* (see note on
4.1), and much in evidence in this Book (see also 8.35, 8.41,
8.47, 8.50). See note on 10.33.
no one can prevent you: A form of expression, and a sentiment,
very frequent in the *Meditations*: see note on 2.9.

8.34 See note on 4.29 for the notion of severance from human society
or universal nature: there is comparably full treatment in 11.8,
where also regrafting is allowed, with reservations. The physical
analogy ('*a severed hand or foot . . .*') doubtless reflects Marcus'
own experience of the field of battle.

8.35 See note on 8.32 and 7.58.

8.36 *always the present*: For this thought see notes on 3.10 and 4.26.
thus stripped bare: See note on 3.11 for the reductive analysis
which Marcus frequently recommends to himself.

8.37 See note on 8.25. A further reflection, in darker and more cynical
tone, on the finality of death and the futility of remembrance.
Panthea: a famed courtesan, mistress of Marcus' adoptive
brother *Verus* (on whom see notes on 1.16 and 1.17.4). *Pergamus*, *Chabrias*, and *Diotimus* (also in 8.25) are unknown: the
latter two may have been favourites/lovers of *Hadrian* (emperor
117–138).
all stench and corruption in a bag of bones: See note on 3.3 for
Marcus' disdainful reference to the material (de)composition of
the body, and note on 4.48.2 for his wider view of all human life
as short and cheap.

8.38 The poet and the context are unknown, and the Greek text here
is not certain.

8.40 *If you remove your judgement . . . immune to pain*: For this
doctrine, frequently rehearsed in the *Meditations*, that hurt or
harm, including physical pain, is only a matter of judgement ('all
is as thinking makes it so'), and that therefore removal or denial
of the judgement removes the hurt or harm, see notes on 2.15,
4.7, and 5.19. For Marcus on pain see note on 7.33.

8.41 Familiar use of the *scala naturae* (5.16n.) leads to further consideration of the right approach to obstacles (8.32n.). For the
sense of 'an unconditional aim' see note on 4.1.
The mind cannot be touched by fire . . . or anything whatever: A
similarly extreme formulation in 4.39 ('Even if . . . your own
body is subjected to knife or cautery, or left to suppurate or

186

mortify, even so that faculty in you which judges these things should stay untroubled'). Compare also 7.68 and 8.51.

'*a perfect round in solitude*': The quotation, repeated in slightly fuller form in 12.3 ('perfect round rejoicing in the solitude it enjoys') and probably alluded to in 11.12, is from Empedocles (fr. B 27.4 Diels-Kranz = fr. B 28.2), a fifth-century BC pre-Socratic philosopher and poet from Acragas in Sicily.

8.44 For Marcus' view of fame and futurity see note on 7.34.

8.45 For '*the god within me*' see note on 2.1.

8.46 The *scala naturae* again (5.16n.). For the limits of natural experience/endurance see 5.18 and note.

8.47 Familiar themes. For judgement as the arbiter and filter of harm/distress see note on 8.40. For the 'no one stops you' mode of expression compare 8.32 and see note on 2.9. For the suggestion of suicide ('*you must depart this life*') see note on 3.1.

8.48 Marcus frequently speaks of the calm and security of 'retreat into yourself': see note on 4.3.1.

a mind free from passions: See note on 8.10 for Marcus on pleasure and passion.

8.49 A characteristically tough prescription, which few could follow. For the death of a child see note on 11.34.

8.50 A robust answer to questions of waste and imperfection in the universe (on which see LS, 54 Q–U). For the circumvention of obstacles see notes on 8.32 and 10.33. For the analogy with crafts ('carpenter or cobbler') see notes on 5.8.2 and 6.35. For the constant recycling and fresh creation in the universe see note on 2.3: the image of economical craftsmanship with finite material is elaborated in 7.23 ('Universal nature uses the substance of the universe like wax . . .').

'*So why are these things in the world anyway?*': An idealistic answer is given in 3.2 and 6.36. 'Even the incidental effects of the processes of Nature have their own charm and attraction' (3.2); 'So even the lion's gaping jaws, poison, every kind of mischief are, like thorns or bogs, consequential products of that which is noble and lovely' (6.36).

8.51 '*They kill, they cut in pieces, they hunt with curses*': The source and context of this quotation, if such it is, are unknown: but the point is clear and familiar, that even the most extreme external circumstances are irrelevant to the preservation of internal tranquillity (see note on 8.28).

a spring of clear, sweet water . . . an everlasting spring: For the reservoir of inner resources see note on 4.3.1, and compare 7.59:

'Dig inside yourself. Inside there is a spring of goodness ready to gush at any moment, if you keep digging.'

8.52 Compare 4.29: '. . . one who does not recognize the contents of the universe is a stranger in it.' This and the next chapter stress the irrelevance of praise (or the lack of it) from the unworthy: for Marcus on praise see note on 4.20.

8.55 For the doctrine that wickedness does true harm only to the perpetrator, not the recipient, see notes on 2.1 and 2.6. Similar in the next chapter.

8.56 *we are born . . . for the sake of each other*: See note on 7.13. Characteristic of Marcus to temper this potentially universal benevolence with the caveat of individual proclivity (see note on 5.3).

8.57 Similar in 8.54. The particular point connecting 'rays' (*aktines*) with 'extend' (*ekteinein*) is in fact false etymology. For the mind's extension see also 9.8, 9.9.1, and 12.30.

8.58 See notes on 2.14 (Marcus on death and the fear of death) and 3.3 (the *post mortem* possibilities).

8.59 A terse summary of obligations argued elsewhere. See note on 7.13 for 'Men are born for the sake of each other': and notes on 2.1, 2.13, and 5.33 for 'either teach or tolerate'.

8.61 See note on 6.53.

BOOK 9

9.1 A careful chapter, drawing together several important themes in the philosophy of Marcus and the Stoics and setting them in the theological context which springs from the essential equation of Nature, Providence, and God (for these and other equivalents see the introductory note to Book 2 and note on 6.44). The language of theology ('sin' is irreverence or impiety) is insistently repeated: an offence against nature (one's own nature or the universal nature of which it is a part) is an offence against god. The offences/sins here discussed are the breach of proper relations/obligations between human beings; deviation from the truth; action or attitude consequent on a mistaken view of pleasure and pain; the attribution of inherent value to 'indifferents'. There is a similar list, in the context of a soul's self-harm, in 2.16.

9.1.1 *rational creatures for the sake of each other*: See note on 7.13 for this central tenet of Marcus' philosophy.

9.1.2 Marcus on truth and truthfulness. From the frequency of reference in the *Meditations*, and the vigour of his expression (e.g. 11.15: 'It should be written on your forehead, immediately clear in the tone of your voice and the light of your eyes . . .'; 3.12: 'a heroic truthfulness in all that you say and mean'), it is clear that Marcus had a passionate, and perhaps unfashionable, love of truth and regarded truthfulness/honesty as one of the defining virtues of the good man (see, for example, 3.6.1, 4.49.2, 10.8, 11.1.3, 12.15).

When Marcus was seventeen, the emperor Hadrian, playing on his name Marcus Annius *Verus* ('the true'), nicknamed him 'Verissimus' ('the most truthful') – which imperial recognition of an early character trait may well have been an effective spur to its future maintenance. Marcus himself attributes his 'love of truth' to the influence of Severus (1.14.1), and admires Antoninus Pius for not keeping 'many matters secret to himself' (1.16.7).

Marcus gives robust expression to this life-long conviction in 6.21: 'I seek the truth, which never harmed anyone.' Truth and justice (as here by the implication of their negatives) are frequently presented as the two essentials of the good life: see for example 6.47 ('In this world there is only one thing of value, to live out your life in truth and justice'), 3.16.2, 12.3.1, 12.29 ('The salvation of one's life lies in . . . applying one's whole soul to doing right and speaking the truth'). A terse summary in 12.17: 'If it is not right, don't do it: if it is not true, don't say it.' For Marcus' insistence on sincerity see note on 11.19.

See also 2.17.2, 4.33, 12.1. Closest to the present passage is 2.16: 'The soul of a man harms itself . . . whenever it dissimulates, doing or saying anything feigned or false.'

For Marcus on veracity see further Brunt, pp. 8–10.

9.1.3   For Marcus on pleasure and pain see notes on 8.10 and 7.33 respectively. The apparent problem of the wicked flourishing like a green bay-tree is easily resolved theologically (see 2.11) and by a proper understanding of 'indifferents', as in 9.1.4–5 below. An allied theme is the glad acceptance of one's lot: see note on 5.8.

9.1.4–5   For 'indifferents' see notes on 2.11.4, 5.12, and 5.20.

9.1.5   *generative powers . . . successive regeneration*: See note on 2.3.

9.2   The familiar image of life as a banquet (see, for example, Horace, *Satires*, 1.1.119, Lucretius 3.938) is given a characteristic twist by Marcus: for him life is a *sickening* banquet.

depart the company of men: On suicide, here implied, see note on 3.1.

plague: Marcus probably has in mind the disastrous infection brought back from Mesopotamia by Verus' armies in 166–7. The plague spread all over the empire, with particularly severe mortality in Rome and among the army. See Birley, pp. 149 ff. The *Historia Augusta* (4.28.4) has Marcus saying on his death-bed, thirteen years later: 'Why weep for me? Think rather of the plague and the communal death.'

9.3   For Marcus' attitude to death, and the arguments he deploys in consolation and/or against fear of death, see note on 2.14. In this chapter Marcus advances two consolatory arguments of widely differing tone: death as one of the functions of nature (9.3.1), and death as the relief from life (9.3.2).

9.3.1 *one further part of nature's will ... one of the functions of nature*: For this argument see note on 6.2. A similar argument from the natural transitions of life in 9.21.
       the child your wife carries: This reads like a personal reference, but we cannot be sure. The last child of Marcus and Faustina, Vibia Aurelia Sabina, may have been born as late as 170 (see Birley, p. 248). For Marcus' children see note on 1.17.4.
       when your soul will slip this bodily sheath: Similar in 10.36: 'that easy slipping of the soul from the body's carapace experienced by those dying at peace'. For the mind/body dualism see note on 6.32.

9.3.2 *rather care for them and tolerate them kindly*: For the duty of care, tolerance, and kindness to one's fellow men (not an easy duty for Marcus) see notes on 5.33 and 9.11.
       out of tune with your fellows: For Marcus' view of his fellows and contemporaries see note on 5.10.1.

9.4   A cardinal tenet of Socratic and Stoic philosophy: see notes on 2.1 and 2.6.

9.7   *keep your directing mind its own master*: Similar exhortations in 2.2 and 9.26. On the 'directing mind' see note on 5.21.

9.9   A closely argued chapter, weaving together Stoic ideas of the four constituent elements, the affinity of like to like, the evolution of society along the *scala naturae* (see 5.16 note – here extended to the astral bodies, *'yet higher things'*); and ending with the picture of a degenerate age, reminiscent of Hesiod.

9.9.1 *to mix and blend with its family*: Compare 12.30 (the mind 'reaches out to others of its kind and joins with them'), and for the mind's ability to permeate, like air or sunlight, see 8.54 and 8.57: similar in 9.8.

9.9.2 See note on 5.1 for Marcus' fondness for lessons drawn from the ordered world of animals.

9.9.3 *They may run from it . . . such is the power of nature*: For the
mastery of nature Marcus may have in mind a saying of Heraclitus (fr. B114 Diels-Kranz). Seneca (*Epistles*, 107.11) puts this
thought in epigrammatic form: 'ducunt volentem fata, nolentem
trahunt' ('Fate guides the willing, drags the unwilling'). This is
part of Seneca's vigorous translation of the *Hymn to Zeus* by
Cleanthes of Assos (331–232 BC), the pupil and successor of
Zeno as head of the Stoa. See LS, 54 I.
a man cut off from man: See note on 4.29 for the concept of
severance.

9.10 *each in its own due season*: See note on 12.35.

9.11 *show them the better way*: For the obligation to educate the
morally unsighted see note on 2.13.
the gift of kindness: Marcus fully recognized the duty of care and
kindness to one's fellows: it did not come easily to him, and
the frequency of reference in the *Meditations* suggests that he
constantly fretted at his record. He found the more passive virtue
of tolerance difficult enough to maintain (see note on 5.33):
active kindness, especially towards those many he judged
unworthy, was a struggle for him, and he knew it.

The philosophical base of the duty of kindness is the kinship
of all men, who share a rational nature (see note on 2.1). Marcus
frequently reminds himself of this moral imperative and its
source: 'caring for all men is in accordance with man's nature'
(3.4.4); 'it is our duty to do good to men and tolerate them'
(5.20); 'treat men, because they do have reason, with social
concern' (6.23); 'Man's joy is to do man's proper work. And
work proper to man is benevolence to his own kind . . .' (8.26).

Marcus knows that he should be kind, wants to be kind,
castigates himself for not achieving his aim (4.37: 'you are not
yet . . . kindly to all people'; 7.13: 'you do not yet love your
fellow men from your heart'), exhorts himself to do better (e.g.
5.5, 6.30, 6.39, 7.63, 8.8, 9.27, 11.13), and sometimes convinces
himself that he is/has been kind (5.31: 'how often you have . . .
been kind to the unkind'; 10.36: 'keep true to your own character
– friendly, kind, generous'; cf. 8.43). His last words on this topic
(11.18.9) ring with conviction and hope: 'Kindness is invincible.'
In fact, kindness and gentleness were notable aspects of Marcus'
public reputation.
The gods too are kind to such people: Similar in 9.27, '. . . the
gods too help them in various ways . . . at least to the objects of

their concern.' See in general note on 6.44 for Marcus on the gods.

who is stopping you: See note on 2.9 for this frequent form of expression.

9.13 *just my own judgements*: For this constant theme, that 'all is as thinking makes it so', see note on 2.15.

9.14 *All things are the same*: Another familiar set of themes: see notes on 2.14.2 and 5.10.1.

9.17 A similar image is elaborated in 8.20.

9.18 For penetration of others' minds see note on 6.53, and for the contemptuous use of 'they/them/their' see note on 3.4.4. Such thoughts were evidently much in Marcus' mind hereabouts: see also 9.22, 9.27, 9.34.

9.19 For the *'process of change'* see note on 2.3.

9.20 See note on 7.29.

9.21 One of Marcus' consolatory arguments against fear of death: see in general note on 2.14. A similar argument from the transitions of life (here extended from the general to the particular changes in Marcus' own life) in 9.3.1: compare also the wider perspective in 12.23.

9.22 See note on 9.18 above, and for *'ignorance or design . . . a kindred mind'* see note on 2.1.

9.23 *a life of social principle*: For this aspect of man's duty see note on 6.7.

9.24 The most scathing of Marcus' judgements on his contemporaries (see note on 5.10.1). The image of 'children squabbling' is used again in 5.33, and the quotation from Epictetus ('tiny spirits carrying corpses', fr. 26 Schenkl) recurs in 4.41. The Underworld in the *Odyssey* (Book 11), to which Odysseus travels to obtain guidance from the dead prophet Teiresias, is a place where the dead maintain a spectral and inane existence.

9.25 For this mode of analysis see note on 4.21.2.

9.26 Compare 9.7 and note.

9.27 *the gods too help them in various ways*: See note on 9.11.
dreams and divination: Marcus himself shared the prevalent (and Stoic) belief in the validity of divine communication through dreams and oracles: see 1.17.9 and note.

9.28 Familiar themes. In sequence see notes on 2.14.2, 5.13 (the cycles of the universe), 4.3.2 (providence or atoms), 2.5 (the need for purpose), 2.3 (successive change and transformation), 4.48.2 (contempt for mortal things).

9.29 This vigorous chapter, with its strong undercurrent of emotion (which seems a characteristic blend of anger, frustration, and self-contempt), is the closest that Marcus comes in the *Meditations* to a statement of political philosophy (other than, indirectly, in his detailed appreciation of Antoninus Pius in 1.16). The chapter is discussed in Rutherford, pp. 172–7.

In the context of eternity the focus can only be the present moment (see 4.26 note), and nature (i.e. reason) the only guide: the quest for approbation or fame is both irrelevant and pointless (see notes on 4.20 and 7.34). There is no room for large ambition – neither the 'big idea' nor the 'big stick'. No point in abstract and impractical theorizing (as in Plato's *Republic*), the attempt to change society by changing minds: no virtue either in dramatic conquest and the mere imposition of power unguided by reason, which leads to a nation of ostensibly compliant slaves. One rational step at a time: '*simple and modest*'.

The universal cause is a torrent: For the image of the rapid river of time/existence see note on 4.43.

How worthless are these little men: See note on 5.10.1 for Marcus' often contemptuous view of his contemporaries. It is not clear to what class of 'little men' Marcus is referring: perhaps toadying courtiers and 'advisers'. Marcus may have these same men in mind in the vitriolic chapter 10.19.

They are full of snot: i.e. they don't even know enough to wipe their own noses. Marcus may have in mind here Thrasymachus' rude taunt to Socrates in Plato, *Republic*, 343a: '. . . [your nurse] lets you drivel on and doesn't wipe your nose when you need it.'

Alexander, Philip, Demetrius: Philip (382–336 BC), king of Macedon, was the father of Alexander the Great (356–323 BC), and almost as successful an imperialist as his son. Demetrius of Phalerum (born *c.*350 BC) was a philosopher (a pupil of Theophrastus) and orator rather than a general, though as a pro-Macedonian he was appointed absolute governor of Athens and held that post for ten years (317–307 BC), until he was deposed by conquest. The Greek text speaks of 'Demetrius of Phalerum', but 'of Phalerum' could well be an intrusive gloss. In that case the reference would be rather to Demetrius 'Poliorcetes' ('the besieger of cities'), 336–283 BC, a major military figure who was also for a time (294–287 BC) king of Macedon, like Philip and Alexander.

9.30 *Take a view from above*: The same conceit in 7.48 and 12.24. For the medley of human experience and universal process thus

observed see notes on 4.32 and 7.3. The familiar point is the
insignificance of any individual human life, both in the wider
world and in the perspective of eternity. See notes on 3.10 and
6.24: for the fickleness of praise and the evanescence of fame see
notes on 4.20 and 7.34.

9.31 *that social conduct which is an expression of your own nature*:
See notes on 5.1 and 6.7.

9.32 *which lie wholly in your own judgement*: For this familiar consolatory thought, central to Marcus' philosophy, see note on
2.15.

grasping the whole universe in your thought: Similar in 10.17,
'Keep constantly in your mind an impression of the whole of
time and the whole of existence', and 11.1.2. Compare Plato,
Republic, 486a, and Lucretius, 1.72–9.

the rapid change of each thing: See note on 2.3.

how vast the gulf of time: See note on 3.10.

9.33 For indifference to the length of life, given the eternal sameness
of things, see notes on 3.7 and 2.14.2.

9.34 *these people*: See note on 3.4.4 for Marcus' frequent contemptuous reference to an unspecified 'they'.

Train yourself to look at their souls naked: For this aspect of
analysis see note on 3.11. Such training will mirror god's ability
to see 'all our directing minds stripped of their material vessels,
their husks and their dross' (12.2). The notion of the inspection/
judgement of souls naked (and possibly scarred) is Platonic
(*Gorgias*, 523c–525a).

9.35 *Universal nature delights in change*: For this central Stoic doctrine see note on 2.3.

So why do you say ... that all those gods between them: The
answer is given tentatively in 9.40 and more firmly in 12.5 (the
fact that things are not otherwise ordered by the gods is a guarantee that they should not be otherwise).

9.36 Reductive analysis in extreme and evidently bitter form. Similar
in 6.13, and comparable in 8.24 (bath-water). See note on 3.11,
and for Marcus' view of the shoddiness of all things temporal,
note on 5.10.1.

9.37 *cause and material*: For this mode of analysis see note on 4.21.2.
For relations to the gods see note on 6.44.

9.38 See note on 2.6 for self-harm. The second sentence is a charitable
softening of Marcus' usual view: cf. 11.18.5 ('You are not even
sure that they are doing wrong ...'), and 12.16.

9.39 The familiar disjunction of the Stoic view of a unitary and unified

universe (see note on 6.38) and the Epicurean atomist theory: for
this disjunction ('providence or atoms') see note on 4.3.2, and
for 'stew' see note on 6.10.

are you herding with the rest: See note on 5.3 for Marcus' insistence on the independence of his own practical and moral will.

9.40 Marcus discusses the nature and rationale of prayer more briefly
in 5.7, 6.44 (see note), and 12.14. His conclusion here, that
prayer is an experiment, has a surprisingly modern ring. See
further Rutherford, pp. 200–205.

if the gods can cooperate with men: Marcus believed in divine
cooperation: see 1.17.6, 1.17.9, 9.11, 9.27.

9.41 This passage of Epicurus (fr. 191 Usener), not preserved elsewhere, is similar in tone to the letter he wrote to Idomeneus on
his deathbed (Diogenes Laertius, 10.22). The founder of the
Epicurean school of philosophy was born in Samos in 341 BC
and died in Athens in 270 BC. Although in the *Meditations*
the Stoic view is often opposed to the Epicurean, especially in
cosmology ('providence or atoms'), this passage of Epicurus is
clearly consonant with Stoic philosophy, and there is a sort of
generosity in Marcus' quotation of the head of a 'rival' school:
Marcus quotes Epicurus on pain, with like approval, in 7.64.

how the mind shares in such disturbances of the flesh: See notes
on 5.12 and 6.32. For the preservation of calm compare 7.28:
'It is in the nature of the rational directing mind to be self-content
with acting rightly and the calm it thereby enjoys.'

Concentrate only on the work of the moment: See note on 4.26,
and compare especially 9.29: 'Do what nature requires at this
moment.'

9.42 In the context of a set of principles or reflections to inform and
moderate his reaction to the faults of others (11.18 is a similar
exercise with specific reference to anger), Marcus draws together
and links several tenets of philosophy or experience recurrent
elsewhere in the *Meditations*.

These are: the inevitability of wrongdoing (see note on 4.6,
and compare 5.17: 'To pursue the impossible is madness: and it
is impossible for bad men not to act in character'); wrongdoing
as involuntary, the result of ignorance (see note on 2.1); the
consequent duty to educate (see note on 2.13); the inability of
any external to do true harm, which is harm to the mind/soul
(see notes on 2.1 and 2.6); kindness as an end in itself (see note
on 5.6); man's proper nature, 'made to do good' (see note on 5.1).

Compare in particular 8.14 and note, and 10.30.

BOOK 10

10.1 A remarkable passage of devotion and aspiration, eloquent of the deeply religious response which Stoic philosophy evoked in Marcus.

all is well and all will be well for you: The idealization of the duty to accept one's lot, an insistent theme: see note on 5.8. Compare Julian of Norwich (born 1343), *Revelations of Divine Love*, ch. 27.13: '. . . all shall be well and all shall be well and all manner of thing shall be well.'

as they dissolve into the generation of others like them: For this central doctrine of Stoic physics see note on 2.3.

10.2 For Marcus' frequent use, in various contexts of argument, of the (inanimate)/animate/rational sequence see note on 5.16.

10.3 Compare 5.18 ('Nothing happens to any creature beyond its natural endurance') and 8.46. Similar in 7.33: 'Unbearable pain carries us off: chronic pain can be borne.'

10.4 For the duty to educate the morally unsighted see note on 2.13.

10.5 The Stoic system was necessarily deterministic. See Long, pp. 164–70 and 198–9; Sandbach, ch. 6; LS, i. 340–43, 392–4.

10.6 *Whether atoms or a natural order*: The familiar disjunction of Epicurean and Stoic accounts of the universe: see note on 4.3.2.

For the kinship of men (a particular application of the wider kinship of all parts of the universe) see note on 2.1. For the interrelation of interest between part and whole, individual and community, see 5.22 and note on 6.54 ('What does not benefit the hive does not benefit the bee either').

10.6.2 *all that his city assigns him*: Marcus will have in mind here the dual citizenship of one's own local city and the 'great city' of the world/the universe. See note on 2.16, and in particular 6.44: 'As Antoninus, my city and country is Rome: as a human being, it is the world. So what benefits these two cities is my only good.'

10.7 A difficult chapter, the thought compressed and the sequence of thought not always clear. The main intention is to assuage fear of death (see note on 2.14 for Marcus' frequent arguments of 'consolation'). Dissolution at death, however understood (i.e. on either the Epicurean or the Stoic view), is part of an eternal and universal process of change and regeneration determined by nature (see note on 2.3); nature is neither improvident nor careless (compare 2.11: a similar argument concerning the gods in 12.5), so there can be no harm for the individual part of nature in this process ('nature' and 'the Whole' are synonymous); even on the Epicurean atomist view, death/dissolution is necessarily part of the working of some natural law, so no cause for complaint. For the Epicurean view of death see LS, 24.

See note on 3.3 for Marcus' consideration of the various *post mortem* possibilities – extinction, dispersal, or survival.

10.7.2 *periodically turned to fire*: For this Stoic belief see notes on 5.13 and 2.14.2.

10.7.3 The purpose and, to some extent, the meaning of this section is obscure. Perhaps Marcus intends a further point of rather austere consolation – that the process of change toward dissolution has been running since birth. 'The influx of food consumed' is set in an apparently different context in 10.26.

10.8 Marcus' starting-point for this chapter may have been a passage of Epictetus (*Discourses*, 2.10), headed 'How is it possible to discover duties from titles?'

10.8.1 *any other indifferent thing*: For 'indifferents' see notes on 2.11.4, 5.12, and 5.20.

you will be a new man: Similar in 7.2: 'You can live once more.'

10.8.2 *half-eaten gladiators*: See note on 6.46.

10.8.3 *the Islands of the Blest*: A mythical paradise at the ends of the earth to which the gods send specially favoured mortals (in Hesiod, *Works and Days*, 167 ff. this is the destination of some 'happy heroes' of the Theban and Trojan wars). An identical concept is the 'Elysian Plain' to which Menelaus is promised translation in Homer, *Odyssey*, 4.536 ff.

retire in good heart: For the notion of retreat or withdrawal into one's own mind as a means of inducing calm or (here) 'regaining control' see note on 4.3.1.

a complete exit from life: For suicide see note on 3.1, and for a discussion of Marcus' thoughts on the appropriate reasons/circumstances for suicide see Sandbach, pp. 51–2, especially the concluding sentences: 'It was basic to Stoicism that intention was everything and achievement nothing. Marcus could not escape the normal human feeling that unless he could execute his purpose he would be a failure.' See also LS, i. 428–9.

10.8.4 *to keep your mind on the gods*: Compare 6.7: 'Let one thing be your joy and comfort: to move on from social act to social act, with your mind on god.' For Marcus on the gods see note on 6.44.

the proper work of man: See notes on 5.1 and 6.2.

10.9 *Farce, war, . . . slavery*: There is no means of knowing what these five exclamatory words meant to Marcus at the time, other than a comprehensive vexation. Further evidence, if that were needed, that Marcus was writing for himself.

those sacred doctrines of yours: See note on 3.13.

what is its essential nature ... who can give it and take it away: For the modes of analysis which Marcus recommends to himself see notes on 3.6.3, 3.11, and 4.21.2. Compare 8.11: 'What is this thing in itself, in its own constitution? What are its elements of substance and material, and of cause? What is its function in the world? What is its duration?'

10.10 *Sarmatian prisoners*: A sardonic addition to the list of men's hunting, doubtless in reference to Marcus' own campaigns against the Germanic tribe of Sarmatians (Iazyges) which resulted in the assumption of the title 'Sarmaticus' ('conqueror of the Sarmatians') in 175.

10.11 *a systematic study*: As recommended in 3.11, where 'Nothing is so conducive to greatness of mind' recurs in identical form. Here, yet more than there, a compendious prescription for the good life, following the law of nature (i.e. reason) and the path of god (compare 12.23).

One so trained has divested himself of his body: A strikingly extreme phrase to connote the triumph of the mind in the mind/body dualism, on which see note on 6.32. See also note on 8.10 on pleasure/passion.

glad acceptance of his present lot: See note on 5.8.

10.12 *consult your best advisers*: See note on 4.12 for Marcus' recognition of the need for help and advice..

10.13 Compare 5.3 (and note) for the rejection of irrelevant criticism, and note on 5.10.1 for Marcus' view of *'these people'*. Similar disgust for 'their' implied habits *'in their bed and at their board'* in 10.19 and 11.18.2.

10.14 Compare the exaltation of sentiment in 4.23 and 10.21.

10.15 *Live it as if you were on a mountain*: Compare 10.23. The point combines the notion of 'retreat' (see note on 4.3.1) with that of the irrelevance of local habitation to wider citizenship of the world (see notes on 2.16 and 10.6.2).

10.17 A similar precept – to weigh the finite in the scale of infinity – in 9.32, 11.1.2.

10.18 For the doctrine of dissolution, change, and regeneration see note on 2.3. For the ambiguity, in this context, of 'death' see 10.7.1. Marcus may have in mind a paradox of Heraclitus equating birth and death (fr. B21 Diels-Kranz).

10.19 Compare 10.13 (see note) and 11.18.2.

10.21 In this remarkable chapter of exalted devotion (see 4.23 note) Marcus begins with a compressed quotation from a famous passage of Euripides (*Chrysippus*, fr. 898).

'*This loves to happen*': Marcus is here using word-play to point and validate what is for him a profound truth (generally the ancient world was ready to attribute deep significance to what we would see as accidental word-associations or puns). The Greek word *philei*, 'loves', can also mean 'tends to, is accustomed to'. Marcus takes the regular, familiar pattern of things as evidence and expression of nature's *love* to create an ordered universe.

10.22 *your service done*: Compare 5.31: 'Remind yourself ... that the story of your life is fully told and your service completed.' For the metaphor of life as a form of military service, from which god will ultimately sound the Retreat (3.5), see note on 7.7.

10.23 Compare 4.3.1: 'Men seek retreats for themselves – in the country, by the sea, in the hills – and you yourself are particularly prone to this yearning.' There, as here, Marcus reminds himself that a change of place is not a change of mind: the most effective retreat is into oneself.

The relevance of the quotation from Plato (*Theaetetus*, 174d) is not immediately clear. In Plato the context is the contrast between the philosopher and the politician/ruler, who can milk his people like a farmer on a larger scale – as isolated, blinkered, and profit-driven as a herdsman on a hill-farm. Marcus is quoting from memory: the immediate 'trigger' is '*on a mountain*', but doubtless Marcus also had in mind the wider context and its possible application to his own position.

10.25 *Law is our master*: For the various and essentially interchangeable ways in which Marcus refers to the governing principle of the universal world-order (Nature, the Whole, God, Law, etc.) see introductory note to Book 2.

See note on 7.33 for Marcus on pain, and note on 11.18 for Marcus on anger.

10.26 One of the warmest chapters in the *Meditations*, blending obvious human emotion with admiration of the causal power of nature. For Marcus on children and their loss see note on 11.34.

10.27 For the eternal sameness of things (a constant theme) see note on 2.14.2.

whole dramas with similar settings: Life as a play (as seen by the actor), and history (as seen by the 'audience') as a repetitive

drama, are common images, of which Marcus makes frequent
use with a characteristically individual twist. The good man's
'play' is always complete, at whatever point he leaves the stage
(3.8, 11.1, implied in 12.36). Other uses of the dramatic metaphor in 6.42, 7.3, 9.29, 11.6.

Croesus: King of Lydia in the sixth century BC, overthrown by
Cyrus of Persia in 547/6 BC. His wealth was proverbial.

10.28 *pure submission is forced on all*: On the force of destiny see
Seneca/Cleanthes quoted in note on 9.9.3. Submission there must
be, but 'rational creatures' (i.e. adult human beings) can choose
to submit rationally, recognizing that their individual lot is part
of and a contribution to the universal good planned by a providential nature. See notes on 5.8, 6.38, and 6.54.

10.29 This thought is elaborated in 12.31.

10.30 Compare 8.14 (and see note) and 9.42. Your offence at others'
wrongs could arise from your own similar mistaken attribution
of value to 'indifferents'.

the man is acting under compulsion: i.e. ignorance. For wrongdoing as ignorance, and the consequent duty to educate, see notes
on 2.1 and 2.13, and compare especially 12.16.

10.31 *When you see Satyrion . . . a parallel in the past*: This seems a
rather odd way of making the common (see note on 2.14) 'Where
are they now?' reflection on human transience and mortality.
The point is that this reflection is encouraged if you compare
living examples of particular types with (long-)dead analogues.

So *Satyrion*, *Eutyches*, and *Hymen* (all otherwise unknown)
must be members of the contemporary Academy (i.e. latter-day
followers of Socrates and Plato). *Eutychion* and *Silvanus* (likewise unknown) must be contemporary Stoics: the sophist *Euphrates* was one of the teachers of Pliny the Younger (c.61–112).
Nothing is known of either *Tropaeophorus* or *Alciphron*. For
Severus see 1.14 and note: he was a friend of philosophy, like
Crito and the historian *Xenophon*, both devoted friends of
Socrates.

mere smoke and nothing: See note on 4.48.2 for this constant
theme. Similar language in 12.27 ('smoke and ashes'), 12.33
('corpse and smoke').

an exercise for . . . reason: For the concept of life as an obstacle-
course for the exercise of virtue/reason see, for example, Epictetus
1.24. A similar thought in 10.33.4 below, and compare 4.1,
where the image of the bright fire recurs. The stomach-simile
again in 10.35.

10.32 See note on 9.1.2 for Marcus on truth and truthfulness.

decide to live no longer: For suicide see notes on 3.1 and 10.8.3.

10.33 On obstacles. See 5.20: 'The mind adapts and turns round any obstacle to action to serve its objective: a hindrance to a given work is turned to its furtherance, an obstacle in a given path becomes an advance'; and the further passages listed in the notes on 4.1 and 8.32. Marcus' precept encompasses both the practical and the ethical exercise of reason. The rational man finds ways to circumvent obstacles in the path of his intended action or to turn them to advantage. But at a deeper level it is in the nature of a rational human being ('man's constitution') to recognize and gladly accept apparent obstacles or 'so-called misfortunes' as part of a wider providential order (see note on 5.8), to recognize that nothing external to the mind (including all that pertains to 'the corpse which is our body') can do it harm without its own consenting judgement (see notes on 2.1 and 2.5), and to enjoy the immunity of his citizenship of the universal city of nature (see notes on 2.16 and 6.54). For 'law' as one formulation of the governing principle of the world-order see note on 10.25.

The image of the roller comes from Chrysippus (see 6.42 note), the third head of the Stoa, after Zeno and Cleanthes, who was both the most prolific and the most definitive figure in the establishment of the Stoic system of philosophy. For the roller-image see LS, 62 C–D.

10.34 *bitten by the true doctrines*: For the importance Marcus attached to his doctrines see note on 3.13. For the 'bite' of philosophy see Alcibiades in Plato, *Symposium* 217e–218a (Marcus' metaphor may well be a reminiscence of this passage).

The quotation, indicative of Marcus' view of the moral/didactic value of some poetry (see 11.6), is a compressed version of *Iliad* 6.146–9. The full text of this famous and much imitated passage is: 'The generation of men is just like that of leaves. The wind scatters one year's leaves on the ground, but the forest burgeons and puts out others, as the season of spring comes round. So it is with men: one generation grows on, and another is passing away.'

For children as 'leaves' – in the same insubstantial and transient category as praise, blame, or fame – see note on 11.34.

All things are short-lived: For this persistent theme see notes on 3.10, 4.48.2, and 5.10.1: and for the inevitable sequence of burial/mourning 4.48, 8.25, 8.37.

10.35 *'my children must live'*: Compare the recommended form of prayer in 9.40, and see note on 11.34.

10.36 *Was he the earnest sage*: Marcus is here referring to the ideal Stoic sage or *sapiens*, an ideal recognized as virtually unattainable and not yet attained, and is presuming the response to the death of such a sage. Though the reference is probably ironic, and Marcus is certainly not claiming for himself any approximation to this ideal, in his formulation of the presumed response Marcus may well be thinking that others see him as 'this schoolmaster'.

For death as the relief from life, and from ungrateful/uncongenial colleagues, see note on 2.14.

that easy slipping of the soul from the body's carapace: See 9.3.1 and note.

My release is like parting from kinsmen: For the kinship of men see note on 2.1.

10.37 *examine yourself first*: See 10.30 and note.

10.38 *that part of us hidden inside*: i.e. our directing mind. See 5.21 ('the ultimate power in yourself') and note. Marcus here gives a new application to his favoured image of the marionette (2.2 note): it is the mind, not the desires of the body, which pulls the strings. For the body as *'vessel'* see also 3.3 and note: similarly 'sheath' (9.3.1), 'carapace' (10.36), 'compound' (11.20.1), 'husk' (12.2).

BOOK 11

11.1 *The properties of the rational soul*: To the extent that the 'rational soul' differs from the 'directing mind' (see note on 5.21) it connotes the directing mind in full accordance with its own nature (i.e. rationality) and attuned to universal nature. It has achieved the state to which Marcus urges his own soul in 10.1.

11.1.1 *Unlike a ballet or a play*: Similar in 3.8 and 12.36. See note on 10.27.

11.1.2 *traverses the whole universe*: For the recommended panoptic view see 9.32 and note.

the periodic regeneration of the Whole: See notes on 2.14.2 and 5.13.

such is the sameness of things: See note on 2.14.2 for this recurrent theme. Compare in particular 7.49: 'So for the study of human life forty years are as good as ten thousand: what more will you see?'

11.2 An extreme (and utterly unconvincing) example of the reductive
      analysis which Marcus frequently recommends and employs. See
      notes on 3.11 and 6.13.

11.3 *the soul ready for its release*: The context suggests that Marcus
      is thinking primarily of voluntary death. See notes on 3.1 and
      10.8.3.

      prepared for whatever follows: See note on 3.3 for Marcus'
      consideration of the *post mortem* possibilities.

      like the Christians: The only mention of the Christians in the
      Meditations. This casual comparison in a brief discussion of the
      ethics, and almost the etiquette, of suicide suggests that at or by
      the time of Marcus' writing the Christians were notorious for
      their defiant choice of martyrdom, given the alternative of recan-
      tation proved by sacrifice made to the emperor. Most non-
      Christians doubtless shared the view in the famous exchange of
      letters (Pliny, *Epistles*, 10.96–7) between Trajan (emperor 98–
      117) and Pliny the Younger (*c.*61–112), then governor of Bithy-
      nia, that the regular refusal of Christians to recant was 'unbend-
      ing obstinacy'. There were persecutions in Marcus' time, most
      notably at Lyon and Vienne in the late 170s: and Rusticus (1.7
      and note), as Marcus' prefect of the city, condemned Justin
      Martyr to his death in 165. See Birley, pp. 202–4 for the Lyon and
      Vienne persecutions, and Appendix 4 for a detailed discussion of
      Christianity in Marcus' time: for wider-ranging consideration of
      the relation between Stoicism and Christianity see Rutherford,
      pp. 256–63.

      The point here is that the decision to terminate one's life
      must rest on something stronger and more deliberate than mere
      enthusiasm for martyrdom (as with the Christians – and indeed
      some Stoics) or the desire to make a dramatic gesture. Closest in
      thought to this passage is 10.8.3: '. . . or else make a complete
      exit from life, not in anger, but simply, freely, with integrity,
      making this leaving of it at least one achievement in your life'.

11.6 A remarkable excursus into literary criticism, firmly in the aus-
      tere Platonic tradition, adopted by the Stoics, of looking primar-
      ily for the moral or didactic value of poetry – 'educational value',
      'useful sayings'.

11.6.1 *on the larger stage of life*: For the image of life as a play see
      note on 10.27, and compare especially the *envoi* in 12.36.

      'Oh Cithaeron!': Sophocles, *Oedipus Tyrannus*, 1391: Cithaeron
      is the mountain in Boeotia on which Oedipus was exposed as a

baby. The other three quotations are repeated in 7.41, 7.38, 7.40: see notes there.

11.6.2 The prime representative of *Old Comedy* is Aristophanes (mid-fifth century BC–386 BC), and of *New Comedy* Menander (*c*.344–292 BC). Eleven of Aristophanes' comedies survive: of Menander's one nearly complete, and substantial portions of six others. Of *Middle Comedy* (the period between late Aristophanes and early Menander) only fragments survive.

Diogenes too adopted this trait: The famous Cynic philosopher (see 8.3 note) was noted, among other things, for his aggressive wit. Marcus clearly approves of 'unbridled frankness', and often displays it himself.

11.7 For Marcus on philosophy, and as philosopher *manqué,* see note on 8.1. There he expresses a different view of the relation/tension between philosophy and his 'walk of life': 'difficult for you now to win the reputation of a philosopher, and besides your station in life is a contrary pull'.

11.8 For the notion of severance see note on 4.29. Regrafting is also allowed in 8.34.

11.9 Good advice to himself. The two virtues urged here – undeviating adherence to principled action, and retention of kindly feelings to one's 'natural kinsmen and friends' (see note on 2.1) – Marcus sometimes found difficult, and cause for self-doubt. He found them yet more difficult in combination. Display of these virtues, and the example thus given, figures large in the admiration and gratitude he expresses to his 'role models' in Book 1: e.g. Apollonius (1.8), Sextus (1.9), Maximus (1.15), Antoninus Pius (1.16.1). For the duty of kindness see note on 9.11.

11.10 *'No nature is inferior to art'*: Evidently a quotation, of unknown poetic source.

the lower in the interests of the higher: One of the conclusions which Marcus draws from the *scala naturae* (see 5.16 note). Compare 5.30, 7.55, and 11.18.1.

here is the origin of justice: A difficult conclusion. Probably Marcus' thought is that justice, being the right application of reason, is thereby the source of all other virtues and the principle of universal nature herself. To deviate from reason, by misattribution of value to 'indifferent things' or inconstancy of principle, is to fail to preserve justice. For 'indifferents' see notes on 2.11.4, 5.12, 5.20, and 8.10.

For the primacy of justice see also 5.34, 9.1.1–2, 12.1.1, 12.24.

11.11 For the thought in this chapter see note on 5.19, and compare especially 11.16.

11.12 *The soul is a sphere*: See note on 8.41 for this allusion to Empedocles. Marcus clearly has in mind the analogue of the sun.

11.13 *That is his concern*: For this 'let him see to it' response see note on 5.25.

   like the famous Phocion: Phocion (402/1–318 BC), Athenian statesman and general known as 'The Good', was condemned to death by hemlock in 318 BC. He was the subject of a biography by Plutarch, in which (and elsewhere) it is recounted that just before his execution he was asked if he had any message for his son: his reply was that his son should bear no grudge against the Athenians for his death ('for their hospitality, which I now drink', in Aelian, *Varia Historia*, 12.49). The version in Aelian admits of irony.

   For the duty to educate the morally unsighted see note on 2.13. For '*our inner thoughts, which are open to the gods' eyes*' compare 12.2.

11.14 For Marcus' frequent and contemptuous reference to an unspecified 'they' see note on 3.4.4.

11.15 For Marcus' love of truth and sincerity, here expressed in striking and passionate language, see notes on 9.1.2 and 11.19. For other examples of physiognomy as indicative of character see note on 7.24.
   Calculated honesty is a stiletto: I have borrowed from C. R. Haines (translation of Marcus Aurelius in the Loeb Classical Library, Harvard, 1916) 'stiletto' for the word *skalme* in the Greek text. As Rutherford observes (notes on Farquharson's translation republished in the Oxford World's Classics series, Oxford, 1989) 'the word is Thracian and should sound foreign and dangerous'. Compare Chaucer (*Knight's Tale*, 1. 1999), 'The smiler with the knife under the cloak'.

11.16 A compilation of familiar doctrines and themes for living through life 'in the best way you can'. For 'indifferents' see notes on 2.11.4, 5.12, 5.20, and 8.10. For recommended modes of analysis see notes on 3.6.3, 3.11, and 4.21.2. For '*things themselves are inert*', unless activated by our judgements of them, see note on 5.19 and compare in particular 4.3.4 and 11.11. For accordant with/contrary to nature see note on 6.33. For the triviality of praise/glory/fame see notes on 4.20 and 7.34. The final sentence adds a pleasant touch of irony.

11.18 In this long chapter, similar in intent to 9.42 (see note), Marcus attempts in a somewhat disjointed series of reflections to argue himself from anger to understanding, tolerance, and kindness in his response to others and their faults – not without some flickers of the old contempt. To this end, as in 9.42, he draws together several doctrines and themes prominent elsewhere in the *Meditations*: on the assumption of a world-order governed by providential nature (see note on 4.3.2, 'providence or atoms'), and therefore 'the lower in the interests of the higher' (see note on 11.10), men were born for each other (see notes on 5.16 and 7.13); the inevitable link between opinion/character and action (see notes on 4.6 and 8.14: compare 11.8, 'Share their stock, but not their doctrines'); wrongdoing as involuntary, the result of ignorance (see note on 2.1); the consequent duty to educate (see note on 2.13); 'all is as thinking makes it so' (see note on 2.15); the inability of any external to do true (i.e. moral) harm (see notes on 2.1 and 2.6); and, in any case, the brevity of human life, 'a mere fragment of time' (see note on 3.10).

The analysis and control of anger was a common subject of ancient moral philosophy (see in particular William V. Harris, *Restraining Rage* [Cambridge, Mass., and London, 2001]), and there are extant essays on this topic by Seneca and Plutarch. Marcus falls broadly within this tradition, but his treatment, as often – since he was writing for himself – is individualistic and sharply personal: see in particular Brunt, pp. 10–14. The anger which bothers Marcus in himself is not, or at least not very much, the ordinary man's anger at real or imagined personal slight or harm, but rather his general irascibility at the faults, deficiencies, and moral blindness of many (most) of his fellows and contemporaries: 'he is preoccupied with righteous indignation' (Brunt). This was a real problem for Marcus, and he hated it. He sets 'a mild temper' as an example given (and by implication a lesson to be learnt) at the very beginning of the summatory Book 1 (1.1). He is conscious of his irascible disposition (1.17.1, 1.17.7, 6.26, 6.57, 8.4, 8.8, 9.42.2, 10.30), and recognizes it as a fault; recognizes too and rehearses, as here, the philosophical arguments against his form of anger (the kinship of men, the involuntary nature of wrongdoing, etc.); and yet the *Meditations* are as full of expressions of anger as of contrary prescriptions and exhortations. In the end Marcus accepts anger as a weakness (11.9, 11.18.10) and kindness as a strength ('invincible', 11.18.9). See also 1.9.3, 2.1, 2.10 (and note), 2.16, 5.28, 7.38, 11.20.2, 12.27.

11.18.2 *at table, in bed, and so on*: See note on 10.13.

11.18.3 *Just as no soul likes to be robbed of truth*: For this paraphrased quotation from Plato see 7.63 and note. The point is
that all people, including wrongdoers, instinctively recognize
good and bad, and the categories of wrongdoing: hence their
resentment at inclusion in these categories. In Farquharson's
words (pp. 415 and 872), 'the homage vice pays to virtue'.

11.18.4 *You yourself have many faults*: Compare 10.30.

11.18.5 An extension of the charitable softening of view in 9.38.
Compare 12.16.

11.18.7 *and become a robber, a rogue*: Compare the implication of
10.10.

11.18.9 Marcus' best word on kindness (see note on 9.11), and a
charming and sensitive practical example of the re-education of
the morally unsighted (see note on 2.13).
not a lecture: Compare the schoolmaster image in 10.36 (and 5.9).

11.18.10 *take them as gifts from the Muses*: Probably just a *jeu
d'esprit*: Marcus has made nine points, and nine is the canonical
number of the Muses. The *Leader of the Muses* (next section) is
Apollo.
Anger is as much a sign of weakness as is pain: For Marcus on
pain see note on 7.33.

11.18.11 *that is asking for the impossible*: A familiar theme: see for
example 4.6 (and note), 5.17, 9.42.1, 12.16.
cruel tyranny: Compare 6.27: 'How cruel it is not to allow people
to strive for what seems to them their interest and advantage!'

11.19 *'This would not be yourself speaking'*: For Marcus' insistence
on sincerity see, for example, 1.15 (Maximus admired for 'the
trust he inspired in everyone that he meant what he said and was
well-intentioned in all that he did'), 6.39 ('. . . but your love must
be genuine'), 11.15 ('It should be written on your forehead . . .'),
11.18.9 (kindness must be 'sincere, not fawning or pretence').
See also note on 9.1.2.
the more divine part of you: For the mind/body dualism see note
on 6.32, and compare especially 3.3 (and note): 'One is mind
and divinity: the other a clay of dust and blood.'
the body and its gross pleasures: For Marcus on pleasure see note
on 8.10.

11.20.1 Compare 10.7.2: 'Dissolution is either a scattering of the
component elements or the change of solid to earth and spirit to
air, so that these too are subsumed into the Reason of the Whole.'
On the elements see LS, 47.

11.20.2 *resentment at any happening*: For the rational duty to accept and welcome all that happens to you see note on 5.8.

justice to men . . . service of god: See note on 5.33 for these 'two commandments'.

11.21 The source of this maxim is unknown. It is possibly Marcus' own formulation, since consistency in life and action was both a Socratic (cf. Plato, *Apology*, 33a) and a Stoic ideal (e.g. Cicero, *On Duties*, 1.111). For the importance of *aim* and purpose see note on 2.5. 'To be always the same man' was a lesson learnt from Apollonius (1.8).

11.22–39 The Book ends with a random collection of short jottings or quotations, not all with clear point or reference, suggesting that Marcus kept a personal anthology or commonplace book. Similar in 7.35–52 and (on a smaller scale) 11.6. See note on 3.14.

11.22 The fable of the town mouse and the country mouse is told in Aesop (297 Halm), Horace, *Satires*, 2.6, Babrius (108). Why the 'hill' mouse in Marcus alone? Perhaps he is thinking of 'life on a mountain' (10.15). Compare 7.3: '. . . the scurries of frightened mice'.

11.23 From Epictetus (2.1.15: cf. 3.22.106), based on Plato, *Crito*, 46c and/or *Phaedo*, 77e.

11.25 A slip of memory (compare the slip in 3.3). The king of Macedon in this story, told by Aristotle and Seneca, was Perdiccas' son Archelaus, who ruled from 413 to his assassination in 399 BC. Archelaus saw himself as a patron of the arts, issuing invitations to distinguished figures: the poets Euripides and Agathon and the painter Zeuxis spent some time at his court.

11.26 Epicurus (fr. 210 Usener), quoted in Seneca, *Epistles*, 11.8.

11.27 For Pythagoras see note on 6.47. A similar thought in 7.47: 'Observe the movement of the stars as if you were running their courses with them.'

11.28 The source of this anecdote is unknown. The literary tradition represents Xanthippe, Socrates' wife, as something of a shrew.

11.30 A fragment of an unknown poet (Fr. Trag. Adesp. 304 Nauck²).

11.31 Homer, *Odyssey*, 9.413: Odysseus relishing his triumph over the Cyclops Polyphemus.

11.32 Hesiod, *Works and Days*, 186, adjusted by Marcus or his source to substitute the metrically equivalent 'virtue' for the original 'them' (i.e. their ageing parents: Hesiod is writing of a degenerate age when men will not even honour their parents).

11.33–8 A sequence of condensed excerpts from Epictetus, especially from *Discourses*, 3.24.86–93.

11.33 Epictetus, 3.24.86–7. For other fig-tree analogies see note on 4.6.

11.34 Epictetus 3.24.88–91. For the comparison with the reaping of corn see the fragment of Euripides quoted in 7.40 and 11.6: 'Ripe ears of corn are reaped, and so are lives.'

Marcus on children and the loss of a child. Although Marcus speaks of learning 'a genuine love for children' from Catulus (1.13), and he and Faustina had to endure the death of seven of their fourteen children in infancy or early childhood (see note on 1.17.4), there is undeniable Stoic coldness in his treatment of what to most ordinary people is, and surely always was, the most important focus of their life – one of the most obvious gulfs between Stoic philosophy and human psychology. Marcus' thanks to the gods for his children are that they 'were not born short of intelligence or physically deformed' (1.17.4) and that he 'found no lack of suitable tutors' for them (1.17.8). He admires Apollonius for being 'always the same man, unchanged in sudden pain, in the loss of a child, in lingering sickness' (1.8). Those who pray 'How can I save my little child?' should rather pray 'How can I learn not to fear his loss?' (9.40), and the initial impression 'that my little boy is ill' should not be elaborated to 'he is in danger' . . . 'and then that is all' (8.49). The most chilling of Marcus' chapters on this subject are 10.34 and 10.35. 'Your children are no more than "leaves"' – as trivial and transitory in the wider scheme of things as praise, blame, or fame (10.34). To say 'my children must live' is equated as counter-factual folly with saying 'there must be a popular acclaim for all I do' (10.35).

His final word is set in the perspective of theology: 'nothing is our own property, but even our child, our body, our very soul have come from that source [i.e. god]' (12.26).

See also Epictetus 1.11.

11.35 Epictetus 3.24.91–2.

11.36 Epictetus 3.22.105. Compare 12.14: '. . . if the flood carries you away, let it take your flesh, your breath, all else – but it will not carry away your mind.'

11.37 Epictetus fr. 27 Schenkl. For the sense of 'conditional' see note on 4.1.

11.38 Epictetus fr. 28 Schenkl. Compare Plato, *Republic*, 352d: 'This is no trivial subject of discussion, but how one should live one's life.'

11.39 This Socratic vignette is not otherwise known.

BOOK 12

Although there are no firm objective criteria for the relative dating and sequence of the twelve Books of the *Meditations* (see Brunt, pp. 18–19, and Rutherford, pp. 45–7), the character and content of Book 12 strongly suggest that it was indeed the last Book to be written, towards – perhaps very close to – Marcus' death. There is much recapitulation, either closely argued or in short headings, of the central doctrines of Marcus' belief and the conclusions of his experience; he writes in this Book as a man more at peace with himself, less vexed with his surroundings, his thoughts predominantly on death and god; the final chapter (12.36) reads like a conscious *Nunc dimittis*.

For Marcus on death see note on 2.14, and for Marcus on the gods see note on 6.44.

12.1 One of the summations in Book 12 of the moral and philosophical principles which guide the 'right way' in life and prepare for peaceful fulfilment in death: comparable summations in 12.3, 12.24, 12.26.

12.1.1 *direct the present solely to reverence and justice*: For the primacy of the present moment as the focus of moral endeavour see note on 4.26. Compare, in this Book, 12.3.2 and 12.26.

so that you come to love your given lot: See note on 5.8.

open and direct in word and action, speaking the truth: See notes on 9.1.2 and 11.19 for Marcus on truthfulness and sincerity.

not what anyone else thinks or says: For the insistent assertion of the independence of one's own moral will see notes on 2.6, 4.12, and 5.3.

the afflicted part must see to its own concern: See note on 7.14.

12.1.2 *the divinity within you*: See note on 2.1, and compare especially in this final Book, in which Marcus' thoughts are much on god, 12.3.2 ('at peace with the god inside you') and 12.26 ('every man's mind is god').

You will no longer be a stranger in your own country: For this thought and form of expression compare 4.29 ('... one who does not recognize the contents of the universe is a stranger in it'), 8.52, 12.13. In darker mood Marcus writes, 'life is warfare, and a visit in a strange land' (2.17.1).

as if bemused by the unexpected: Compare 4.46 (Heraclitus), 'their everyday experience takes them by surprise', and 12.13.

12.2 *minds stripped of their material vessels*: See notes on 3.11 and 9.34. Our 'inner thoughts' are 'open to the gods' eyes' (11.13).
clothes, houses, reputation . . . stage scenery: i.e. 'indifferents', for which see notes on 2.11.4, 5.12, and 5.20.

12.3 For the mind/body dualism, much to the fore in these first three chapters of Book 12, see note on 6.32. For the 'directing mind', and the equation of 'mind' and 'self', see note on 5.21. Marcus here presents the ideal state of the directing mind, 'pure and liberated'.

12.3.1 *the external vortex encircling us*: A reference, unique in the *Meditations*, to Empedocles' theory that the earth is held at the centre of the universe by the rapid circular movement ('whirl') of the heavenly bodies: the inclusion of this reference presumably springs from the Empedoclean context of Marcus' thought in this chapter.

12.3.2 *Empedocles' 'perfect round rejoicing in the solitude it enjoys'*: See note on 8.41.
seek only to perfect this life you are living in the present: See note on 4.26, and compare 12.1.1 and 12.26.

12.5 The argument, that the providential reason of the gods guarantees that the way things are is the way things should be, is closely parallel to that in 10.7.1 (nature is neither improvident nor careless). Compare 2.3 ('The works of the gods are full of providence') and 2.11.
perpetual extinction rather than some return to existence: See note on 3.3 for Marcus' contemplation of the *post mortem* possibilities. His own position is agnostic, though perhaps with an emotional leaning towards some form of survival. Stoic doctrine allowed at best only limited survival of the individual soul after separation from the body, a doctrine reflected, with the agnostic conditional, in 4.21: '. . . if souls live on . . . They continue for a time, then change, dissolve, and take fire as they are assumed into the generative principle of the Whole.' See further Rutherford, pp. 212–14 and 248–50; Sandbach, pp. 82–3.

12.6 'Practice' is essential to the moral 'progress' which is the Stoic's best aim short of the (unattainable) status of 'sage' (*sapiens*). See Long, pp. 199–209. For practice see also 5.5 ('And yet even this can be worked on') and 5.9 ('Do not give up in disgust or impatience . . .').

12.7 Familiar themes, here mere headings *pour mémoire*. See notes on 3.10, 4.48.2, 5.10.1.

12.8 More headings. For reductive analysis ('*causation stripped bare . . . ulterior reference*') see note on 4.21.2. For Marcus on pain, pleasure, death, fame see respectively notes on 7.33, 8.10, 2.14, 7.34. For '*all is as thinking makes it so*' see note on 2.15.

12.9 See 7.61 and note for the alternative image of the wrestler.

12.10 See note on 4.21.2.

12.11 *to welcome all that god assigns him*: See note on 5.8.

12.12 For human wrongdoing as involuntary see note on 2.1. For the absence of blame compare 8.17 ('There is no blame').

12.13 See note on 12.1.2. For the absurdity of surprise see 4.6 note, and 5.17, 8.14–15, 9.42.3, 11.18.11, 12.16.

12.14 Three models of the universe – a variant on the familiar 'providence or atoms' alternatives, for which see note on 4.3.2. '*A providence open to prayer*' is a softening, though not a denial, of '*the compulsion of destiny*'. Marcus clearly believed in the efficacy of prayer (see 6.44, 9.40), not as a means of influencing or changing destiny (no Stoic model of the universe admits that possibility), but as collaboration with god in the achievement of moral progress – 'the gods are with us and share our lives' (6.44). For Stoic determinism see note on 10.5.

but it will not carry away your mind: A strong statement of the mind/body dualism (see note on 6.32). Compare Epictetus quoted in 11.36: 'No thief can steal your will.' For the autonomy of the directing mind even in '*an ungoverned welter*' compare 9.28: 'The Whole is either a god – then all is well: or if purposeless – some sort of random arrangement of atoms or molecules – you should not be without purpose yourself.'

12.16 Further extension of the charitable softening of view begun in 9.38 ('If he did wrong, the harm is to himself. But perhaps he did not do wrong') and continued in 11.18.5 ('You are not even sure that they are doing wrong').

For the fig-tree analogy see note on 4.6, and for the absurdity of '*wanting the bad man not to do wrong*' note on 11.18.11. For wrongdoing as involuntary, the consequence of a 'state of mind', see note on 2.1, and compare in particular 10.30 (the wrongdoer 'is acting under compulsion – what else can he do? Or, if you can, remove the cause of his compulsion'). For the consequent duty to educate/cure see note on 2.13.

12.18 For this method of analysis, more fully discussed in 3.11, see notes on 3.11, 4.21.2, and 9.34.

12.19 *you have within you something stronger and more numinous*: i.e. your directing mind (see 12.3 and note on 5.21), 'the divinity within you' (12.1.2: see note on 2.1).

a mere puppet on their strings: For this favoured image see notes on 2.2 and 10.38.

12.20 For Marcus' insistence on a clear aim in every action, impulse, or thought see note on 2.5.

12.21 For the central Stoic doctrine of change, dissolution, and regeneration see note on 2.3.

12.22 *all is as thinking makes it so*: This constant theme (see note on 2.15) is particularly insistent in this last Book: see also 12.8, 12.26.

remove your judgements . . . and then there is calm: For this frequent consolatory or therapeutic application of 'all is as thinking makes it so', based on the philosophic principle that externals can only hurt with the assent of our own judgement (which can and should be withheld), see notes on 2.15, 4.7, and 5.19. For the means of inducing calm see also note on 4.3.1.

12.23 For Marcus' arguments against fear of death see in general note on 2.14. Closest to the argument in this chapter are those in 9.3.1 and 9.21, though here Marcus widens the perspective to 'god's own path' (cf. 10.11) and the ultimate identity of the individual and the universal interest.

constant changing . . . keeps the whole world ever young and fresh: See note on 2.3, and compare especially 6.15 ('Flows and changes are constantly renewing the world, just as the ceaseless passage of time makes eternity ever young').

12.24 *nothing aimless*: See 12.20 and note on 2.5.

our constitution and . . . dissolution: See note on 2.17.2, and compare in particular 4.5: 'Death, just like birth, is a mystery of nature: first a combination, then a dissolution, of the same elements.'

lifted up to a great height: The same notion in 7.48 ('view earthly things as if looking down on them from some point high above') and 9.30 ('Take a view from above . . .'): see note on 9.30. Such an aerial or 'cosmic' perspective would confirm the triviality and sameness of all things human – '*monotony and transience*'. For the eternal sameness of things (a constant theme) see note on 2.14.2.

human activity and . . . all its variety: Elsewhere Marcus gives colourful lists expressive of the miscellany of human life and activity: 4.32.1, 7.3 (and see note), 7.48, 9.30.

the great surrounding host of spirits: It is not clear what category of spirits/beings Marcus has in mind in this unique passage. Probably not the stars and planets, since they are visible from earth (cf. 12.28); he may be reflecting the ancient and persistent belief that tens of thousands of 'spirits', something intermediate between human and divine, populate the earth (Hesiod, *Works and Days*, 252) or the air (as the Pythagoreans believed: Diogenes Laertius, 8.32); or he may be thinking of the 'souls migrated to the air', the population problem which he addresses in 4.21 ('You may ask how, if souls live on, the air can accommodate them all from the beginning of time'). This last seems the most likely context for Marcus' thought here, which is on the utter insignificance of any individual life in the sweep of eternity, 'the gulf of immeasurable time both before and after' (4.3.3).

12.25 Compare in particular 4.7: 'Remove the judgement, and you have removed the thought "I am hurt".' For this tenet of Stoic philosophy, frequently rehearsed in the *Meditations*, see notes on 2.15, 4.7, and 5.19. For the *'who is there to prevent . . . ?'* type of exhortation see note on 2.9.

12.26 A concentrated *vade mecum* recapitulation of many of the central tenets of Marcus' philosophy: similar in 4.3. Almost the whole of the philosophy of the *Meditations* is summarized in Book 12: and almost the whole of Book 12 is summarized in this chapter.

12.27 *where is it all now? Smoke and ashes . . . a story forgotten*: Familiar themes: see notes on 2.14 and 4.48.2. Closest are 10.31 and 12.33 ('All else . . . is just corpse and smoke').

Fabius Catullinus . . . Velius Rufus: 'This whole class of examples' seems to be of those who entertained grandiose but ultimately inane ambitions and/or life-styles. *Tiberius*, born 42 BC and emperor AD 14–37, was notorious in the historical/literary tradition (Tacitus, *Annals*, 4.57, 67; Suetonius, *Tiberius*, 39–45) for the depravity of his semi-retirement in Capri in the final years of his reign. *Fabius* may be the evidently long-lived Fabius mentioned in 4.50; nothing is known of *Lusius Lupus*; *Stertinius* may be the rich doctor of Naples mentioned in Pliny, *Natural History*, 29.5; *Velius Rufus* was a correspondent of Fronto (2.86–8 Haines), but otherwise unknown.

Baiae (modern Baia) was a fashionable resort on the coast of Campania; *Capri*, a small island in the Bay of Naples, was a luxury imperial preserve.

The pride that prides itself on freedom from pride: Farquharson (p. 428) appositely quotes Coleridge, *The Devil's Thoughts*, vi:

> And the Devil did grin, for his darling sin
> Is pride that apes humility.

12.28 One of Marcus' strongest affirmations of belief in, and reverence for, the gods. See note on 6.44, and compare in particular 2.11.2 ('But they [the gods] do exist, and they do care for humankind'). On this chapter see the discussion in Rutherford, pp. 209–12.

visible to our eyes: i.e. as the heavenly bodies.

12.29 'Salvation' in proper analysis, truth, and good deeds. For analysis into material and causal see note on 4.21.2. For Marcus on truth and truthfulness see note on 9.1.2. For '*a linked succession of good deeds*' and the joy in their accomplishment see 6.7 (and note): 'Let one thing be your joy and comfort: to move on from social act to social act, with your mind on god.'

12.30 For the unity of the cosmos, here supported by argument from the *scala naturae* (see note on 5.16), see in particular 4.27, 4.40 ('Think always of the universe as one living creature, comprising one substance and one soul'), 9.8, and note on 6.38.

the gravitation of like to like: Compare in particular 9.9.1 ('All things which share some common quality tend to their own kind . . .'), again in the context of the mind's special ability to 'mix and blend with its family'.

But the mind has this unique property: For the ability of the mind/universal mind to permeate (like the air, like sunlight) see 8.54 and 8.57, and compare 9.8, 9.9.1.

12.31 For the thought compare 10.29: 'Consider each individual thing you do and ask yourself whether to lose it through death makes death itself any cause for fear.'

12.32 Familiar themes of temporal and geographical insignificance (see note on 3.10), to focus the mind on the only true importance in life. The thought is rephrased, in more vigorous language, in the next chapter.

12.33 For the directing mind see note on 5.21.

corpse and smoke: Compare 10.31 ('. . . look on human life as mere smoke and nothing') and 12.27: see in general note on 4.48.2.

12.34 Marcus is doubtless thinking of Epicurus: see 9.41 and note. For the Epicurean view of death see LS, 24, and especially Epicurus, *Letter to Menoeceus*, 124: 'Accustom yourself to the belief that death is nothing to us. For all good and evil lie in sensation, whereas death is the absence of sensation.'

12.35 *what comes in its own proper season*: The proper season is that determined by nature. Compare 9.10, 12.23 ('The time and the term are assigned by nature'), and especially 4.23: 'Universe, your harmony is my harmony: nothing in your good time is too early or too late for me. Nature, all that your seasons bring is fruit to me.'

for a longer or a shorter time: See note on 3.7 for indifference to the length of life, a theme continuing into the final chapter.

12.36 An eloquent and moving *envoi*, 'full of reserved emotion' (Farquharson, p. 430), and carefully composed to conclude the *Meditations* in contentment and peace.

a citizen in this great city: i.e. the 'great city' of the world/the universe. See note on 2.16.

a comic actor: For the metaphor of life as a play see note on 10.27, and compare especially 11.1.1.

Marcus died on 17 March 180, a month short of his fifty-ninth birthday, in military quarters near Sirmium in Pannonia (modern Sremska Mitrovica in Serbia). His final illness was short – only a week or so – and the exact cause of his death is not known.

Index of Names

Names of people (including gods and peoples) are given in Roman: names of places or geographical features are given in *italics*.

References are to Book and chapter (e.g. 1.3) or Book, chapter, and sub-section (e.g. 1.17.3).

Not all the passages cited *name* the referent. For example, Marcus refers to his mother several times, but never by her name, Domitia Lucilla: those references are given under the heading 'Lucilla', but there are also cross-references to Lucilla and other family members under the heading 'Marcus' family'. Similarly many of Marcus' literary or philosophical quotations do not name the author. There are several quotations from Homer, for example, but Homer is nowhere named: and other authors are sometimes named, sometimes not. Generally, I have not made any distinction in this Index between named and un-named references. Where a reference is uncertain, or marginal at best, it is included in brackets.

Most of the names in the *Meditations* are treated in the notes (even if that treatment has to take the form 'otherwise unknown'). References to the notes are indicated by 'n.' after the chapter reference (e.g. 8.31n.), with the more important notes marked in bold (e.g. **1.16n.**).

Index of Quotations

This Index lists both direct quotations and those passages of other authors which either clearly or probably lie behind Marcus' thought and/or expression at various points – allusions, reminiscences: the references to such passages are enclosed in brackets.

Many of the passages quoted or alluded to survive now only as fragments, for some of which Marcus himself is the sole testimony. These fragments are identified by their list-number in the current standard collection of the fragments of each author (or class of authors) made by modern scholars. The relevant collection to which reference is made is given by the name of the editor(s) after the first reference: e.g. Diels-Kranz, Nauck².

References to the *Meditations* are to Book and chapter, or Book, chapter, and sub-section. Many of the quotations and allusions here listed are explained or discussed in the notes on the relevant chapters.

bar

Quotations (or possible quotations) of unknown source:

General Index

The nature of the *Meditations* is such that a fully comprehensive index would be almost as long as the work itself, and therefore of limited value. This General Index (which excludes for the most part the proper names listed in the Index of Names) aims to strike a reasonable balance between completeness and utility. Many of the notes contain synoptic treatment and/or a mini-index of the point or issue discussed, and all the references there listed are not always reproduced in the General Index: for any entry the more important chapters and/or notes (often with further references) are given in **bold**. Users of this Index may therefore wish to turn first to the emboldened references in any entry (for example **2.14n.** for Marcus on death). I hope that this combination of Index entries and references to synoptic or mini-indexing notes will provide as full coverage as is practical.

Readers seeking to recapture a striking phrase or image remembered from their reading of the *Meditations* can find it a needle-in-haystack task. For that reason I have included in this Index a good number of otherwise trivial entries which may aid that search (e.g. 'bath-water', 'cucumber', 'puppies', 'rubbish-dump'). References are to Book and chapter (e.g. 1.3) or Book, chapter, and sub-section (e.g. 1.17.3). References to the notes are indicated by 'n.' after the chapter reference (e.g. 2.1n.). For ease of reference the headings of some fifty major entries are given in bold capitals.

Acceptance of one's lot: **5.8n.**, 10.1n.
Actor: 3.8, 12.3
  See also Dramatic analogies
Advice, correction, help: **4.12n.**, 6.30.2 (Antoninus), 7.12n.
Affection: 1.9.3 (from Sextus), 1.11n. ('Patricians' short of human affection), 6.30.1, 10.1
  See also Love (of fellow men), 'Two commandments'

– the body as 'vessel', etc.: 3.3n., 10.38n.
  See also Pain, Pleasure(s), Tripartite division
'Bogies': 11.23
Bones: 'all stench and corruption in a bag of bones', 8.37
Books/study: 1.7.3, 2.2n., 7.67, 8.1n., 8.8, 11.29; 'the food of learn-
  ing', 4.30
– Marcus' own writings/compilations: 3.14n.
  See also Philosophy
Box: 7.23
Boxer: 12.9
Brambles: 8.50
Branch, severed and regrafted: 11.8
Bread, baking of: 3.2.1
Breaker of horses: 6.16.1
Breath: 2.2, 3.1, 4.4, 5.4, 6.15, 8.54, 12.3, 12.30; 'our little breath',
  5.33
– soul as breath: 12.24
– foul breath: 5.28
  See also Tripartite division
Bubble: 8.20
Bull: 11.18.1
Burial: *see* Mourning
Busy: never say 'too busy', 1.12

'Caesarified': 6.30.1
CALM: 4.3.1n., 5.2, 7.28, 7.33, 7.68, 7.75, 8.28, 9.41, 11.18.10,
  12.22
– the mind's preservation of calm: 4.39, **6.32n.**, 7.28, **7.33n.**, **7.68n.**,
  8.28 ('clear sky and calm voyage'), 9.41
Candle: 8.20
Care: *see also* Kindness
– gods' care for men: 6.44n.
– care of self: 1.17.4, 3.14
Carpenter: 8.50
Catamites: 3.16.1, 5.10.1n., 6.34
  See also Homosexuality
Causal and material: in analysis, 3.6.3n., **4.21.2n.**; in eschatology,
  7.10
Causal power of nature: 10.26; 'the divine cause which is the source
  of all that happens to men', 8.27
Chance: 3.11.3, 12.24
  See also Fortune, Luck

See also 'All is as thinking makes it so', Externals, Harm, Pain

completed', 5.31, 10.22; service to the 'divinity within us', 2.13;
service to god, 6.44n.
  See also Duty
Severance: **4.29n.**
Severed limbs: 8.34
Sexual matters: 1.17.2, **1.17.7n.**, 3.2.3, 3.7, 3.16.1, 5.10.1n., 6.13n.
– presumed habits of others in bed: 3.4.4, 10.13, 10.19, 11.18.2
  See also Catamites, Homosexuality
Shamelessness: 9.42.1
Ship's captain: 6.55, 8.15
Shoddiness of things temporal: **4.48.2n.**, **5.10.1n.**, 8.24
Shortness of life (people and things): 2.6, **3.7n.**, **3.10n.**, **4.48.2n.**,
  5.10.1n., 10.34, 11.18.6; long life no advantage, 4.50
Shuttle: 10.38
Sickness: *see* Illness/disease
Silver: 9.36
SIMILES: ball thrown up, 8.20; boxer, gladiator, 12.9; children
  accepting all they are told, 4.46; children squabbling, tantrums,
  5.33, 9.24; doctors and their instruments, 3.13; eye, feet, 9.42.4;
  feet, hands, eyelids, teeth, 2.1; fire, 4.1, 10.31, 10.33.2–3; horse,
  dog, bee, 5.6; lamp, 4.19, 12.15; limbs, 7.13, 7.19; masons, 5.8.2;
  mill, 10.35; olive, 4.48.2; ophthalmia, 5.9; pig at sacrifice, 10.28;
  puppies, 5.33, 7.3; rocky headland, 4.49.1n.; roller, 10.33.2–3;
  drifting sands, 7.34; schoolboy, 5.9; shuttle, pen, whip, 10.38;
  stomach, 10.31, (10.35); stone thrown up, 9.17, 10.33.3; unwashed,
  11.15; vine, 5.6; wax, 5.33, 7.23; wrestling, dancing, 7.61
  See also Images
Simplicity of living: 1.3, 1.5, 1.6, 1.7.2, 1.16.8 (Antoninus), 1.17.3,
  3.11.2, 5.5, 5.9, **6.30.2n.**, 7.31, 7.67 ('the happy life depends on
  very little'), 10.1, 10.9, 12.27
Sin(s): **2.10n.** (Theophrastus), **9.1n.**
– sin/error as ignorance, **2.1n.**; a sort of blindness, 2.13
  See also Good and evil
Sincerity: 8.5, **11.19n.**
  See also Honesty, Truth/truthfulness
Slaves: 1.16.8, 1.17.7, 3.2.3, 6.14, 10.25, 11.30
– slaves to ambition, 8.3; slaves to needs, 10.19
Sleep: **2.1n.**, 4.46 (Heraclitus), 5.1, **6.2n.**, 6.31, 6.42 (Heraclitus),
  7.64, 8.12 (sleep 'shared with dumb animals'), 10.13
Smith: 5.1.3
Smoke: ' "The fire smokes and I leave the house" ', 5.29; 'human life

PENGUIN CLASSICS

CITY OF GOD   ST AUGUSTINE

'The Heavenly City outshines Rome, beyond comparison. There, instead of victory, is truth; instead of rank, holiness'

St Augustine, Bishop of Hippo, was one of the central figures in the history of Christianity, and *City of God* is one of his greatest theological works. Written as an eloquent defence of the faith at a time when the Roman Empire was on the brink of collapse, it examines the ancient pagan religions of Rome, the arguments of the Greek philosophers and the revelations of the Bible. Pointing the way forward to a citizenship that transcends the best political experiences of the world and offers citizenship that will last for eternity, *City of God* is one of the most influential documents in the development of Christianity.

This edition contains a new introduction that examines the text in the light of contemporary Greek and Roman thought and political change. It demonstrates the religious and literary influences on St Augustine and his significance as a Christian thinker. There is also a chronology and bibliography.

Translated with notes by Henry Bettenson with an introduction by Gill Evans

PENGUIN CLASSICS

PENSÉES   BLAISE PASCAL

'If we submit everything to reason our religion will be left with nothing mysterious or supernatural'

Blaise Pascal, the precociously brilliant contemporary of Descartes, was a gifted mathematician and physicist, but it is his unfinished apologia for the Christian religion upon which his reputation now rests. The *Pensées* is a collection of philosophical fragments, notes and essays in which Pascal explores the contradictions of human nature in psychological, social, metaphysical and – above all – theological terms. Mankind emerges from Pascal's analysis as a wretched and desolate creature within an impersonal universe, but who can be transformed through faith in God's grace.

This masterly translation by A. J. Krailsheimer conveys Pascal's disarmingly personal tone and captures all the fire and passion of the original. Also contained in this volume are a comparison between different editions, appendices and a bibliography.

Translated with an introduction by A. J. Krailsheimer

THE STORY OF PENGUIN CLASSICS

Before 1946 ...'Classics' are mainly the domain of academics and students, without readable editions for everyone else. This all changes when a little-known classicist, E. V. Rieu, presents Penguin founder Allen Lane with the translation of Homer's *Odyssey* that he has been working on and reading to his wife Nelly in his spare time.

1946 *The Odyssey* becomes the first Penguin Classic published, and promptly sells three million copies. Suddenly, classic books are no longer for the privileged few.

1950s Rieu, now series editor, turns to professional writers for the best modern, readable translations, including Dorothy L. Sayers's *Inferno* and Robert Graves's *The Twelve Caesars*, which revives the salacious original.

1960s The Classics are given the distinctive black jackets that have remained a constant throughout the series's various looks. Rieu retires in 1964, hailing the Penguin Classics list as 'the greatest educative force of the 20th century'.

1970s A new generation of translators arrives to swell the Penguin Classics ranks, and the list grows to encompass more philosophy, religion, science, history and politics.

1980s The Penguin American Library joins the Classics stable, with titles such as *The Last of the Mohicans* safeguarded. Penguin Classics now offers the most comprehensive library of world literature available.

1990s The launch of Penguin Audiobooks brings the classics to a listening audience for the first time, and in 1999 the launch of the Penguin Classics website takes them online to a larger global readership than ever before.

The 21st Century Penguin Classics are rejacketed for the first time in nearly twenty years. This world famous series now consists of more than 1300 titles, making the widest range of the best books ever written available to millions – and constantly redefining the meaning of what makes a 'classic'.

The Odyssey continues ...

The best books ever written

PENGUIN (🐧) CLASSICS

SINCE 1946

Find out more at www.penguinclassics.com